Tony Hall

The ABZs of Adventist Youth Ministry

North American Division Edition

Stuart Tyner

Preface by José Vicente Rojas
Introduction by Ron Whitehead

Book design: Stuart Tyner
Cover design: V. Bailey Gillespie

Tyner, Stuart.
    The ABZs of Adventist Youth Ministry

ISBN# 1-57756-066-3

Contributors

The author and publishers thank the following lay and professional youth ministry leaders and organizations for their significant contribution to this resource, suggesting topics, researching and writing entries and examining the manuscript, as well as for providing a continuing, shining example of Christ-centered, grace-oriented excellence in youth ministry.

Adventist Colleges Abroad
Adventist Frontier Missions
Adventist Youth to Youth
Tony Anobile
John Anthony
Denise Badger
Mark Bond
VirLynn Burton
G. Alexander Bryant
Patti Cabrera
Ann Calkins
Lance Campbell
Melvin Campbell
Carol Cannon
Paul Cannon
Steve Case
Jon Clark
Fred Cornforth
Dave Cress
Daniel L. Davis
Ray Descalso
Mark Driskill
Rich DuBose
Brian Dudar
Ruben Escalante
Wendy Finlay
Brad Forbes
Barry Gane
Timothy Gillespie

V. Bailey Gillespie
Mike Goetz
Janine Goffar
Group Publishing
Richard Guerrero
Paul Hafner
John Hancock
Edwin Hernandez
Home Study International
Gary L. Hopkins
Jackie James
Paul Jensen
Terry L. Johnsson
Tim Lale
Mark C. Lynch
A. Allan Martin
Norm Middag
Erin Tyner Miller
Heather Miller
Todd Miller
Cyril Millett, III
Phil Muthersbaugh
Willie Oliver
Dick Osborne
Don Pate
Lori Peckham
Ron Pickell
Greg Porter
Shannon Quishenberry
Humberto Rasi
Joelle Reed

Paul Richardson
Curtis Rittenour
Carl Rogers
Ken Rogers
José Rojas
Phil Rosburg
Susan Ross
John Rudometkin, Jr.
Celeste Ryan
Dan Savino, Jr.
Beth Schaefer
Mark Schiefer
Graeme Sharrock
Ella Simmons
Lincoln Steed
Gary Swanson
Gerry Thompson
George Tichy
Chary Torres
Cindy Tutsch
Jennifer Tyner
Roger Wade
Rona Wadkins
Ron Whitehead
Allan Williamson
Randal Wisbey
Bob Wong
David Wong
Bill Wood
David Wood
Anita Youngberg
Youth Specialties

Adventist Youth Ministry

North American Division Edition

Stuart Tyner

Table of Contents

• Preface

José Vicente Rojas
Director, North American Division Teen and Young Adult Ministries
Executive Director, Adventist Youth Service Network

The purpose of youth ministry in North America is outreach. All across the continent, successful youth ministries are reporting that they are performing outreach through service projects in the community, help for needy people, Bible study teams, Magabooks, or any one of many other powerful evangelistic activities.

The reason for this is that the most effective youth ministry today is rooted in a dynamic, affirming, Christ-centered youth program at the local church. When your youth group is the best place to be, an evangelistic phenomenon occurs because your youth will bring their friends, and many will stay. Now more than ever, our churches and campuses are the most strategic locations for the sharpest youth ministry to occur.

This book is a must have for all youth leaders.

People like you are at the forefront of a movement that God has launched. As you lead in your youth or young adult group, you need the best resources to accomplish what God has planned for you. This book, *The ABZs of Adventist Youth Ministry*, is a must-have for all youth leaders. Here you will find just what you need.

The North American Division extends special thanks to the Hancock Center for Youth and Family Ministry at La Sierra University for the excellent job they have done in creating this valuable resource for you. Many youth ministry professionals have examined the manuscript and contributed to the rich practical contents of this book.

...the right book, for the right people, at the right time...

As you go through the pages, cross-referenced with a huge variety of youth ministry issues, I know that you will feel as I do: this is the right book, for the right people, at the right time, to aid the most powerful youth and young adult ministry movement this world has ever seen.

Go with courage. This battle is not yours, it is the Lord's!

Preface

Introduction

Ron Whitehead
Associate Director, NAD Teen and Young Adult Ministries
Director, Center For Youth Evangelism

Who? What? Where? Why? Life is full of questions.

And so are youth and young adults in the Seventh-day Adventist Church. "Why am I an Adventist Christian?" "What's so important about evangelism?" "How can I make a difference?"

Many youth and young adults desire to know Christ more fully and to make a difference in the world around them. But many don't know how. As youth leaders, we can help in the search for answers when we understand basic fundamentals and put them into action. So where do we start?

This book, *The ABZs of Adventist Youth Ministry*, is a great place to begin! On be-half of all the congregational

...this is a great place to begin!

and campus youth leaders in North America (and around the world) let me thank Stuart Tyner, Bailey Gillespie, John Anthony and all the other members of the Hancock Center team for a job well done!

The ABZs will guide you to ideas, places and people that have answers. From A to Z, this resource is packed with information that will connect you to the world of Adventist youth ministry. This book is premised on the idea that we in fact have the necessary people to do what needs to happen in youth and young adult ministry in churches across the continent. What we need most is to come together like never before in a network of trained leaders who will lead church- based and campus-based ministry.

To aid in this process, the Center for Youth Evangelism has developed seven core principles for excellence in youth ministry leadership. These seven insightful principles, when applied within a Christ-centered, grace-oriented, relational ministry, form a dynamic curriculum direction and structure for successful local ministry.

seven core principles for excellence in youth ministry leadership

The "Seven Principles for Youth Ministry Excellence" provide simple yet effective answers to difficult youth ministry questions. They are intended to appeal to a large variety of

Introduction

church and conference youth ministries, regardless of culture, age, or demographics. You may wish to add other leadership principles which have empowered your specific ministry. But we believe that these basic essentials will strengthen your leadership, develop a clear direction, and assist you in inviting young people to join God's unstoppable army.

- *Seven Principles for Youth Ministry Excellence*

1. **Principle One: Grow Spiritually..** We have never met an effective youth leader who does not have a deep personal walk with God. Powerful youth leaders are committed to personal spiritual growth through regular prayer, Bible study, and fellowship.

2. **Principle Two: Learn Leadership Skills.** To stay on the cutting-edge, youth leaders that excel tend to show constant growth and improvement in their leadership skills. They subscribe to at least one leadership journal, read youth ministry materials, and attend leadership-training events. They are also mentored by experienced youth leaders.

   constant growth and improvement

3. **Principle Three: Nurture Relationships.** Successful youth leaders focus on the experiences of people rather than relying only on programs. They identify all active and inactive youth and contact them outside of Sabbath events. They also staff their ministry properly (one leader per seven youth).

4. **Principle Four: Empower Youth for Leadership.** Youth leaders that excel perceive their youth as the church leaders of today. They don't wait until an undefined tomorrow to give teens and young adults ownership of their youth group and church. They mentor them, provide them the resources, and then release them to leadership among their peers.

5. **Principle Five: Plan.** A good youth leader plans. Jesus did. He clearly sketched out to his team where he was going and how they could get there with Him. Jesus did not claim to know all the details, but He certainly pointed to the big picture and acted toward goals on a daily basis. Likewise, effective youth

Introduction, continued

leaders plan their ministry with "youth day" worship services, a budget, calendar, regular evaluation process, and spiritual/ topical goals they plan to cover.

6. **Principle Six: Communicate.** Effective youth leaders create awareness and find support for their youth group by constantly communicating. They make sure other church leaders, parents, and the community are well informed on the youth ministry events and accomplishments.

> ## life changing experiences that make the gospel come to life

7. **Principle Seven: Mobilize for service.** Engaging youth in church ministries, community outreach, and world evangelism is a must for effective youth leaders. Vigilant leaders constantly seek to provide environments for youth to have life-changing experiences that make the gospel come to life. Each time a young person gives away what God has given them, they receive more in their own lives.

These seven principles are proving to be a powerful guidance and support to successful youth ministry. Hundreds of youth and young adult leaders, the growing youth ministry army in the trenches, are confirming their effectiveness as they carry them out! That's why the North American Division Teen and Young Adult Ministries Department is emphasizing their importance. Those who are still working to develop power-ful youth ministries can now embrace a solid curriculum for leadership!

> ## a solid curriculum for leadership

Imagine if every youth leader in the North American Division applied principles, such as "The Seven Principles for Youth Ministry Excellence," in their youth and young adult groups. If church leaders were to delegate significant authority to youth who truly need permission to lead, how much more would our churches grow? If we give Adventist youth a vision, equip them with skills, affirm them, provide resources for them, and work with them to develop action plans to live out their faith, how much sooner will our task on earth be finished?

"With such an army of youth, rightly trained, might furnish, how much sooner will the message of a crucified, risen, and soon-coming Savior be carried to the all the world!" (Ellen White, *Christian Service*, 30).

This is your opportunity to be a part of the movement of youth and young adult ministries quickly spreading across the land. Remember that each step you take toward the goal of a vibrant ministry is dependent on your commitment to Christ and how that relationship translates into leadership.

each step is dependent on your commitment to Christ

Each page in *The ABZs of Adventist Youth Ministry* will assist you in that journey. You will find in these pages that you are not alone, and that countless others are also growing in their ability to lead. The rich variety of youth ministry organizations listed in this book will also provide you with many specialized support mechanisms when you need them most.

Your moment has come, welcome to the *ABZs of Adventist Youth Ministry*!

Notes:

_____

_____

_____

_____

_____

_____

_____

_____

_____

_____

_____

_____

_____

_____

_____

_____

_____

_____

Introduction, continued

How to Use this Resource

The ABZs of Adventist Youth Ministry is dedicated to the expanding team of committed youth ministry leaders, church by church, school by school, conference by conference, who daily face the ever-changing, never-ending, always complicated challenges of youth ministry.

And, oh, what a ministry it is! New frustrations every day. Fresh personalities. Innovative techniques. Complex issues. Delicate relationships. Infrequent rewards. Constant change. Not enough time or appreciation. Too many demands and pressures.

The ABZs of Adventist Youth Ministry is meant to help alleviate some of those pressures, not add to your burden by producing one more thing you ought to read. This isn't a comprehensive discussion of any one youth ministry dynamic or a one-stop solution to any particular problem. You shouldn't sit down and devour it cover to cover in one sitting. Rather it is a one-challenge-at-a-time, quick-read reference, a practical guide, an encyclopedic overview of this demanding ministry aimed at an ever-moving target, the kids who motivate and inspire us.

Here are three ways to begin using the book.

Three Ways to Put the ABZs to Work for You

1. **Explore the Entries.** Just open the book and begin exploring. Or look for topics that interest you. Start on any page, apply the content to your youth group, then read related entries and see where your exploration takes you.
2. **Search the Index.** Read through the Index (beginning on page 281), column by column, until you come to topics that discuss the needs you know are present in your youth group. Meet your needs before going on to explore new ideas.
3. **Consider Ministry Situations.** In the interactive table of contents you'll recognize 25 types of ministry situations. Find the situations which best describe your responsibilities. Start with these entries, then move to new possibilities.

The ABZs of Adventist Youth Ministry also employs a graphic signal we've grown accustomed to on the internet: the hyper-text transfer protocol of underlined, blue text. On the web all we'd have to do is click on this text and off we'd fly to a related cyber-site. Here, the highlighted text indicates the presence of an entry elsewhere in the book on that specified topic. (Unfortunately, you'll have to turn there, not just click.) As you follow your interests through the *ABZs*, be sure to look up these additional discussions which relate to the topic you're exploring.

When we first began talking about this type of resource, we wondered if we could find one youth ministry dynamic for each letter of the alphabet, twenty-six unique dynamics to write about. As you can see the list has grown. There are now 200 topics we've included, and doubtless we could find more.

Here are some tips about navigating around each of those entries.

Guide Words

Precise Entries

Bibliographies

Hyper Text

Discussion

Highlights

Additional Entries

Practical Ideas

---

page 88

The ABZs of Adventist Youth Ministry

Discussion

In most conversations with teens, especially in teaching situations (such as Sabbath School lesson study), the rule is that discussion is better than lecture. Discussion helps you hear the concerns of the person or group with whom you're talking. And discussion helps keep the subject focused, encouraging you to speak to real needs.

The Three Best Ways to Kill a Discussion

1. **Lecture for twenty minutes,** then ask the kids, "Now, do you have any questions?"
2. **Look for one, and only one, right answer** – "What one word best describes the character of God?" "Righteous." "NO." "Merciful." "NO!" "Love." "That's it!"
3. **Belittle an answer you don't agree with** – "Who's your favorite Bible character?" "Joseph." "Oh, come on, you've been saying 'Joseph' ever since you were a little kid. Why don't you grow up and choose a better character?"

The Three Best Ways to Get a Discussion Going

1. **Begin with a question.** Don't wait for someone to ask. Make the question easy to answer. Appreciate the answer you receive.
2. **Ask questions to specific people.** Don't expect volunteers.
3. **Divide your youth into small groups.** Give an assignment that can be worked on together. Appoint a spokesperson for each group. ("The person with the longest hair will be the spokesperson this time.") Establish a time limit and hold to it (three minutes or five minutes, depending on the assignment). Pay attention to the answers.

More Great Advice
Ken Davis, *How To Speak To Youth* (Loveland, CO: Group, 1986);
David Lynn, *High School Talk Sheets* (Grand Rapids, MI: Zondervan, 1985, and 1988);
David Lynn and Mike Yaconelli, *Amazing Tension Getters* (Grand Rapids, MI: Zondervan, 1987;
Edward N. McNulty, *Controversial Topics for Youth Groups* (Grand Rapids MI: Zondervan, 1981,
Stephen Parolini, *Controversial Discussion Starters* (Loveland, CO: Group, 1988);

Also See: Active Learning; Boredom; Climate Issues; Involvement; Learning Styles.

Now you're ready to explore. Look for ways to balance your youth ministry budget. Find how to plan a master calendar. Discover how

How to Use this Resource, continued

you can lead a successful song service, prevent youth ministry burn-out, organize a mission trip, create a youth council, provide creative programming, work with your pastor, and so much more.

- *Look for these Specific Ministry Dynamics*
  15 qualities of a successful youth leader
  14 actions to take for at-risk teens
  13 youth ministry newsletters, magazines and studies
  12 article ideas for your newsletter
  11 ways to warm up your church
  10 fund raising ideas
  9 parts you play in discipline
  8 things you can do about violence
  7 ways to build attendance
  6 keys to success in preventing drug use
  5 ways to enrich Bible study
  4 secrets of AYS planning
  3 ways to deal with criticism
  2 things to do right after youth church
  and the one, essential foundation for all youth ministry

The Table of Ministry Situations is built around the following 25 youth ministry situations and responsibilities.

- *25 Ministry Situations*

  A. You're a new youth leader
  B. Youth ministry resources
  C. Ministry elements:
    a. Spiritual life
    b. Programming
    c. Teaching
    d. Social Activities
    e. Finances
  D. Targeted ministries:
    a. Understanding teens
    b. Junior High ministry
    c. Adventists in public school
    d. Small church
    e. Young adults

  E. Additional ministries
  F. Adventist education
  G. At-risk behaviors
  H. Communicating
  I. Counselling
  J. Cultural diversity
  K. Family issues
  L. In need of training
  M. Music
  N. SDA Church; history and function
  O. Service; Outreach
  P. Standards
  Q. Worship

You've just been nominated
by your church to be the
New Youth Leader.
Quick! Read these entries first.

New Youth Leader

Table of Ministry Situations

Ministry Situations, continued

You're most interested in the
Spiritual Life
of your youth. Meditate on these entries.

You're looking for the best available youth ministry
Resources.
Search these entries.

Spiritual Life

Resources

You plan, prepare and schedule the youth ministry **Programming** at your church. Begin here.

Programming

You have the responsibility for **Teaching** the youth. Study these entries.

Ministry Situations, continued

Teaching

Ministry Situations, continued

You're a party animal! Here's how you can lead out in the
Social Activities
of your youth group.

You're in charge of the money. Put these entries at the top of your list. They're about the
Finances
of youth ministry.

Sometimes you just can't figure the kids out! These entries on
Understanding Teens
will be enlightening.

Your primary responsibility is for

Junior High Ministry.

Add these entries to your other ministry situations.

Adolescence	5	
Baptism	40	
Junior High Ministry	139	Junior High Mi...
Pathfinder Ministries	171	

Acceptance		
AMiCUS	3	
Campus Advent	29	
Dialogue	54	Public School
SDA Students in Public School	86	
Worldview	197	
	251	

A large portion of your youth are attending

Public School

Get better acquainted with the information on these pages.

You lead out in the youth ministry activities of a

Small Church.

Add these entries to your list.

Building Your Youth Group	52	
Pathfinder Ministries	171	Small Church
SDAs in Public School	197	

Your primary work is with

Young Adults.

Here are entries about resources especially for them.

Adventist Colleges and Universities	11	
	22	
	23	
AIA	29	Young Adults
AIDS		
AMiCUS	10	
Adventist Colleges Abroad	54	
Campus Advent	74	
CQ: *Collegiate Quarterly*	86	
Dialogue	117	
Generation X	256	
Young Adults		

Ministry Situations, continued

Ministry Situations, continued

You're looking for exciting **Ministries** for your youth. Check out these ideas.

Additional Ministries

You want to know more about **Adventist Education.** The textbook starts with these entries.

Adventist Education

You're concerned about your youth being exposed to
At-Risk Behaviors.
Study these entries.

At-Risk Behavi

You've been asked to tell the youth ministry story in your church. Start with these entries, which are all about
Communicating.

Communicating

Ministry Situations, continued

Ministry Situations, continued

You have the gift and the training for youth ministry **Counselling.**

Think about these dynamics.

Counselling

You want to strengthen the rich **Cultural Diversity** of your youth group. These entries will assist you.

Cultural Diversity

You want to support the families of your youth.

These **Family Issues** discussions can help.

Abuse	2
Adolescence	5
Adoption Services	8
Attachment	33
Climate Issues	58
Confidentiality	67
Dating	79
Death and Dying Issues	82
Distancing	89
Divorce	93
Effectiveness Factors	99
Faith Development	103
Family Worship	105
Generations	116
Parents	170
Standards	213
Television	226
Values	238

Family Issues

You feel the need for **Training.**

Consult these resources.

Adventist Communication Network	12	Hancock Center Symposium	131
Center for Creative Ministry	55	National Black Youth Resource Center	163
Center for Youth Evangelism	56	PlusLine	179
Conference Youth Director	66	Three:20 Zone	228
Giraffe University	122	Youth Specialties	274
Group	128	Youth Summit	275
Hancock Center for Youth and Family Ministry	130		

Training

Ministry Situations, continued

Ministry Situations, continued

They always turn to you for
Music.
Listen to these entries,
note by note.

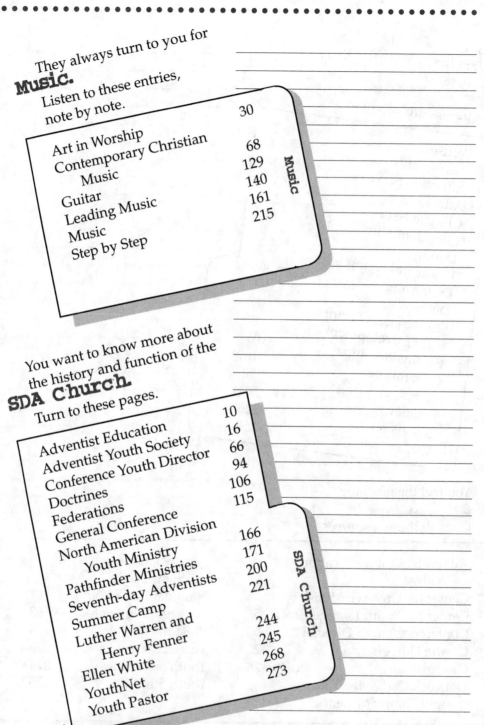

Music

You want to know more about
the history and function of the
SDA Church
Turn to these pages.

SDA Church

The ABZs of Adventist Youth Ministry

North American Division Edition

• AAYMP

The purpose of the AAYMP, the North American Division's Association of Adventist Youth Ministry Professionals, is to enhance <u>youth ministry</u> by fostering professional growth from a <u>Seventh-day Adventist</u> perspective, engaging in supportive interaction and promoting spiritual renewal.

Anyone who serves the youth of the Seventh-day Adventist Church in a professional capacity is eligible for membership in this organization. This includes youth directors on the conference, union, division and <u>General Conference</u> levels, <u>youth pastors</u>, Bible teachers, academy and college chaplains, dormitory deans, resource centers and professional youth organizations.

The Association holds an annual convention, generally in conjunction with professional growth events such as the North American Division Ministries Convention, NAD Youth training event, or a <u>Youth Specialties</u> National Convention.

• *The Mission Statement of the AAYMP*

1. To network youth ministry professionals.
2. To enhance professional growth through educational in-service opportunities.
3. To identify people who possess special gifts and recruit them to professional youth ministry service.
4. To advocate the hiring of youth ministry professionals on conference, church and institutional staffs. (See: <u>Conference Youth Director</u>)
5. To promote the spiritual growth, retention and involvement of <u>teens</u> and <u>young adults</u> in ministry.

For more information, contact Allan Williamson, Director of Youth Ministries for the Southern Union, and President of the AAYMP.

AAYMP
%Allan Williamson
Southern Union Conference of SDAs
3978 Memorial Drive
Decatur, GA 30032
Phone: (404) 299-1832.

AAYMP

• Abuse

Abuse is a broad term which refers to any form of maltreatment, including neglect, or physical, sexual or emotional <u>violence</u>.

Apart from random criminal activity, abuse usually is perpetrated by someone who is close to the victim and in a position of power or control, such as parents, stepparents, care-givers, clergy, or teachers.

Victims of prolonged *sexual* abuse usually develop low self-esteem, a feeling of worthlessness, an abnormal perspective on sexuality (specialists refer to being "sexualized," which may result in promiscuity or sexual dysfunction) and often become abusive themselves. The abused person may become withdrawn and mistrustful of adults, may experience acute loneliness, and may resort to heavy drug abuse and other self-destructive behaviors, including becoming suicidal.

• Responding to Abuse

1. If an individual even hints in a vague way that abuse has occurred, encourage him or her to talk freely.
2. Take the report seriously. Positive resolution of the trauma is more likely when the abused is listened to and understood.
3. Assure the individual that he or she did the right thing in telling. There may be guilt (especially if the abuse involves a family member) or fear of reprisal.
4. Offer the person protection and promise to take steps immediately to see that the abuse stops.
5. Report any suspicion of abuse. If the abuse is within the family, report it to the local Child Protection Agency. If the abuse is outside of the family, report it to the police or district attorney's office. The family physician should be consulted. Usually, the person should also have a psychiatric evaluation to determine the need for ongoing professional help.
6. Early in the healing process forgiveness may be too heavy a burden to place on the shoulders of the abused. But assure the abused that the abuse cannot separate them from the love of God (See Romans 8:35-39).

☞ **Also see**: Counselling; Self-esteem Issues; Sexuality Issues; Suicide; V iolence.

Sources: The National Center on Child Abuse and Neglect, US Department of Health and Human Services; The Canadian Society for the Investigation of Child Abuse; The American Academy of Child and Adolescent Psychiatry.

Abuse

• Acceptance

Many of the most tragic stories kids tell about their <u>church</u> experience deal with the issue of acceptance (*non*-acceptance would be a more accurate way of saying it). Youth have been turned away at the door of the church by greeters who insist they are not dressed properly. Drama groups have been lectured from the front of the church about the unacceptably of drama. Music groups have been interrupted mid-song and told that God doesn't like their music. Kids repeating memory verses from contemporary translations have been told that they were in error for not learning from the "right" <u>Bible versions</u>.

The bottom line for this non-acceptance seems to be the notion that God is honored by only traditional forms of <u>worship</u> and only certain worshippers, and that only a few know who and what God accepts.

The Christian ideal presents a very different picture. "Stop passing judgment on one another," Paul tells us in Romans 14:13. "Who are you to judge someone else's servant?" We must not condemn people who behave differently than we do, *because God has accepted them* (Romans 14:3, 4). The Christian <u>community</u> supports, it does not tear down.

"If you have any encouragement from being united with Christ, if any comfort from His love, if any fellowship with the Spirit, if any tenderness and compassion, then make my joy complete by being like-minded, having the same love, being one in spirit and purpose," (Philippians 2:1, 2).

"May the God who gives endurance and encouragement give you a spirit of unity among yourselves as you follow Christ <u>Jesus</u>, so that with one heart and mouth you may glorify the God and Father of our Lord Jesus Christ. Accept one another, then, just as Christ accepted you, in order to bring praise to God," (Romans 15:5-7).

• *Three Ways to Show Acceptance*

1. **Be Single-Minded in Greeting.** Greet young people by looking straight into their eyes and not at their clothing, hairstyle, makeup, jewelry, etc. Express your delight at their presence.
2. **Demonstrate Unity.** Include your youth in your planning, your programming, your outreach – your ministry.
3. **Celebrate <u>Diversity</u>.** Be intentional about variety and diversity. For example, plan a musical worship service that includes many musical styles of praise.

☞ Also see: Church; Climate Issues.

• Active Learning

Active learning is a non-passive approach to learning. It is acquiring knowledge through participation. Contemporary educational research confirms the view that people learn most efficiently when they are engaged in interaction rather than in merely receptive or passive activities.

"In contrast, passive learning occurs when teachers explain and tell (the 'now I told you; now you know' paradigm) and students primarily listen. In these settings, we often hear students ask, 'Do I need to learn this? Will it be on the test? Tell me what I need to know.' The student's role is to be the recipient of information, while the teacher is the 'knower,' or giver of information."[1]

"Passive teaching assumes that students are 'empty vessels,' or 'blank slates.' Active teaching assumes that students are meaning-makers, active constructors of their own knowledge; that they bring to each learning experience a reservoir of information from which they will draw as they try to understand."[2]

What is true for teachers in formal education situations is also true for <u>youth ministry</u> leaders in religious education settings. While the experience of God in worship leads to *knowledge* of God, the primary mode of knowing is by *participation*.

• Active vs. Passive Learning

Circle each statement below which models active learning.
1. "Tell me what you know about the <u>Sabbath</u>."
2. "Today I'm going to give you a <u>Bible study</u> on tithing."
3. "Let's brainstorm ideas and questions about <u>prayer</u>, organize our responses into categories, and prioritize our discussion."
4. "How have you experienced God's presence in your life?"
5. "Please take notes on my lecture this morning."
6. "Here's a study sheet with the dates you need to memorize."
7. "What do you think would happen if this story took place on your campus this week?"

☞ **Also see:** Curriculum; Involvement; Learning Styles.

1   Shirley Ann Freed, "Encouraging Active Learning," in the *Journal of Adventist Education* February/March, 1995, 4.
2   Ibid, 5.

Answers: 1, 3, 4, 7

• Adolescence

Adolescence is the period of life through which we pass as youth and <u>young adults</u>. The period is associated with rapid physical, psychological, and social changes.

- ### • The Three Stages of Adolescence
    1. Early adolescence (earliteens from ages 12 to 15).
    2 Middle adolescence (the high school years, ages 15 to 18).
    3. Late adolescence (young adults, from around 18 to 22).

There are two primary and dramatic developments which take place during this period of life.

The first is the physical-sexual maturing which changes our appearance and the way our bodies work. Girls usually experience these types of changes about two years earlier than boys.

- ### • Four Physical Changes During Adolescence
    1. A spurt in physical growth.
    2. The maturation of the reproductive organs.
    3. Changes in the endocrine system.
    4. The development of secondary sex characteristics.

The second development is cognitive – the change in the way we think, which affects the way we see ourselves, others, and the world around us.

- ### • Five Life Tasks of Adolescence
    1. Consolidating individuality – becoming who we are.
    2. Becoming independent from our parents – including moving from subscribing to our parents' faith to owning our own faith.
    3. Establishing and maintaining peer relationships.
    4. Developing a sexual identity.
    5. Preparing for a lifework.

In the book, *The Complete Book of Youth Ministry* (Moody Press, 1987), Byron Klaus identifies the most difficult problems occurring during adolescence with which youth ministry leaders need to be prepared to deal.

Adolescence

Adolescence, continued

- *The Seven Most Difficult Adolescent Problem Areas*
  1. Substance abuse (See: <u>At-risk behaviors</u>)
  2. Premarital sex (See: <u>Sexuality issues</u>)
  3. Abortion (See: <u>Sexuality issues</u>)
  4. Crime (See: <u>Violence</u>)
  5. Child <u>abuse</u>
  6. <u>Suicide</u>
  7. <u>Eating disorders</u>

- *Strategies for Working With Adolescents*
  1. **One-on-One**. Remember that the most effective ministry takes place on a one-on-one basis. Adolescents will not remember everything you teach them in a Sabbath School <u>lesson study</u>, and they won't always respond exactly as you'd like them to, but they will relate to you. Your relationship with them is what determines your lasting influence.
  2. <u>Acceptance</u>. Adolescents can read our hearts. We must learn to love them for who they are — treasured children of God — and not for what we can turn them into.
  3. **Challenge**. Encourage your youth to ask questions. Help them explore their faith in a positive way, in a supportive environment, even when you don't know all the answers and have to join in the search. (See: <u>Faith Development</u> and <u>Faith Maturity</u>.)
  4. <u>Involvement</u>. Provide as many ways as possible for your youth to be involved in your <u>youth ministry</u>, in the planning and preparation for programs, in service projects, in worship. (See: <u>Climate Issues</u>.)
  5. **Serve their Parents**. In many cases (for example, see: <u>Family Worship</u>) the best thing we can do for our youth is to be of service to their parents. Help them understand what their adolescent children are experiencing and show them the best way to deal with pressing adolescent issues. (Also See: <u>Parents</u>.)

☞ **Also see:** Attachment; Codependency; Confidentiality; Teens.

• Adopting a Small Church

Newberry, Algonac, Grove, Milford... We all know them – the tiny churches whose membership has never exceeded 35 and are now hanging on by their fingernails.

And the sad reality is that though they may have the message they just don't have the critical mass that would be attractive to most people and growth looks humanly impossible.

Therefore, why not kill two birds with one stone...(although "kill" might not be the best term to use with regard to a struggling little church!?!?) Once a month (or once a quarter) why not let the kids be servants? Why not allow them to cut their teeth in church leadership with folks who are almost guaranteed to be less critical... Why not choose a small, out-of-the way church and take over!

- ## • Five Reasons to Adopt a Church:
  1. **Variety.** Brother Donaldson has taught the Sabbath School lesson there every <u>Sabbath</u> for 16 years straight and they've heard Aunt Tillie's offertory a thousand times!
  2. **Newness.** The fresh air your youth will bring to the little congregation will make up for a ton of inexperience.
  3. **Experience.** In your standard youth setting when does Kimberly or Jason get baptized into sermon delivery? The saints of Podunkville would love to hear the Montez sisters' duet or Eric's first trumpet solo!
  4. **Vibrancy.** Adopting a tiny church may just serve as a life saver for both parties - a dying church may find some vibrancy.
  5. **Discovery.** Your kids may find *their* church (even if it's not Podunkville)!

- ## • How To Adopt a Church
  1. **Ask your pastor** or your conference ministerial secretary about churches that need to be adopted.
  2. **Choose a church** and visit it with several members of your youth group. If you decide this is the church to adopt, set up a meeting with the church's head elder. Tell the elder about your plans and ask for an appointment with the church board.
  3. **Present detailed plans** including schedule, budget, goals and benefits. Pray that the board will welcome you with open arms.

• Adoption Services

"I'm pregnant."

These two words can be the beginning of one of the most extraordinary times in a young couple's life together. The joys of becoming a parent, the thrill of the birth, the delight at every advancement in the new life – nothing else quite compares.

But an announcement of pregnancy also can be one of the most discouraging moments young people will ever experience. If the pregnancy is unwanted, either because of bad timing early in a marriage, or because there is no marriage, only three options present themselves to the mother and father: having an abortion (see: <u>Sexuality Issues</u>), keeping the child themselves, and placing the child for adoption.

• Are You Ready to Be a Parent?

1. Are you willing to give the next 18-20 years of your life to be responsible for your child?
2. Can you raise a child and still meet your own school, career and social needs?
3. Can you meet all the responsibilities of being a parent without having to depend on your family to take over for you?

If a young parent answers no to any of these questions, then they should seriously consider adoption as the best and most loving life-giving choice for themselves and their child.

Adoption is a legal procedure which places a child with adoptive parents who raise the child as a member of their own family. The child legally becomes a permanent member of the adoptive family.

Adoption may also be the answer for couples who are unable to have biological children. Couples wanting to adopt a child must apply and be accepted as prospective adoptive parents by a government approved agent. A thorough home study is done to ensure that the couple will be able to give proper care and love for the child.

Wanting to provide a secure family for a child reveals both love and maturity. Getting married because you are pregnant is widely recognized as a poor basis for building a loving family. Marriage failures are high for those who marry under such pressures.

For more information, contact: Adventist Adoption and Family Services, 60400 SE Belmont Street, Portland, OR 97215, (503) 232-1211.

Adoption Services

• ADRA International

The Adventist Development and Relief Agency (ADRA) is an independent, humanitarian agency established by the <u>Seventh-day Adventist</u> Church in 1956 with the specific purpose of individual and community development, and disaster relief. As a nongovernmental organization (NGO) ADRA helps people without regard to age, ethnicity, or political or religious affiliation.

• ADRA At Work
1. ADRA works for the poor in over 150 countries.
2. ADRA assists almost 15 million people a year in its five core portfolios: basic education, economic development, food security, primary health and disaster preparedness and response.
3. ADRA and its NGO partners in Sudan serve approximately 56,000 people per month in areas of basic health care.
4. ADRA's 1998 Kyrgyzstan Greenhouse Project is providing additional food and income for 200 Tadjik refugees.
5. Since 1995, ADRA has shipped more than $4.3 million worth of food aid famine-stricken North Korea.
6. Adventist Community Services (ACS), ADRA's U.S. branch, initiated 100 volunteer, community-based tutoring/mentoring projects this year for underprivileged children in the U.S.

The ADRA Office of Volunteers enables young and old alike to go into the world's most needy places to experience direct involvement with people in crisis. It's not only a chance for lending a helping hand but also for learning how other cultures live, working side by side with local people.

If members of your youth group are interested in a life of <u>service</u>, ADRA provides some of the very best opportunities available through the Adventist Church.

ADRA International Central Office
   12501 Old Columbia Pike
   Silver Spring, MD 20904
   Phone: (301) 680-6380 (Administrative Offices)
      (301) 680-5122 (Volunteer Office)
      (301) 680-6355 (News and Information)
   FAX: (301) 680-6370

ADRA International

Adventist Colleges Abroad *(sidebar, rotated)*

• Adventist Colleges Abroad

Within the <u>Seventh-day Adventist</u> network of education, Adventist Colleges Abroad (ACA), established in 1962, assists students in acquiring language skills, cross-cultural sensitivity, a global outlook on life and a sense of mission to other peoples of the world through specifically designed educational opportunities in international settings.

Because ACA is a consortium of Adventist colleges and universities in North America affiliated with international Adventists colleges, students receive the credits they earn through their own school at home. In addition, most loans and scholarships available on home campuses (including asistance for dependents of denominational employees) also are available for students in ACA programs.

Students take the grammar, composition, conversation, culture, civilization and literature courses necessary to complete minors and most major requirements in French, German and Spanish, or courses in Chinese (Mandarin), Italian, Portuguese, or Swahili. General education courses in art, music, physical education and religion are also available. In addition, students may choose from other courses available on the campus of enrollment.

Students who cannot spend a full academic year abroad may achieve a portion of the benefits of the experience by enrolling in ACA's Summer Language Abroad program.

• *Eight Beautiful ACA Campuses*
1. Argentina
2. Austria
3. Brazil
4. France
5. Greece
6. Italy
7. Kenya
8. Spain

Adventist Colleges Abroad
   Phone: (301) 680-6444
   FAX: (301) 680-6464
   e-mail: 104474.304@compuserve.com

• Adventist Colleges and Universities

There are fourteen Seventh-day Adventist colleges and universities in North America. When your youth begin to talk about going to college, get in touch with the Enrollment Services people at the numbers below, request an information packet and arrange for a visit.

- ### • Five Reasons to Choose an Adventist College
  1. The Adventist educational system is dedicated to deepening a relationship with Jesus. That's why the school system was founded. Jesus is at the center of our worldview, at the heart of our mission statements, at the core of our curriculum.
  2. Adventist schools understand our need to worship.
  3. Adventist schools invite you into a family.
  4. Adventist schools create opportunities to serve.
  5. Adventist schools provide quality education. The faculty members are outstanding. The teacher/student ratio is just right.

NAD Schools:	Phone:	http:
Andrews University	1-800-253-2874	www.andrews.edu/index.html
Atlantic Union College	1-800-AUC-2030	www.atlanticuc.edu/
Canadian University College	1-800-661-8129	www.rtt.ab.ca/rtt/cuc
Columbia Union College	1-800-835-4212	www.cuc.edu
(From Maryland)	1-800-492-1715	
Florida Hospital College of Health Sciences	1-800-500-7747	www.fhchs.org/
Kettering College of Medical Arts	1-800-433-KCMA	www.erinet.com/janmic/ kmchome.html
La Sierra University	1-800-874-5587	www.lasierra.edu
Loma Linda University	1-800-422-4558	www.llu.edu
Oakwood College	1-800-824-5312	www.oakwood.edu
Pacific Union College	1-800-862-7080	www.puc.edu
Southern Adventist University	1-800-SOUTHERN	www.southern.edu
Southwestern Adventist University	1-800-433-2240	www.swac.edu
Union College	1-800-2280-4600	www.ucollege.edu/
Walla Walla College	1-800-541-8900	www.wwc.edu

☞   Also see: Adventist Colleges Abroad; Home Study International.

Adventist Colleges and Universities

Adventist Communication Network

• Adventist Communication Network (ACN)

The Adventist Communication Network (ACN) is a service of the North American Division that provides denominational <u>resources</u> for local churches – a linkage that uses satellite technology to bring together and improve communication within the <u>Seventh-day Adventist</u> Church in North America.

- ## • Five ACN Benefits to Local Churches
  1. ACN provides training events.
  2. ACN links evangelistic meetings to all churches who wish to participate and minister to their communities.
  3. ACN provides outreach seminars on health, family life, and spiritual topics for local churches
  4. ACN makes it possible for local church members and leaders to participate in major events.
  5. ACN delivers news and mission reports and other inspirational and informational reports for use in local churches on <u>Sabbath</u> or during midweek meetings.

- ## • Three ACN Programs
  1. **First Wednesday.** A monthly program providing inspirational and informative news and mission reports about the worldwide Seventh-day Adventist Church and its members.
  2. **Lifestyle Live.** An educational series providing churches with outreach programs.
  3. **Cross Training.** A workshop series to train local church leaders and volunteer ministry coordinators that provides job descriptions, creative ministry ideas, and cutting-edge resources.

For more information, including specific titles and schedules for ACN programs, contact ACN at the following numbers.

Adventist Communication Network
    12501 Old Columbia Pike
    Silver Spring, MD 20904
    Phone: 1-800-ACN-1119, ext. 7 or (301) 680-6315
    FAX: (301) 680-6464
    CServe: 74617.1575@compuserve.com

• Adventist Education

The first <u>Seventh-day Adventist</u> school opened in Battle Creek, Michigan in 1872, a decade after the official organization of the Church. The principal of that first school was Goodloe H. Bell. The school building was a 20-foot by 30-foot building which originally had been built to house the press of the Battle Creek Sanitarium.

Today the Seventh-day Adventist Church operates the second largest church-sponsored school system in the world, second only to the Roman Catholic Church.

• The Number of SDA Schools in North America
1. K-8   698
2. K-9   67
3. K-10   140
4. K-12   59
5. 9-12   52

• The Number of Teachers Employed in the System
5,578 during the 1999/2000 school year

The North American Division Office of Education sees Christian education as the response of parents and the Adventist church <u>community</u> to God's instruction about the nurture and training of His children. The NAD Adventist education system is committed to strengthening education that enables God's children to study every aspect of His Word and His world as citizens of His kingdom.

Christian education in the Adventist tradition is deeply rooted in Christ, is as broad as the scope of creation and culture, and is alive with the energy of students who are learning to be and become everything that God intends them to be as they serve Him joyfully and faithfully.

Write the numbers below of your nearest Adventist schools.

Academy:	Elementary:
Name: _____	Name: _____
Address: _____	Address: _____
Phone #: _____	Phone #: _____
Principal: _____	Principal: _____

• Adventist Frontier Missions

David Howard, chronicler of student involvement in the history of missions, observed that students have been involved in every significant new development in missions throughout the history of the Christian church. Thus it's perhaps not surprising to learn that Adventist Frontier Missions found its beginning among students.

In the fall of 1984, two students at the Adventist Theological Seminary in Berrien Springs, Michigan, began meeting in one of the student's homes to learn more about missions and to promote an interest in the subject among other seminary students. About a year later, in September of 1985, the students officially organized a new Seventh-day Adventist mission agency and called it Adventist Frontier Missions.

In March, 1987, AFM sent out its first missionary family, who went to serve the Ifugao people in the Philippines. Since that time, many of the AFM missionaries have been young people. "We send student missionaries who are in their late teens and early twenties," says AFM, "but even our career missionaries are going to the field in their twenties and thirties. God can use the strength, idealism, and zeal of youth to do mighty things for Him."

• *Examples of Unreached People Targeted by AFM*

1. The Uygurs of northwestern China
2. The Mien of northern Thailand
3. The Afghan refugees in Pakistan
4. The people of Mongolia

AFM provides a way for any church to directly participate in missions, by sending missionaries or by supporting missionaries through prayer and giving. Contact AFM for information about how your church youth group can be involved.

Adventist Frontier Missions
PO Box 346
Berrien Springs, MI 49103
Phone: 1-800-YES-4AFM or (616) 473-4250
FAX: (616) 473-4375

• Adventist View (now called View)

View magazine (formerly known as *Adventist View*) is a bimonthly Christian lifestyle magazine created by, for, and about <u>young adults</u> ages 18-35. Founded in 1992 by the <u>North American Division Youth Ministries</u> department, *View* provides readers with a forum for the discussion of issues, interests, needs, and experiences. Every issue's three major features (spiritual, life, and current events) are surrounded by thought-provoking editorials, columns, and letters. To keep abreast of young adult interests, there are news articles, service calls, and reviews of the latest music, books, resources and Web sites.

In early 1998, *CyberView* was launched to afford a cutting-edge venue to pro-actively target technology-savvy young adults, especially collegiates, not only in North America but around the world. In addition to the features of the print magazine, *CyberView* offers all the interactive advantages of the Internet.

View is more than just a magazine, it's a young adult ministry that includes young adult retreats and events, service trips, a video magazine called *VTV*, and monthly discussions on the *CyberView* online forum.

• Three Goals of View
1. Help readers know Jesus in a real and relevant manner.
2. Promote the experience of community in the church.
3. Foster and facilitate Christian service to the world community.

View
12501 Old Columbia Pike
Silver Spring, MD 20904
Phone: (301) 680-6315
FAX: (301) 680-6464
E-mail: gonzce@nad.adventist.org
http://cyberview.adventist.org.

Notes:
_____
_____
_____

Adventist View

Adventist Youth Society (AYS)

Understanding the strong connection between the community provided by a youth group and long-term church membership, early Seventh-day Adventist administrators and youth leaders sought to build an active society for the younger members of a local church.

In 1879, two young Adventists, Luther Warren and Henry Fenner, established a local Adventist society for boys in Hazelton, Michigan (girls were soon admitted!). Twelve years later, a 16-year-old young man in Wisconsin, Meade MacGuire, formed a similar society.

At Union College in Nebraska in 1893, church members established a Young People's Society of Christian Service. The goal of this new group was "to secure the increased spirituality of the young people, their enlistment in all missionary activity through existing channels of work, and their elevation to a higher plan of living and thinking."

About the same time, A. G. Daniels was forming a youth society in Adelaide, Australia, and Ellen White was appealing to the General Conference from Australia to organize the work for the young people of the church.

Ding the first decade of the 20th century, the Church responded. At a meeting in Mount Vernon, Ohio, July 10-20, 1907, the new Young People's Department of the General Conference choose the name, "Young People's Society of Missionary Volunteers," and the name was adopted at the General Conference Session of 1909. Soon "MV Societies" were springing up in churches all across the world.

The MV Society's Purpose
1. **Aim.** "The Advent message to all the world in this generation."
2. **Motto.** "The love of Christ constraineth us."
3. **Pledge.** "Loving the Lord Jesus, I promise to take an active part in the work of the Young People's Missionary Volunteer Society, doing what I can to help others and to finish the work of the gospel in all the world."

Through the years the MV Society expanded to include devotional, educational, outreach and fellowship activities. Among the most enduring of MV activities was the weekly MV meeting. Officers of the Society planned programs which emphasized Christian ideals, missions, church history, methods of service, cultural subjects and nature topics.

Adventist Youth Society

Today, we generally refer to these meetings as Adventist Youth Society meetings, or simply as AYS. In hundreds of churches in the North American Division and around the world, AYS meetings continue to be a strong and central part of the local youth ministry program.

- ### Four Secrets of AYS Planning
  1. **Start Planning Early.**
  2. **Advertise the Program.** Be creative. Capture your market's attention. Use posters, flyers and bulletin announcements as well as personal invitations.
  3. **Develop Creative Programming.** Use <u>drama</u>, outdoor trips, videos and films, Bible quizzes, guest speakers and panel discussions. Ask your pastor to answer questions. Have the various ministries of your church put on an informative program about their work. Exchange programs with an AYS team from another church. Let the youth talk about their issues.
  4. **Follow-up.** Especially after dealing with life issues.

- ### Four Common AYS Pitfalls
  1. **Waning Interest.** Identify the natural point when things are slowing down and do something special during those times.
  2. <u>**Burnout.**</u> Don't try to do everything on your own. You need a support staff.
  3. **Failing to Meet Goals.** Set both long- and short-term goals for your AYS ministry, and determine to meet those goals.
  4. **Lack of Communication.** Remember to talk to your pastor, your church board, and your friends in the congregation.

Remember, you are AYS leaders all week long, not just on <u>Sabbath</u>.

Notes on AYS Meetings:

_____
_____
_____
_____
_____
_____
_____
_____

Adventist Youth Society, continued

Adventist Youth to Youth *(vertical left margin)*

• Adventist Youth to Youth

Adventist Youth to Youth is a positive peer prevention program which uses local clubs led by youth with the support of adult advisors to reach other youth with a drug-free living message. The program is sponsored by the General Conference Health and Temperance Department.

Positive...

The program focuses on positive alternatives to handling problems so that the use of alcohol, tobacco, and other drugs is seen as unnecessary and undesirable. The program features personal support and encouragement of all participants. Positive interpersonal communication is taught.

Peer...

Youth are trained to take initiative to teach and encourage other youth in choosing to live drug-free.

Prevention...

The objective is to help youth make a personal commitment to abstaining from alcohol, tobacco, and other drugs, or to stop using them if they have begun experimental or casual use.

- ### • Five Adventist Youth to Youth Program Elements
  1. **A totally drug-free message.** Because using a mind-altering drug is always risky, there are no messages saying the "responsible use" or "moderate drinking" is all right.
  2. **Youth orientation.** This is youth speaking to other youth rather than adults speaking to youth. Youth are actively involved in leading the program activities.
  3. **Drug-free living is fun.** The youth leaders of this program show other children and youth that living free of drugs is more fun and profitable than depending on drugs.
  4. **Personal support.** Through small Family Groups where confidentiality, honesty, and positive interaction are the ground rules, youth feel acceptance and the freedom to learn how to be good friends with others and with God.
  5. **Honor, dignity, respect for self and others.** This philosophy is the ethical foundation of Youth to Youth. It gives value and honor to each person as a child of God. It builds in each person a deeper sense of self-respect and self-worth.

Why do we need Adventist Youth to Youth?

Worldwide surveys of Adventists, among both youth and adults, confirm that significant problems exist in understanding and practicing abstinence from alcohol, tobacco, and other drugs.

We live in an addictive age, as predicted by the apostle Paul (2 Timothy 3:1-5) and encouraged by characteristics of today's global village. Media promotion of illegal drugs is pervasive and persuasive, subtly influencing even non-drinking Christians to accept social drinking as harmless.

To counter these threats the Adventist church has begun the Upholding Abstinence Initiative. Among its objectives will be to educate every member on the abstinence beliefs of the church and the advantages of drug-free living; to involve every youth in making a personal commitment to abstinence as a lifestyle, and in sharing that lifestyle with their peers and younger children. The Adventist Youth to Youth program is a major strategy to achieve these objectives.

Research on prevention shows that strategies using the influence of peers for positive prevention have greater potential for success. They make the decision to stay drug free attractive to undecided youth and also provide positive role models for younger children.

- ### Six Keys to Success in Preventing Drug Use
    1. A **"drug-free"** message vs. a "responsible or social use" message is an absolute must.
    2. **Hold up young people** as responsible, capable, and positive role models.
    3. **Emphasize the positive** benefits of being drug-free rather than the negative effects of drug use.
    4. Always **involve youth** in planning, organizing, and performing the program.
    5. All activities must be specially **oriented towards teenagers.**
    6. **Offer quality training** for youth leadership development.

Adventist Youth to Youth
  Andrews University
  Berrien Springs, MI 49104-0211
  Phone: (616) 471-3558
  FAX: (616) 471-6611
  iadd@andrews.edu

• Adventists On-line

In 1994 the <u>General Conference</u> of <u>Seventh-day Adventists</u> established an on-line meeting place for computer users on CompuServe, and called it Adventists On-line.

If you have a computer, a modem, and a phone line, you can join the meeting place (known as the Adventist Forum) and keep in touch with other members. There is a monthly charge for access to the on-line service through CompuServe. There is an additional monthly fee for unlimited access to all discussion and library areas.

• 22 Discussion and Library Areas

1. Adventist News
2. <u>ADRA</u>
3. Adventist Review
4. Bible/Theology
5. Church Outreach
6. Education
7. <u>Ellen White</u>
8. General Info
9. Health/Medical
10. Mission
11. Pastoral Practices
12. <u>Prayer</u>/Announcements
13. SDA Periodicals
14. <u>Service</u> Openings
15. Singles Network
16. Spanish/Hispanic
17. <u>Teen</u> Talk
18. Town Hall
19. Women's Ministries
20. <u>Young Adults</u>
21. GC Administration
22. NAD Administration

Call 1-800-260-7171 to request your membership packet. Or visit the Adventist Forum web site at http://online.adventist.org.

AdventSource

Advent*Source* produces and distributes quality <u>resources</u> for <u>Seventh-day Adventist</u> ministry leaders. A complete supply of print, video, and material resources can be accessed simply by calling Advent*Source* at 1-800-328-0525.

- ## Free AdventSource Catalogues
  1. <u>Youth Ministries</u>
  2. Children's Ministries
  3. Family Life
  4. Community Services
  5. <u>Pathfinder Ministries</u>
  6. <u>Stewardship</u>
  7. <u>Sabbath School</u>
  8. Church Growth
  9. Women's Ministries

If you need fresh ideas for youth ministry, innovative <u>service</u> projects, <u>discussion</u>-starter videos, great retreat formats, information about "the coming revolution in youth ministry," interactive <u>Bible studies</u> for <u>SDA students in public school</u>, grace-oriented worships for home, school and church, a music ministry start-up kit, customized youth group <u>T-shirts</u>, and more … contact Advent*Source*.

Advent*Source* has all the current Adventist youth ministry authors *all under the same roof* - along with recommended youth resources from other Christian publishers.

The professional customer service representatives at Advent*Source* can also refer you to Adventist individuals or organizations who specialize in youth ministry.

Advent*Source*
  5004 Prescott Avenue
  Lincoln, Nebraska 68506
  1-800-328-0525; (402) 486-2519
  FAX: (402) 486-2572
  www.adventsource.org

AdventSource

• AIA

AIA (the Adventist Intercollegiate Association) is the official North American Division organization for representing the collective thoughts and opinions of student governments of the Seventh-day Adventist colleges and universities which are members of AIA.

AIA promotes, opens and coordinates channels of communication among the student governments of these institutions of higher learning. AIA assists member student governments in becoming more effective, beneficial and responsive to the social, scholastic, and spiritual needs of their respective students by facilitating and sharing ideas which relate to student government programs and projects.

The mission of the AIA is to be the voice of collegiate Christian leadership with a vision for fostering unity and service that impacts our communities.

• *The Vision of AIA*
1. To promote community service projects.
2. To provide opportunities for interacting and networking among Adventist students.
3. To promote fellowship and idea-sharing between Adventist youth.

AIA held its first convention in 1950 on the campus of Southern Missionary College (now Southern Adventist University). The convention has been held on an annual basis since then and each year seeks to provide a common bond among the student leaders of NAD institutions of higher education.

Notes:

_____

_____

_____

_____

_____

_____

AIA

• •

• **AIDS**

"I am going to be extremely blunt. This virus does not care how old you are, what color your skin is, your religion or how much money you have. If you do not protect yourself you can die." — Anonymous AIDS patient

Acquired Immune Deficiency Syndrome. AIDS. A subject that is difficult to talk about, especially to teens. And, especially Christian teens. According to the latest statistics available, AIDS is now the fifth leading cause of death among people aged 15 to 24. Nearly one fifth of all high school students have had four or more sex partners. Every year, the highest rate of STD cases reported occur between the ages of 15 to 24.

Everyone suffers the devastation of this illness – male and female, young and old, straight, bisexual and gay, rich and poor, and members of every religious, ethnic or cultural backgrounds. Unfortunately, teens get AIDS. Youth are recognized as one of the segments of the general population with the fastest increasing rate of HIV infection.

AIDS is a disease caused by the human immunodeficiency virus (HIV) that destroys the body's natural ability to fight illness. When this virus causes a breakdown in the body's immune system, it allows diseases such as rare cancers and pneumonias to develop. HIV is transmitted through exposure to blood, semen and vaginal secretions. As many as 1.5 million Americans are believed to be infected with HIV. Some of them have AIDS, but most have no symptoms at all, and many do not know they are infected.

No one actually dies of AIDS – it's usually one or more of the nearly 25 known AIDS-related illnesses that eventually causes death to occur. Currently, there is no known cure for AIDS. Today adolescents of both genders face a serious risk of HIV infection. When adolescents take certain risks, they are more likely to become infected.

• *These Are the Most Important Facts about AIDS:*

1   Adventist teens get AIDS.
2. AIDS is fatal.
3. You can get AIDS from use of even one contaminated needle or one sexual act with a partner who has HIV/AIDS.
4. Condoms can prevent AIDS.
5. Risk of AIDS is increased by:
    • An increased number of sexual partners.

AIDS

- Sharing needles for tattoos or intravenous drugs, such as heroin or cocaine (and even steroids).
- Any sex without condoms.
- Alcohol and other drug use (sex is more impulsive and use of condoms less likely if under the influence of alcohol or other drugs).
- Being born by a woman infected with the virus.
- Having a blood transfusion with infected blood.

Fortunately, HIV infection is preventable. Knowledge about HIV is an important aspect of prevention. Parents should educate their children and also work closely with schools, churches, youth organizations, and health care professionals to ensure that children and teens receive sex education and preventive drug abuse courses which include material on HIV.

If a young adult shows signs of drug abuse or premature sexual activity, these are reasons for immediate intervention. Evaluation by a professional psychiatrist can be an important first step in helping a family respond effectively to high risk behaviors of their children.

Remember that teens with AIDS need the same kind of concern you would offer anyone dealing with an illness. Feelings of isolation, fear, anger and anxiety are common. Many persons with AIDS, including teens, are discriminated against, subjected to ridicule and rejection and even suffer acts of physical violence. Be a good listener and a supportive ally. Continue to include them in social activities that you previously enjoy together.

Here are a few of the available resources which will help youth leaders in working with individuals directly affected by AIDS.

- **AIDS Resources**
  1. Department of Health Education at (908) 932-7710
  2. U.S. Public Health Service (800) 342-AIDS
  3. AIDS National Interfaith Network
     110 Maryland Ave., NE, Suite 504
     Washington, DC 20002 Phone: (202) 546-0807
  4. Dealing with an AIDS-related death:
     Churches, hospices, other health care organizations and community agencies often sponsor seminars and support groups for the bereaved.

AIDS, Continued

5. AIDS Memorial Quilt:
    The Names Project (Quilt)
    310 Townsend St. #310
    San Francisco, CA 94107
    (415) 863-5511

Resources about AIDS and HIV:
- *201 Things You Should Know About AIDS and Other Sexually Transmitted Diseases* by Jeffrey S. Nevid and Fern Goffried
- *AIDS and HIV-Related Diseases: An educational guide for professionals and the public* by Josh Powell and Amy Bourdeau
- *AIDS: Trading Fears for Facts* by Karen Hein and Theresa Foy DiGeronimo
- *The Essential AIDS Fact Book* by Paul Harding Douglas and Laura Pinsky
- *The HIV Drug Book* by Project Inform, Donald Abrams, editor
- *Living Proof: Courage in the Face of AIDS* by Carolyn Jones
- *Risky Times: How to Be AIDS-Smart and Stay Healthy* by Jeanne Blake, Beth Winship and Jerome Groupman
- *Ryan White: My Own Story* by Ryan White and Ann Marie Cunningham
- *What You Can Do to Avoid AIDS* by Earvin "Magic" Johnson

Notes About AIDS:

_____
_____
_____
_____
_____
_____
_____
_____
_____
_____
_____
_____
_____
_____
_____

AIDS, continued

Alcohol

Seventh-day Adventists consider maximum health to be one of the greatest blessings God has given His children here on earth. We also realize that one of our enemy's strongest endeavors is to destroy our wellness in as many ways as possible, turning happy, healthy, productive lives into bitter, disease-infested, wasted experiences.

One of the strongest agents for destruction of our well-being, our judgement and our values is alcohol. This drug is even more destructive because its use not only injures the individuals who use and abuse it, it also is the source of untold pain and heartache for the victims of alcohol-related accidents and violence.

In Canada, about 10% of the population suffers from alcoholism or drug addiction. In the U.S., about 10 million people under the age of 21 regularly use alcohol. Six and a half million American children under the age of 18 years live in households with at least one alcoholic parent. While purchase and public possession of alcohol by people under the age of 21 is illegal in all 50 U.S. states, approximately 2/3 of teens who drink report that they find ways to buy their own alcoholic beverages. The economic cost of alcoholism is more than $1 billion annually.

Mass media contributes to the impression that alcohol use is part of a sexy, successful life, and we are never more susceptible to the blatant messages of advertising or the subliminal messages of media than we are during our teen years. (56% of students in grades 5 to 12 say that alcohol advertising encourages them to drink.) Take the time with your youth group to explore media portrayals of alcohol use.

And, as in the discussions you have about tobacco and other standards issues, remember not to make this an issue of God's love. There is plenty of biblical evidence to prove that God loves the alcoholic. It is the result of alcohol use that brings pain to our Heavenly Father.

- Who Drinks?
  1. The ages 18-21 is the period of heaviest alcohol consumption.
  2. Sixty-four percent of high school seniors have used alcohol.
  3. First use of alcohol typically begins around the age of 13.
  4. Approximately 8% of eighth graders, 21% of tenth graders, and 33% of twelfth graders report they have been drunk during the last month. 63% of high school seniors report that they have been drunk on at least one occasion.

Alcohol

5. Among teenagers who binge drink, 39% say they drink alone, 58% drink when they are upset, 30% drink when they are bored, and 37% drink just to feel high.

What are the Health Risks?

1. Alcohol and other drug use at an early age is an indicator of future drug or alcohol problems.
2. Use of alcohol and other drugs is associated with the leading causes of death and injury among teenagers and young adults (motor-vehicle crashes, homicides, and suicides).
3. Alcohol contributes to 100,000 deaths annually, making it the third leading cause of preventable mortality in the U.S. after tobacco and diet/activity patterns.
4. Even moderate consumption of alcohol is associated with stroke, cancer, birth defects, harmful interactions with medications, heart disease, and psychological problems.
5. Heavy and chronic drinking can harm virtually every organ and system in the body, is the single most important cause of illness and death from liver disease, depresses the immune system, results in a predisposition to infectious diseases, can lead to inadequate functioning of the testes and ovaries, resulting in hormonal deficiencies, sexual dysfunction and infertility, is related to a higher frequency of menstrual irregularities.
6. Each year between 4,000 and 12,000 babies are born with the physical signs and intellectual disabilities associated with Fetal Alcohol Syndrome.
7. Alcoholics are 16 times more likely than others to die in falls, and 10 times more likely to become fire or burn victims.
8. Estimates suggest that alcohol is associated with as much as 65% of adult drownings.
9. Up to 40% of industrial fatalities can be linked to alcohol.
10. Nearly one-fourth of all persons admitted to general hospitals have alcohol problems or are undiagnosed alcoholics being treated for the consequences of their drinking.

Drinking and Driving

1. At the current rate of accidents, two out every five people in America will be involved in an alcohol-related crash at some time in their lives.

Alcohol, continued

Alcohol, continued

2. About 45% of the more than 40,000 total annual traffic fatalities in the U.S. are alcohol-related.
3. Drivers under the age of 25 are more likely than those 25 or older to be intoxicated in a fatal crash.
4. Alcoholics are nearly five times more likely than others to die in motor vehicle crashes.
5. It is estimated that someone is injured in an alcohol-related driving accident EVERY 33 SECONDS.

- *Drinking and Violence*
  1. Almost half of college students who are victims of campus crimes said they were drinking or using other drugs when they were victimized.
  2. Researchers estimate that alcohol use is implicated in one- to two-thirds of sexual assault and acquaintance or "date rape" cases among teens and college students.
  3. One survey of high school students found that 18% of females and 39% of males say it is acceptable for a boy to force sex if the girl is stoned or drunk.
  4. More than half of domestic violence cases in the U.S. involve alcohol.
  5. Alcohol is typically found in the offender, victim or both in about half of all homicides and serious assaults, as well as in a high percentage of robberies.

- *Three More Reasons Not to Drink*
  1. A clear relationship exists between alcohol use and grade-point average among college students: students with GPAs of D or F drink three times as much as those who earn As.
  2. Fetal alcohol syndrome (FAS), which can occur when women drink during pregnancy, is the leading known environmental cause of mental retardation in the Western World.
  3. Separated and divorced men and women are three times as likely as married men and women to say they had been married to an alcoholic or problem drinker.

Sources: Centers for Disease Control; Mothers Against Drunk Driving; National Center for Health Statistics; National Clearinghouse for Alcohol and Drug Information; National Council on Alcoholism and Drug Dependence; National Institute on Alcohol Abuse and Alcoholism; The Renascent Centres, Toronto, Canada; U.S. Department of Health and Human Services; and USA Today.

• AMiCUS

The Adventist Ministry to College and University Students (AMiCUS) seeks to meet the spiritual, intellectual and social needs of <u>Seventh-day Adventist</u> students on secular campuses worldwide.

Since its establishment in 1988, AMiCUS has sought to provide interdepartmental coordination and support for this important sector of our membership. AMiCUS facilitates student retreats and fellowship opportunities, trains campus chaplains and ministers in university centers and supervises the publication of *Dialogue*, a network journal published in English, French, Portuguese and Spanish for free distribution among these students.

In North America, three departments and their directors cooperate in this ministry: Youth Ministries, Adventist Chaplaincy Ministries, and Education.

• *Five AMiCUS Strategies*

1. Strengthening the faith commitment of these students to Seventh-day Adventist beliefs and <u>values</u>.
2. Providing opportunities for Christian fellowship.
3. Preparing students to deal with the intellectual challenges that arise in a secular environment.
4. Developing leadership abilities.
5. Training for outreach and witnessing on the campus, in the community and in the world at large.

AMiCUS has published a source book on *Adventist Ministry on the Public University Campus* with ideas on how to start and carry out a successful campus program.

AMiCUS
    12501 Old Columbia Pike
    Silver Spring, MD 20904
    Phone: (800) 226-5478
    FAX: (301) 622-9627
    CServe: 104472.1154@CompuServe.com

☞ **Also see:** Campus Advent.

AMiCUS

• Art in Worship

There is very little that inspires hearts and touches souls as much as art. Whether it is basking in the inspiration of an artist's interpretation or actually taking part in creating art, art draws us closer to our Creator, the greatest Artist of all. Our worship needs to be filled with beauty and artistry. Each of us needs to encounter God holistically, not just with our heads and our words, but also with our hearts and emotions.

Accomplished, polished, professional artists can lead us, through the power and beauty of their medium, to a deeper understanding of God. But art is not for professionals alone. Every person is an artist. New artists also experience the joy of creating, of discovery, of taking risk. They learn more about themselves and more about God.

• Seven Ways to Incorporate the Arts in Worship

1. **Still life and Props**. Use a big, wooden cross, mannequins, posters, banners – anything that illustrates the theme.
2. Music. Explore a wide variety of musical styles.
3. **Signing**. Find someone who is skilled at sign language and ask them to interpret the music and scripture reading.
4. **Creative Dramatics**. Skits, plays, reader's theater. (See: Drama.)
5. **Drawing**. A pastor relates this experience: "I watched a girl draw the face of Jesus on a huge piece of white paper during the time of praise singing. We were part of the creation."
6. **Collages**. Choose a theme (this probably works best for Sabbath School). Ask a simple question: "What is your picture of God?" "What is grace?" Hand out construction paper, scissors, glue and lots of old magazines. Each person cuts out pictures they feel fit the theme and pastes their collection on paper. Display the collages. Talk about the messages.
7. **Dance**. If it would be appropriate for your church family, invite a Jewish youth group to come and demonstrate Davidic (Old Testament) dance. The expressive, worshipful dances are done in a circle, forming a sense of unity and community.

• More Great Discussion About Art in Worship:
✔ Dennis Benson, *Creative Worship in Youth Ministry* (Loveland, CO: Group, 1985).
✔ Gloria Durka and Joanmarie Smith (eds.), *Aesthetic Dimensions of Religious Education* (New York, NY: Paulist Press, 1979).
✔ Judith Rock and Norman Mealy, *Performer as Priest and Prophet: Restoring the Intuitive in Worship Through Music and Dance* (San Francisco, CA: Harper and Row, 1988).
✔ Janet Walton, *Art and Worship: A Vital Connection* (Wilmington, DL: Michael Glazier, 1988).

Art in Worship

• At-Risk Behaviors

Contemporary youth are a <u>generation</u> at risk due in part to rapidly changing social conditions which threaten the quality of families, congregations, and schools. High percentages of North American Division youth are involved with choices that seriously compromise their health and well-being and that endanger their ability to lead productive adult lives. (See: "A Generation At Risk," in *Valuegenesis: Faith in the Balance,* pages 254-268.)

Ten such "at-risk" behaviors have been identified by civic and social organizations who study teens. They are listed below.

- ## Ten At-Risk Behaviors
    1. <u>Alcohol</u> use
    2. Binge drinking
    3. Marijuana use
    4. Cocaine use
    5. <u>Depression</u>
    6. Attempted <u>suicide</u>
    7. Shoplifting
    8. Getting into trouble at school
    9. School <u>violence</u>
    10. Sexual promiscuity

- ## Fifteen Actions to Take for At-Risk Teens
    1. Begin one-to-one counselling sessions with problem youth.
    2. Establish an ongoing recovery team of adults who are trained to counsel, approach, and intervene with youth. Make them available on a round-the-clock basis. (Also see: <u>Counselling</u>.)
    3. Develop a "reading rack" of materials for youth, designed to discuss at-risk behavior, and place it each <u>Sabbath</u> in the youth room.
    4. Begin meetings with parents to teach them how to identify at-risk behavior and provide reading material to assist them in coping with these problems.
    5. Schedule regular educational in-service programs for the youth of the church which explore <u>sexuality issues</u>, drug use and intervention.

At-risk Behaviors, continued

6. Develop an <u>Adventist Youth To Youth</u> program in your school.
7. Invite youth to experience Christian education. Research shows this "protection" is both helpful and useful.
8. Invite people involved in abortion clinics and planned parenthood programs, police officers and drug counselors to participate in a series of programs aimed at at-risk behavior problems.
9. Establish a protocol regarding how to approach someone who is having at-risk problems (i.e., if the problem is an <u>eating disorder</u>, identify people in the congregation who have had victory over similar problems).
10. Set up a phone conference with Paul Cannon of <u>the Bridge</u>. Have Paul interview some of his youth with you by speaker phone during one of your meetings. Phone: (502) 777-1094; FAX: (502) 777-1062.
11. Contrast scenes from major <u>movies</u> which show the glamour of drug and alcohol use with some media that shows the opposite. Discuss feelings, attitudes and results of at-risk behavior.
12. Discuss the role of advertising in at-risk behaviors.
13. Take *Time*, *Newsweek* or any other news magazine and select an article about at-risk behavior and youth. Talk about the "pathways" people take to end up in the state described in the articles.
14. Discuss the motivations to stop at-risk behaviors (i.e., fear, love, punishment, etc.). Ask, "What would it take to get you to stop doing something that was hurting you?"
15. Acquaint two youth with a counselor who knows other young people who have attempted suicide. See if you can go with them to interview one or more of these individuals. Use your video camera, if possible, and then report what you discovered about motivations, reasons and changes.

☞ **Also see**: Alcohol; Codependency; Tobacco.

Notes:

_____
_____
_____
_____

• Attachment

During <u>adolescence</u>, young people naturally begin to establish their own identity. They *distance* themselves from their relationship with their parents and other authority figures, while still needing their love and support. And they *attach* themselves to people and things outside of their own families, by creating meaningful relationships with others, particularly their peers.

In a <u>community</u> of faith, youth between the ages of thirteen and nineteen often experience this attachment transition by questioning and critically challenging their childhood faith. This questioning usually includes views of God, the Bible, their church doctrines, their parent's faith, <u>standards</u>, etc. Unfortunately, in response to this necessary process of distancing or detachment (see: <u>Faith Development</u>), parents and adults in the church often become defensive and critical of the adolescent. Such a response offers many adolescents a ready excuse to become detached from the church altogether.

<u>Youth ministry</u> seeks to provide a climate in which the process of <u>faith maturity</u> can take place, an atmosphere in which young people feel safe to ask questions, and a relationship which models and encourages their *attachment* to a meaningful, personal faith. Current studies in "attachment behavior" (often referred to popularly as "bonding") suggest that the church can function like a spiritual parent. Church <u>youth leaders</u>, in particular, can nurture and care for young people through the time of these normal and to-be-expected struggles.

• *Five Characteristics of Attachment*
1. The attached person (the adolescent) seeks proximity (closeness) to the caregiver (the church).
2. The spiritual caregiver provides nurture and protection (a haven of safety in which the adolescent comfortably can explore his or her faith).
3. The caregiver provides a sense of security (a secure base — always there, always accepting).
4. The idea of separation (from the church) causes anxiety in the attached person.
5. Loss of the attachment figure (the caregiver) would cause grief in the attached person (the young person).

Attachment

- ## Seven Ways to Keep Your Youth Attached
  1. Take time to be with them.
  2. Ask them questions about their homes, jobs and lives.
  3. Involve them in church life and leadership.
  4. Don't express disapproval of their exterior expressions of detachment (even if you can't stand them!), especially their choices of clothes, hairstyles, jewelry and music.
  5. Look for the good in them.
  6. Keep on hugging them and patting them on the back.
  7. Attend their performances. Applaud their involvement.

- **More Great Discussion About Attachment:**
  - ✔ Roger Dudley and Janet Leigh Kangas, *The World of the Adventist Teenager* (Washington, DC: Review and Herald, 1990).
  - ✔ Roger Dudley and H. Phillip Muthersbaugh, "Social Attachment to the Seventh-day Adventist Church among Young Adults," in *Review of Religious Research*, Vol. 38, No. 1, September, 1996, 38-49.
  - ✔ David Lynn, "Research Briefs," in *Youthworker* (Fall, 1993), pages 111, 112.
  - ✔ Duffy Robbins, *The Ministry of Nurture* (Grand Rapids, MI: Zondervan, 1990).
  - ✔ Denny Rydberg, *Building Community in Youth Groups* (Loveland, CO: Group Books, 1985).
  - ✔ Bradley J. Strahan, *Parent, Adolescents and Religion* (Cooranbong, New South Wales: Avondale Academic Press, 1994).
  - ✔ Merton P. Strommen, *Five Cries of Youth, New and Revised Edition* (San Francisco, CA: Harper & Row, 1988).

☞ Also see : Climate Issues; Distancing; Teens.

Notes on Attachment:

_____

_____

_____

_____

_____

_____

_____

_____

_____

_____

_____

_____

_____

_____

_____

_____

Attachment, continued

• Attendance

It's difficult to predict when <u>teens</u> will show up to a meeting you've planned, or if they'll show up at all! The big attendance question is always, "Where are my friends going?". Other programs impact your attendance: Does another church have a more interesting meeting planned? Is the academy choir or band on a trip? Did someone host a late meeting last night? Is it one of those mornings just to sleep in?

Fortunately, however, there are things you can do to build attendance, and to take a little of the mystery out of the situation.

• Seven Attendance Builders

1. **A Membership List.** Who's part of your <u>youth group</u>? Start with the kids who attend every meeting. Ask them who should be added to the list. Don't forget kids who are away (boarding academy students, students who live part of the time with family in another town). Include phone numbers.

2. **Personal Invitations.** Let your kids know you want them at your meetings. Ask them to attend. Invite kids to invite other kids.

3. **Fun Events.** Plan events that the kids will really enjoy; <u>pizza</u> feeds, game nights, one-day <u>service</u> projects, etc. The more you build your youth <u>community</u>, the easier the attendance challenges become.

4. **Warm Greetings.** When the kids arrive, be sure to greet them warmly. They've accepted your invitation (as opposed to being made to show up). Show how delighted you are to see them.

5. **Early Bonuses.** If your attendance problem is tardiness, begin to build some early bonuses into your program. For example, serve hot chocolate and donuts fifteen minutes before your <u>Sabbath School</u> begins. Or plan a bring-your-favorite-song time before the program. Play the songs and find out why each song is a favorite.

6. **Deeper <u>Involvement</u>.** Poor attendance sometimes indicates you're doing too much of the work yourself. Involve the kids in all aspects of the programing. Let the ministry become theirs, not just yours.

7. **Follow Up.** After a program write short notes to the kids who attended telling them how thankful you are for them and for their interest. Keep the notes short and to the point. Hopefully you'll have lots of notes to write!

• AVANCE

The incredible growth of the Latino <u>Seventh-day Adventist</u> church in North America (estimated at 128% in the last decade) presents many challenges and opportunities, especially to <u>youth leaders</u>. In order to provide a fuller and more accurate understanding of the Latino family, a national study called AVANCE (meaning advance) was conducted and completed in 1994. This study was a follow up to the *<u>Valuegenesis</u>* study conducted by the North American Division.

Sponsored by the NAD and most of our Universities and Colleges, the AVANCE study represents the largest national survey among Latinos within a denomination ever undertaken. A total of 77 churches representing all of the Unions in the Division participated in the study, resulting in a total of 3, 306 respondents. The study was planned and conducted by a group of eight Latino Adventist scholars and is based at Andrews University.

The purpose of the survey was to assess the religious, educational, family and cultural life of Latino youth.

- • *Three Areas of AVANCE Assessment:*
  1. **Issues of religious experience** involve a level of <u>faith maturity</u>, understanding of <u>grace</u>, devotional life, church loyalty, orthodoxy, church climate, pastoral relationships.
  2. **Issues surrounding family life** involve family togetherness, understanding, modeling, discipline, <u>family worship</u>, authoritarianism, and family limits.
  3. **Issues related to culture** involve cultural identity, level of acculturation, language speaking ability, and generational differences. The value and impact of Christian education is evaluated and contrasted to public education.

- • *Major AVANCE Findings:*
  1. Latinos have a strong commitment to the Seventh-day Adventist church and it's teachings. This commitment is exemplified in high levels of church participation and loyalty. At the same time, there is need for greater understanding of God's unconditional love and grace.
  2. The Latino family exhibits high levels of unity and understand-

AVANCE

ing, while at the same time experiencing the vicissitudes that comes from a majority living in poverty.

3. There is also a high degree of interest in pursuing <u>Adventist education</u> as a family and individual goal. Yet the majority of youth attend public schools and universities.

4. While expressing a high degree of interest in attending an <u>Adventist College or University</u>, the majority of Latino youth are unaware and unacquainted Adventist educational institutions of higher education in their own Unions.

5. The acculturation process among both adults and youth has a negative effect on their religious experience, family life and <u>at-risk behaviors</u>. Thus, the higher acculturated individuals are at risk of increased secularization and resultant apathy toward religious belief and values.

6. Churches that have bilingual programming, warm climate, grace-filled ministry, active social life, and caring pastors are the ones who are more likely to be effective in ministering to the second and third generation.

These and many other interesting findings will be published in various publications designed to disseminate the <u>research</u> results. Among them are a series of eight bilingual newsletters to be distributed among Latino church members and non-Latino church leaders in the NAD.

For more information on the publications and ongoing research contact Dr. Edwin Hernandez at the number below.

Dr. Edwin I. Hernandez
   Vice President for Academic Affairs
   Antillean Adventist University
   Box 1188
   Mayaguez, PR 00681
   Phone: (787) 834-9595, ext. 2212

Notes:

_____

_____

_____

_____

_____

AVANCE, continued

• Baby Boomers

Baby Boom generation individuals ("Baby Boomers") were born from 1946 through 1964. The parents of your <u>youth group</u> members are most likely Boomers.

This generation (more than 78 million Americans), now adults, grew up during the Vietnam War, the Civil Rights Movement, the assassinations of John and Robert Kennedy and Martin Luther King, Jr., the Watergate affair, the introduction and establishment of television, computers and rock music and the first space missions to the moon and beyond. Whatever Boomers do turns into an epidemic, simply because of the enormity of this generation.

In society at large, such notables as Bill Clinton, Spike Lee, Steven Jobs, Bill Gates, Jane Pauley, Steven Spielberg, George Lucas, Woodward and Bernstein, Oprah Winfrey and Jay Leno are Boomers.

• Five Shaping Forces For Boomers

1. Enormous changes in technology
2. Unprecedented economic growth
3. Skepticism about large organizations (business, education, government, religion)
4. An overall level of education that is higher than any other generation, before or since
5. Great expectations from their parents and teachers

Despite delayed marriage and high divorce rates, nearly two-thirds are currently married. Boomers appear to be more worried and pessimistic about foreign relations. They are more likely than other adults to believe that anything labeled "natural" is better, to own personal computers, and to feel stress and tension at the end of the day.[1] Canadian studies indicate that, although Boomers don't smoke as much as other generations, they don't exercise enough and their cholesterol is too high.[2]

Virtually all Boomers (96 percent) were raised in a religious tradition, but usually dropped out of church as soon as they could. "Some boomers are now revising their religious practices as they settle into careers and raise families. Roughly one-third of those who dropped out have returned to religious activities... Baby boomers who are taking a new look at religion are likely to be in their 40s and to have school-aged children."[3]

Baby Boomers

- ## *What Adventist Boomers Want From Their Church*
  1. A church that is guided by <u>values</u>
  2. Supremacy of <u>spirituality</u>
  3. Leadership integrity
  4. Creativity
  5. Quality driven <u>programming</u>
  6. Shared vision
  7. Clear mission
  8. Simplicity in lifestyle
  9. Safe people with whom to share their struggles
  10. Effectiveness in addressing social needs and issues of justice
  11. <u>Technology</u> that makes ministry easier so that they can be serviced personally
  12. Effective <u>youth ministry</u> for their children

The majority of Adventist Boomers have left local churches over the past two decades. Experts on this generation observe that about 20 percent want nothing to do with the church ever again and 20 percent have stayed in the church for a variety of reasons. That leaves fully 60 percent of the 400,000+ who were educated in Adventist academies, colleges and universities who might still be interested in connecting with Adventist people again.

They attend alumni gatherings, camp meetings, special events and holiday church services. While there, they are fully aware of all the subtleties of acceptance or rejection. If they sense that things have changed since their last memory of the church, they are willing to give it another try. If they perceive exclusive and judgmental attitudes, they are gone from sight for months or years before they "check out" the church again.

For information, training or resources on creating an environment that attracts this important generation to church fellowship and leadership, see the listing in this book for the <u>Center for Creative Ministry</u>.

1   Patricia Braus, "The Baby Boom at Mid-Decade," in *American Demographics*, April, 1995.
2   Mario Toneguzzi, in the *Calgary Herald*, January 31, 1996.
3   Wade Clark Roof, "The Baby Boom's Search for God," in *American Demographics*, Dec. 1992.

Baby Boomers, continued

• Baptism

Baptism is a personal, Christian response to the <u>grace</u> of God. It has two meanings in our religious life: 1) baptism shows our public commitment to <u>Jesus</u> Christ; 2) for <u>Seventh-day Adventists</u>, baptism also includes joining a <u>community</u> of believers to accomplish a specific mission. With baptism comes church membership.

Baptism identifies <u>teens</u> with Jesus, their Lord. In fact, the baptized person so closely identifies with Jesus' death, burial, and resurrection, that there is, after the baptism, a unique union with God. Paul says,

". . . Don't you know that all of us who were baptized into Christ Jesus were baptized into his death? We were therefore buried with him through baptism into death in order that, just as Christ was raised from the dead through the glory of the Father, we too may live a new life." Romans 6:3,4.

A contemporary illustration of the mystical power of baptism is that of citizenship. When people become citizens of a country, they choose to become closely associated with their new country.

• *Three Crucial Understandings About Baptism*

1. **Don't baptize youth too early.** The average age of baptism is around 10.8 years in the Adventist church. If you can help youth wait until they are old enough to understand the symbolism of their personal act of commitment, the chances of their appreciating what they are doing is increased.

2. **Include more than <u>doctrines</u>** in your baptismal studies. While doctrines are important, they are only a part of the Christian experience. Focus on Jesus, His grace to us, the Holy Spirit's power to help, and their own personal understanding of what it means to "be" a Christian fully surrendered to God's will. Remember baptism includes identification with Jesus and church membership. Don't neglect relationship for information!

3. **Don't use manipulative techniques** to get decisions. God works in people's lives in the quiet of their souls and through the power of the influence of dynamic leaders, through personal crisis, and through the encouragement of friends. Public demonstrations of commitment which are rushed or emotionally based may only produce teens who regret the decision the next day. Growth in Christ often takes some time.

Baptism

• Baptismal Courses

As you look for study material to help lead your youth prepare for baptism, consider the following resources.

✔ *A Reason to Believe: What Being an Adventist is All About*
Chris Blake, Editor, (Hagerstown, MD: Review and Herald, 1993).
This study guide, heralded as the "first Seventh-day Adventist church-sponsored youth doctrinal/baptismal course anyone has seen for a long, long time," provides a unique approach for older teenagers as they explore the fundamental beliefs and practices of the Adventist church through story format, short activities and Bible study. The guide also contrasts Adventist beliefs with the beliefs of other world religions.

✔ *It's My Choice: Junior Baptismal Guide*
Steve Case, (Hagerstown, MD: Review and Herald, 1996).
This guide presents a balanced approach to Christian experience. It is an excellent guide for junior high students who want to begin to learn about Bible study and their church.

✔ *Walking on the Edge*
Stuart Tyner and V. Bailey Gillespie, (Lincoln, NE: AdventSource, 1996).
These interactive study guides for Adventist youth in public education aid in giving teens a clear view of who Adventists are and what Adventist believe. In addition, the 13 studies give useful information about the challenges Adventist youth face as they live Christian lives in their unique, secular environment. Adaptable for daily, personal devotions, for in-depth exploration of topics, and for small group study.

Additional Baptismal Studies:

_____

_____

_____

_____

_____

_____

_____

Baptismal Courses

• BAYDA

In the 1970s, the Caucus of Regional <u>Conference Youth Directors</u> took a bold step to accomplish together something that couldn't be done separately. The Caucus desired to meet the particular needs of <u>Seventh-day Adventist</u> African-American youth who had not been able to be a part of the large, division-wide conventions that were available for other Adventist youth. So the Caucus decided to hold a major youth gathering, sponsored by the Caucus, and invited black youth from across the North American Division.

The first United Youth Congress was held in Little Rock, Arkansas. It was such a success that the Caucus decided to hold another major youth event every five years. Since that first meeting other Youth Congresses have been held in Detroit, Atlanta, New Orleans, St. Louis and St. Petersburg. The Congresses are now held every four years and are attended by thousands of youth.

The Youth Congresses include seminars and workshops, parades, temperance oratorical contests, and a Bible Bowl competition (the National Bible Bowl is now an annual event, with two age categories, 16-22 and 23-35). The St. Louis event included an outreach visit to every high school and junior high in the St. Louis area, with a challenge to live a drug-free life.

In 1991, the Caucus changed its name to BAYDA, the Black Adventist Youth Directors Association. Members of BAYDA include the Youth Directors of all Regional Conferences in the NAD, the Chaplain of Oakwood College, and Youth Directors from Greater New York Conference and three conferences in the Pacific Union, Southeastern California, Southern California and Central California. BAYDA is the official sponsor of the <u>National Black Youth Resource Center</u> at Oakwood.

For more information about BAYDA contact Oakwood College at 1-800-824-5312.

Notes:

_____

_____

_____

_____

_____

_____

BAYDA

• Bible Classes at Adventist Academies

The curriculum material for <u>Seventh-day Adventist</u> Academy Bible classes (grades 9-12) is called *The Crossroads Series*. Students are required to take one Bible class each year they attend the Academy.

- *Freshman Year. Book One.*
  1. **God's Word and Your Life.** Focuses on the Bible.
  2. **God's Gifts: Creation and Salvation.** The Creation and the <u>Sabbath</u>, the sin problem and God's response to sin.
  3. **God and the Human Family.** The experiences of the families of Adam, Noah, and Abraham.
  4. **God, You and Your Family.** This unit explores God's love for all people and how following His guidance, with the help of the Holy Spirit, leads to better relationships.

- *Freshman Year. Book Two.*
  1. **Jesus and His World.** The four gospels, the land and the people of Christi's time. Especially the early life of <u>Jesus</u>.
  2. **Jesus and His Kingdom.** The early ministry of Jesus.
  3. **Jesus and His People.** The ministry of Jesus from the feeding of the five thousand up to the final week of His life.
  4. **Jesus and the Cross.** The final week of Jesus' life, including the crucifixion and resurrection and ascension.

- *Sophomore Year. Book One.*
  1. **Life and Times of Israel:** The <u>Gospel</u> in Story and Symbol. The history of God's people from the exodus through the period between the Old and New Testaments.
  2. **Christ and the Church:** The Gospel Lived and Shared. The New Testament church. The book of Acts is the major source of the content of this unit with support from the book of Galatians and also Corinthians and Thessalonians.

- *Sophomore Year. Book Two.*
  1. **Christianity as a World Religion:** The Gospel in Prosperity and Adversity. The history of the Church from 70 AD to the early 1800s. The final section explores the impact on the Christian

Church of revolution, revival, expansion, and other challenges amidst conflict.

2. **Adventism and the Second Coming**: The Gospel in Final and Full Proclamation. The Millerite movement as a source of Seventh-day Adventist heritage and history through the contemporary Seventh-day Adventist Church.

- *Junior and Senior Years. Basic Core Units.*

  1. **Daniel and Revelation.** A Christ-centered study which stresses Christ's presence in the practical life and in prophetic events leading to the Second Coming.
  2. **John.** A contextual study of the life of Christ with the purpose of helping students develop devotional attitudes and habits.
  3. **Doctrinal Studies.** A systematic study of the fundamental beliefs of the Seventh-day Adventist Church.
  4. **Marriage and Family.** A study of biblical principles of relationships and their application to marriage and family life.
  5. **Philosophy of Life** and **Contemporary Moral Issues.** The development of a biblical philosophy of life and personal lifestyle within the context of biblical principles and contemporary moral and ethical issues.

- *Junior and Senior Years. Supporting Units.*

  1. **Romans.** A study of Christ's substitutionary sacrifice that provides the basis for pardon, reconciliation and spiritual growth.
  2. **Hebrews and the Sanctuary.** A study of the symbols and services of the ancient sanctuary and their Christ-centered fulfillment in the book of Hebrews.
  3. **Contemporary Religions and World Views.** An introductory study of world views, contemporary denominations, religious movements and cults and world religions as viewed from a biblical perspective.
  4. **Friendship and Dating.** A study of Romans from a Christian perspective of self-understanding, and the dynamics of friendship and dating.
  5. **Meeting Life's Challenges.** This unit is designed to assist students in applying the principles and concepts from the other units of study in the Crossroads Series to the issues and challenges of everyday living.

(Curriculum as Revised 8/22/96)

Bible Classes, continued

• Bible Study

It is particularly humbling to think about the Bible as God's Word. The God of the universe, capable of thundering the eternal message throughout the heavens or painting a clear message of love on the clouds, chose instead to use a medium as human as the local newspaper to share His message of salvation and <u>grace</u> with you and me.

And it is just because God chose to use such a common expression of communication that the Bible has the potential to meet our very personal needs. It speaks to us right where we live.

• *Five Ways to Enrich Teen Bible Study*

1. **Show Respect!** The Bible is God's story. Teach teens that the Bible is not just any book. Talk about it being special.

2. **Read large sections!** When people tell a story, they want you to hear the whole thing. Take time to read larger portions, and take time to read the context. Watch the complete story unfold in a grand way. Then specific applications make sense.

3. **Be creative!** Try some of these methods with your group.
   a. **The Biographical Method.** Use your Bible to discover a particular person in Scripture. Research all the verses about that person and study his or her life and growth in faith.
   b. **The Devotional Method.** Pick a portion of your Bible to study, and prayerfully think about it until the Holy Spirit shows you a way to apply it to your life.
   c. **The Inductive Method.** Let the text be your guide. Try not to read anything into the text, and see what themes and questions naturally come to you in the text.
   d. **The Issue-Centered Approach.** This works particularly well with teens. Find a text or chapter of the Bible that deals with a specific issue (e.g.. Forgiveness – Ps 32; God's love – 1 John 4:9; Worship and praise – Heb 13:15, etc.).

4. **Start!** Nothing happens unless you begin. Encourage teens to start. It doesn't take long to hear God's message.

5. **Share!** Don't study all alone. Teens need relationships, models, and a chance to express themselves. (See: <u>Small Groups</u>)

- **More Great Advice on Bible Study:**
- ✔ V. Bailey Gillespie, *To Make Us Wise* (Boise, ID: Pacific Press Publishing Association, 1996).
- ✔ Brian Dudar, Associate Youth Director of the Carolina Conference, has created a practical, interactive product for studying Bible passages called *REDS* (Read, Examine, Discover, Share). Phone him at (704) 535-6720 for information about how you can utilize these guides.

Bible Study

• **Bible Versions**

The books of the Bible originally were written in Hebrew, Aramaic and Greek. The Old Testament was in place during the time of Jesus. But the New Testament canon, or official grouping of books, was debated until almost 400 AD. During the last 1,500 years, the Bible has been translated over and over again into local, common languages, making it available for people everywhere, not just for biblical scholars or clergy.

Jerome translated the Bible into Latin in the 4th century, much to the delight of the Christians living in the Roman Empire. John Wycliffe, whom we call "the morning star of the Reformation," was persecuted for translating the Bible into English a thousand years after Jerome (1380s). The Puritans produced a version known as the Geneva Bible in 1560. The King James Version, first published in 1611, is still a favorite among many English-speaking Christians (a fact which often causes tension between older church members who prefer the KJV and younger members who want a newer version).

Twentieth century *translations* include the Revised Standard Version (1946-1952), the New English Bible (1961-1970), the New International Version (1973-1978), and the New King James Version (1982). Popular *paraphrases* include The New Testament in Modern English by J. B. Phillips (1958, revised 1972), The Living Bible (1971) and The Message Bible (1993).

• *Three Reasons to Read a New Version of the Bible*
1. **To honor the spirit of the Reformers.** The great, inspired goal of the Bible translators of the Middle Ages was to bring the Bible to the people in the everyday language of the time, in order that we all might understand the Bible through the experiences of our lifetime.
2. **To keep from segregating the spiritual life.** When the source of our religious experience speaks to us in a language form that we never use in any other area of our lives, we subconsciously receive the message that the spiritual dimension belongs in one compartment of our life, and that the other dimensions have little to do with the spiritual.
3. **To allow the Holy Spirit's impressions.** Sometimes we're so familiar with a passage that we don't even think about its

Bible Versions

meaning. We need to take fresh, new looks at the Scriptures, allowing the Holy Spirit to impress us anew with the marvelous meaning in the passages we read.

- *Five Versions – Same Verse (2 Corinthians 2:14)*
    1. **King James Version**: "Now thanks be unto God which always causeth us to triumph in Christ, and maketh manifest the savor of his knowledge by us in every place."
    2. **New Jerusalem Version**: "Thanks be to God who always gives us in Christ a part in his triumphal procession, and through us is spreading everywhere the fragrance of the knowledge of himself."
    3. **New International Version**: "Thanks be to God, who always leads us in triumphal procession in Christ and through us spreads everywhere the fragrance of the knowledge of him."
    4. **Phillips**: "Thanks be to God who leads us, wherever we are, on Christ's triumphant way and makes our knowledge of him spread throughout the world like a lovely perfume!"
    5. **The Message Bible**: "In Christ, God leads us from place to place in one perpetual victory parade. Through us, he brings knowledge of Christ. Everywhere we go, people breathe in the exquisite fragrance."

- *Exploring Bible Versions*
    1. Ask your <u>youth group</u> to read a Bible passage in several different versions. Discuss the similarities and differences. How do the nuances of the different phrases help us better understand the passage? Do you think it's most helpful to stick to just one version or to explore several?
    2. Take a Bible passage that is built on observation or description (for example, Proverbs 15:17 or 24:3, 4). Discuss the meaning of the passage. Now ask each of your youth group members to paraphrase the passage, to write it again, but in their own words, making the meaning come to life in their own setting. Then ask each member to share his or her paraphrase. Discuss the different applications of the meaning. Explore why there are such different versions among your group of the same passage.

Bible Versions, continued

- ## Boredom

The most feared word in <u>youth ministry</u>! A foolproof test of whether or not your kids are involved, whether your <u>discussion</u> is relevant, or whether your methods are up-to-date and interesting.

- ### *Three Ways to Know if You're Boring:*
  1. The kids go to sleep while you're talking!
  2. You go to sleep while you're talking!
  3. The kids quit showing up whenever you're scheduled to talk!

- ### *Four Word Games to Play with Boredom*
  1. Acrostic:

Before	Because	B _____
Order	Only	O _____
Reigned	Rigid	R _____
Even	Educators	E _____
Dimwits	Dream	D _____
Offered	Of	O _____
Musings	Mousetraps	M _____

  2. Multiple Words from BOREDOM:
     or, ore, dome, red, rob, bed, ...

  3. Bible Characters from BOREDOM:
     Balaam, Othniel, Rehoboam, Ehud, Delilah, Obadiah, Micah

  4. Searching
     for
     BOREDOM:

     ```
     B B D F H M L N P R B
     M O D E R O B C D O E
     R R R A B D C D R S F
     G E H E K E Q E R O S
     Q D R S D R D D T U V
     B O R E D O M W X Y Z
     A M A C M B M D E F G
     ```

☞ **Also see:** Active Learning; Involvement; Learning Styles.

Boredom

• The Bridge

The Bridge is a private, nonprofit residential treatment center for young adults and adults suffering from compulsive and addictive disorders. Located in rural south-central Kentucky, the Bridge was originally founded in 1974 as a ministry of reconciliation for troubled young adults from conservative religious backgrounds. It has now evolved into one of the few extended-care facilities to provide in-depth treatment for chemical dependence and codependence simultaneously.

• Sixteen-day Workshop

The sixteen-day codependency workshop is for individuals who have grown up in painful family systems where addiction, abuse, or neglect have robbed them of the ability to love and care for themselves appropriately.

• Ninety-day Treatment Program

The extended (ninety-day) treatment program is for persons who are experiencing major life problems due to addictive and compulsive behaviors such as alcoholism, drug addiction, sexual compulsions, relationship addiction, workaholism, and eating disorders. Clients must be eighteen years of age or older and willing to take full responsibility for their recovery.

The staff of the Bridge is a multi-disciplinary team of skilled professionals composed of a program director, certified chemical dependency counselors, a chaplain, an outdoor education instructor, a life skills counselor, houseparents, and a consulting psychiatrist and physician. These professionals work cooperatively to develop and monitor an individualized treatment plan for each client.

For eligibility requirements, admission procedure, fees and services, sample daily schedule, and current program and workshop schedule, contact the Bridge at the following numbers.

The Bridge
   1745 Logsdon Road
   Bowling Green, KN 42101
   Phone: (502) 777-1094

The Bridge

• Budget

We're acquainted with a few Adventist churches that have the luxury of generous <u>youth ministry</u> budgets, including a couple of churches with larger budgets than some conference youth departments!

For most of us, however, the reality is just the opposite. If we've been allotted $300 a year - $25 a month - from the church budget, we're lucky. Usually, most of the money that *goes into* youth ministry *comes out* of the pockets of the <u>youth leader</u>. As much as your board agrees that youth ministry is important, it just seems there's never quite enough money for all the youth ministry you'd like to accomplish.

• *Three Principles of the Church Budget Process*

1. **Budgets Define Ministry.** Examine a local church's budget and you can find what the church considers to be ministry, and specifically how that ministry is defined. (One conference youth ministry budget with which we're familiar set aside $85,000 for the summer camp program and $1,500 for the rest of the activities of the youth director for the rest of the year. It's obvious how that conference defined youth ministry.)

   How does your church board define ministry? How much of that definition is about youth ministry? Talk to your pastor about his or her understanding of where work for the youth fits in to the mission and ministry of the church.

2. **Budgets Reveal Commitment.** Where there is a small youth ministry budget, one of three things usually has happened:

   a.) the church board has never stopped to consider its commitment to youth ministry;

   b.) the church board has had a bad experience with youth ministry and is hesitant about recommitting money; or,

   c.) the church board has become openly hostile to youth ministry and doesn't think it has a place in the church.

   Work individually with church board members. Explore their feelings about youth ministry. Talk to them about their own children. Share your vision for youth ministry in your church. Speak of youth ministry in evangelistic terms. Talk about meeting felt needs, baptisms, retention and long-term loyalty to the church. Don't approach the *board* until you have significant support from individual *board members*.

Budget

3. **Budgets Create Interest.** People who give money to a project naturally want to know of the success of that project. Church boards which designate a portion of the church's budget to youth ministry want to know how the program is going. This financial interest presents a wonderful opportunity for you to talk about youth ministry. Take time at every board meeting to list current activities, youth involvement and positive outcomes.

But don't be afraid to admit mistakes and discuss failures, as well. Don't allow money to become the driving force in your ministry! Learn from mistakes, even when they are costly in terms of the church's finances. But don't resign in despair if a project goes over-budget or doesn't return the benefits for which you were hoping.

Find out from your church administration how the church handles the budgeting process, when the proposed budgets are expected, how the proposed budgets will be presented, and who will make the ultimate decision on budget allocations. Keep your expectations low at first. It's reasonable for the church to want to see time and energy commitments on your part and to be able to point to success stories.

Keep careful records of your expenses. Establish a base line of spending per youth group member according to this year's membership. Then increase your budget requests for general operating expenses in proportion to the growth you experience.

- *Three Sources of Alternative Funding*
  1. **Involve your youth in <u>fund raising</u>.** Besides being excellent sources of income, events such as car washes, bake sales and bike-a-thons are great fun!
  2. **Solicit individual donations.** Invite five couples in your church who could each donate $100 a year to youth ministry to come to your house for a special dinner. Have your youth prepare and serve the meal and then make an appeal for dessert. (Okay, *after dessert* would be just fine.)
  3. **Search for youth-friendly local businesses.** Many local businesses make surplus supplies available to worthwhile endeavors (like youth ministry groups). Look for ways to get donated or discounted office supplies, food (from grocery stores and restaurants), tickets, and recreational equipment.

Budget, continued

• Building Your Youth Group

Think of <u>youth ministry</u> as building a house. As <u>youth leaders</u> we're really the general contractors of the project. We bring in experts to do the technical work, yet we're the jack-of-all-trades. We're ultimately responsible for the house.

Did we start with the right plan? Did we read the terrain right so the house doesn't fall in a big storm? Did we choose the right materials? Did we hire the right crew to do the job successfully? Did we discover what was important to those who will live in the house so that they'll want to stay?

• Five Items Needed to Build a Youth Group "House"

1. **Create the Blueprint.** You have to have a plan of attack. If you don't know where you're going you'll probably never get there. Create a personal plan of action. Select your goals. Establish a time limit. Include such goals as: "Within 3 months I'll identify five kids to make up the core of my <u>small group</u> ministry."

2. **Stay Organized.** Youth ministry doesn't follow a 9 to 5 schedule. It's either stay organized or waste a lot of time. Keep a log of what you do everyday and the hours each activity takes.

3. **Identify Leaders.** This can be vital. However, too often we rely on two or three kids to do all the work. Keep track of how many times you've asked Erica to sing, and Joe to organize the praise band, and Elisa to take care of the prayer time. Utilize everyone's talents. A <u>spiritual gifts</u>-based ministry lets everyone in on the action.

4. **Make Friends.** Set up "integrity friendships," to use the Willowcreek phrase. Consistency, accountability, trust, integrity – these are words that must describe your relationships.

5. **Be Consistent with Your Meetings.** The teens should know that at whatever day and time you invite them to a meeting, you *will* show up and have something of quality prepared for them. You can't build a consistent attendance if the kids can't count on you.

☞ **Also see:** Attendance; Climate Issues; Community; Youth Group; Youth Ministry Philosophy.

Building Your Youth Group

• •

• **Burnout**

You're the person who gives 110%! You play your <u>guitar</u> for every song service. You teach the Sabbath School <u>lesson study</u>. You direct the <u>drama</u> team. You open your house for Saturday night parties. You drive the van on outings. You're a friend, a counsellor, a pastor, a cook, and a maintenance person. You plan meetings, arrange dates, buy supplies and pick up kids who can't yet drive.

And, oh-by-the-way, you have a *real* job, a spouse, and a family!

AND YOU'VE ABOUT HAD IT! You don't think you can keep up the pace. And even if you could, you're not sure the kids even notice what you do, much less appreciate it. Besides, every time you plan an activity that really seems to work with the kids, somebody in the church complains to the pastor that you're leading the youth in the wrong direction. Maybe you ought to just quit and let someone else take over.

You're experiencing a classic case of <u>youth ministry</u> burnout!

• *Five Ways to Prevent Burnout*

1. **Build a** <u>Master Calendar</u>. Keep your youth activities reasonable. Don't overschedule. Reserve days every week for *family* activities, and refuse to schedule anything else on those days.

2. **Involve Your Youth.** Don't do all the work yourself! <u>Involvement</u> of the youth is one of the key foundations of successful youth ministry. Let your youth become part of the planning and the preparing, as well as the presenting of all your programs.

3. **Recruit** <u>Volunteers</u>. Search for volunteers among the parents of your kids, young married couples, new, enthusiastic Adventists, and alumni of your youth group. The more you can share the responsibility, the less likely you'll feel overwhelmed.

4. **Learn to Say No.** You are a wonderful youth worker and you accomplish more than most. But you aren't Superman or Superwoman. You can't do it all. So figure out your priorities, do as much as you can, and learn to politely and firmly say no to everything else.

5. **Save Family Time.** Don't put youth ministry above your family.

☞   **Also see:** Criticism.

•   **More Great Advice on Burnout:**
✔   Dean Feldmeyer, *Beating Burnout in Youth Ministry* (Loveland, CO: Group, 1989).

Burnout

- ## Campus Advent

Campus Advent, organized in March, 1991, is the association of <u>Seventh-day Adventist</u> campus ministries on public and private colleges and universities in the North American Division (not owned by the Seventh-day Adventist Church).

- ### Eight Reasons Why Campus Advent Exists
  1. To support existing Adventist ministries on college and university campuses.
  2. To network existing ministries together through a national association.
  3. To encourage the development of campus ministries where there is no Adventist presence.
  4. To encourage the involvement in this ministry of:
     a. Adventist students
     b. Adventist professors and staff
     c. Campus ministry workers
     d. Local Adventist lay leaders and pastors
  5. To recruit and train staff to serve in campus ministry positions.
     a. Student taskforce workers
     b. Chaplaincy training
     c. Lay church leadership involvement
  6. To organize annual association retreats for planning, fellowship and training.
  7. To publish a <u>newsletter</u> of campus ministry news and information.
  8. To educate the church at large about the needs of Adventist students and the potential of Adventist ministry on non-Adventist college and university campuses.

☞ **Also see:** AMiCUS; *Dialogue*; SDA Students in Public School.

Notes:

_____

_____

_____

_____

Campus Advent

Center for Creative Ministry

The Center for Creative Ministry supports leaders of congregations, church planting projects and other ministries in their outreach and nurture through information, resources, training and consultant relationships.

Formerly known as the Baby Boomer Ministries Resource Center (since 1988), the Center has broadened its generational/ministry focus to include children. The Center is a privately funded and managed parachurch ministry fully recognized by the Seventh-day Adventist Church in North America.

- **Four Training Experiences**
    1. **Satellite Training.** Available at locations with satellite downlink equipment.
    2. **Live Events.** The Center lists training event sites and dates.
    3. **Teleconference Training.** You can become part of a training event via teleconference technology.
    4. **Speaker's Bureau.** If you are planning an event, the Center can deliver qualified and highly recommended presenters.

- **Four Consulting Services**
    1. **Phone Contact.** Available by appointment, Senior Consultants will give encouragement and insights for your situation.
    2. **Accreditation Team.** The Center sends a team of specialists to your setting to evaluate your situation and suggest new directions, identify problem areas and provide written and verbal reports.
    3. **External Board.** Research-based information, strategic planning and encouragement, especially for church-planting situations.
    4. **Applied Research.** Specialized research reports, or application of general research to your situation.

Center for Creative Ministry
Phone: (800) 272-4664 or (402) 420-7710
FAX: (402) 437-9502
CServe: 74617.2600@CompuServe.com
www.creativeministry.org

Center for Creative Ministry

• Center for Youth Evangelism (CYE)

The CYE is located at the SDA Theological Seminary at Andrews University, Berrien Springs, Michigan. In operation since 1977, and formerly known as the Youth Resource Center, the CYE's mission is "to develop and provide the methods, resources, and leadership necessary to train young people in effective youth-to-youth evangelism." An active participant in the North American Division's YouthNet initiatives, the CYE is one of three NAD resource centers devoted to the study and application of youth ministry.

The CYE mission influences everything the Center is involved with, whether it be research projects, training events, or youth ministry resource development

• Current CYE Ministries
1. Giraffe Society - a pro-active youth leader's society
2. Giraffe News - a youth leader's "How To" publication
3. Giraffe University - a training event for youth leaders
4. Youth Summit - for high school students
5. YouthNet eXtreme Rig - a national travelling ministry
6. NAD International Pathfinder Camporee - "Discover the Power," Aug 10-14, 1999, Oshkosh, WI
7. Young Pioneer Training - (See: YouthNet)
8. Academic Youth Ministry Studies - For MA or D.Min. degrees
9. Resource Development - for youth leaders and parents

The Center for Youth Evangelism invites you to use their 800 number if you need any help with youth ministry. The hours are Monday through Thursday from 8:30 am to 5 pm, and Friday from 8:30 to noon, eastern standard time.

Center for Youth Evangelism
8903 US 31
Berrien Springs, MI 49103-0904
Phone: (616) 471-9881 or 1-800-Youth-2-U
FAX: (616) 471-9883
e-mail: cye@andrews.edu
http://www.andrews.edu/CYE

Center for Youth Evangelism

• Church

A discussion with youth about *church* could focus on people in every country of the world, in every faith and in every denomination who respond to the winning whispers of God's grace and choose to become members of "the body of Christ," (1 Corinthians 12:27).

Or the discussion could center on *Church* (with a capital C), a denomination, an institution, an organization with a system-wide structure, an established creed or set of doctrines, a voted mission statement, and a group of employees dedicated to fulfilling that mission.

Or the discussion could be about *the local church* in which we hold membership and where we usually attend on Sabbath.

But, most likely, a discussion with teens about *church* will be about *the worship service*, the "eleven o'clock hour," the time when we sing, pray, take up an offering and listen to a pastor preach a sermon.

Here are ten dynamics that youth say will transform church from "boring" into an exciting, positive influence in their lives.

• *Ten Ways to Transform Your Church Service*

1. **Energy.** The rhythm of the service is up. It makes us feel like the congregation really believes.
2. **Informality.** We know the people there, and they know us. We're not trying to impress each other. We're comfortable, not uptight.
3. **Creativity.** We hear familiar stories from the Bible, but with a new insight. We're not stuck in the ruts of routine. We vary the order.
4. **Practicality.** We want an application to real life. How will this relate to me this week?
5. **Challenge.** We don't want pat answers and cliches. We want to think about this, find the principles, be challenged.
6. **Relevancy.** Sometimes the illustrations have to come from our world, not just the world of older adults. Speak to our needs, too.
7. **Sincerity.** The pulpit shouldn't become political. We don't mind sincere emotion. We want the message to come from the heart.
8. **Contemporary.** Please listen to the beautiful music that's been written in our lifetime. Speak in language we understand.
9. **Uplifting.** We definitely want to leave church with hope and peace and a closer walk with God.
10. **Variety.** Sometimes you'll find us holding a worship service outside, or with a small group of our friends. We love variety.

Church

Climate Issues

Valuegenesis asked the youth of the <u>Seventh-day Adventist</u> Church to think about the local <u>church</u> they attended and respond to fifteen statements about that church. From these responses, a list of issues emerged which indicated how a faith <u>community</u> (a home, a church or a school) can effectively minister to its youth.

One group of those issues is called "climate issues," and they represent an area which are "crucial to explore," and "desperately needed in local congregations." (See: Roger Dudley and V. Bailey Gillespie, *Valuegenesis: Faith In the Balance* [La Sierra University Press, 1992],185.)

In the church there are four climate issues: warmth, <u>acceptance</u>, <u>involvement</u>, and the encouragement of thinking.

• Four Church Climate Issues

1. **Warmth**. Is your church friendly? Does it feel "warm" to the youth? Do your youth feel at home in the church? Are they well known by the adults in the church? As they grow older, do your youth feel more or less warmth? Do strangers feel welcome in your church?

2. **Acceptance**. Do your youth feel they can be themselves at church? Or do they have to conform to other people's norms? Do your youth look forward to going to church? Do they go to church because they want to go or because they are forced?

3. **Involvement.** Do your youth take part in the planning, the preparing and the presenting of the Sabbath School program? Are your lesson studies characterized by lecture or discussion? Do your youth have a part in the worship services? Are they active in other church activities?

4. **Thinking**. Would your youth say they learn a lot at Sabbath School and church? Are they being challenged to think, to ask questions and to find the reasons for their faith? Would they say that their church expects people to learn and to think?

• Sixteen Ways to Warm Up Your Church

1. Ask a team of youth to greet people at the door of the church.
2. Create a banner to welcome a family to church on <u>Sabbath</u>. Change the name of the family each week.
3. Remember birthdays.

4. Call people by their first name.
5. Arrange for several members of your youth group to drive elderly members to Sabbath School.
6. Take pictures of church social activities and create a "We're Having Fun" bulletin board in the lobby of the church.
7. Video the arrival of church members at church. Play the video on a monitor in the church lobby next week.
8. Interview church members and use the information to write a story for your church <u>newsletter</u>.
9. One week have all the youth attend Sabbath School in the Kindergarten Division, helping out in the music, the stories and the <u>lesson study</u>.
10. Buy boutonnieres for every man in your church over 50. Have the youth present the flowers when people arrive for church.
11. Get your youth together one evening during the week and bake dozens of cookies, then package the cookies in plastic bags, six to a bag (choose a variety of cookies for each bag). Have the youth present the cookies to families as they're leaving church.
12. Persuade a number of older members to host a Sabbath evening get together in one of their homes. You bring the refreshments, but ask the members to tell the kids stories of when they were growing up or when they were teens.
13. Photograph families in your church in candid poses. Then scan the photos and, using a program like PhotoShop, turn the photos into line drawings. Print copies of the drawings on newsprint, creating a church coloring book for the church's children.
14. One Sabbath a month during the worship service, recognize a church family that has had a positive influence on someone in the church. Praise God for the family's impact and present them with flowers.
15. Have your youth write short letters of encouragement or appreciation to a member of your youth group.
16. We sometimes use the phrase, "I love you this much," accompanied by widely spread arms. Help Kindergarten kids in your church make a poster that says, "We love <u>Jesus</u> this much." Use a roll of butcher paper and have each kid lay down on the paper with arms open wide, touching the fingers of the next person. Outline each child with a colored marker, then help the kids color clothes and hair, and make eyes and big smiles.

Climate Issues, continued

• Clip-Art

If you're really fortunate, you have one or more great young artists in your <u>youth group</u>, kids who can take an idea and illustrate it to capture everyone's attention. These future art majors make your life a lot easier whenever you need to communicate.

• Seven Ways to Utilize Art Work
1. To create a "corporate image" for your youth group, including logo, letterheads, envelopes and business cards.
2. To add to post cards, thank-you notes, birthday cards and seasonal greeting cards.
3. To use in brochures, bulletins and printed programs.
4. To illustrate your <u>newsletter</u>.
5. To advertise an upcoming event through posters, invitations and announcements.
6. To create tickets for programs.
7. To incorporate into the design of your <u>T-shirts</u>.

But if you *don't* have an artist in your group it doesn't mean that all your publications have to be dry and boring. Clip-art comes to the rescue!

Clip-art is already-created art work (both illustrations and type) that you cut and paste (either electronically or manually) to give your publication that professional look you're hoping for. You'll find youth ministry clip-art available in a wide variety of art styles (from cartoons to fine art) on CD-ROMs, computer programs, and in dozens of clip-art books.

When you use clip-art books, most clip-art veterans recommend photocopying the art work you select (instead of cutting it out of the book), reducing or enlarging it to fit your layout, then cutting the art piece out, leaving a margin of white space around the illustration. Place the art on the page, then be creative in wrapping the text around the art. Carefully glue the art in place, and finally photocopy your layout to produce your master copy.

☞   **Also see:** Art in Worship; Communicating; Printing Your Material.

Clip-Art

• Clown Ministry

Want to energize your kids? Need to find a way to get your shy <u>youth group</u> members involved? Why not start a clown ministry! Clown ministry (where kids dress in clown costumes and makeup and perform skits, play <u>games</u>, and just have fun with children) can be a fun and exciting way to cheer-up people and share one's faith at the same time. And what's more, your kids will love it!

• Four Steps to Creating a Clown Ministry

1. **Recruit a team of 4-7 teens.** Choose those who might be too shy to get up in front of people, but who would be willing to "hide" behind some face-paint.
2. **Create costumes.** You can find face-paint at your local toy store or craft house (and during Halloween, it's everywhere!). Purchase clown outfits at a local costume shop, make them yourselves, or have the Community Services people lend you a hand. Or, if you're really low on cash, have your kids look in their parent's closets!
3. **Find skit material.** You can find great clown ministry skits at your local Christian bookstore in the youth section. Or be really brave and write your own. Look for skits with easily understood themes, such as <u>grace</u>, love, <u>acceptance</u>, and salvation. It would also enhance your "sell-ability" if you found some skits promoting drug-prevention.
4. **Practice, Practice, Practice.** Spend quality time learning to dress-up, paint faces, and perform your skits.

• Where to Show Off Your Team

1. Go to a convalescent home in costume and hand out flowers.
2. Contact the preschools in your local area and ask if you can do a skit for them.
3. Do children's stories for local churches.
4. Learn a skit about drug prevention and present it for the elementary schools in your community.
5. Visit your local hospital.
6. Check with your Public Broadcasting TV Station and ask if they could film your team doing one of the above activities. It will make a great, positive feature story for them.

Clown Ministry

- **Codependency**

Chemical dependence and other addictive diseases reach with destructive power into the heart of many Christian families. Unprecedented numbers are suffering from the effects of alcoholism, workaholism, sexaholism, eating disorders, etc. Parents, pastors, and church leaders are concerned about ministering appropriately to these individuals.

It is now recognized that conservative Christian families are highly susceptible to dependency disorders. Their addictions are as devastating as alcoholism, but much more subtle and difficult to diagnose. And when addictions occur in a family system, they predispose the next generations to addictive behavior as well.

If parents become preoccupied with drugs, food, gambling, work, sex, success, caregiving, etc., their emotional availability to their family is minimized. They cannot nurture their family as they otherwise might. Their children are left emotionally hungry – codependent.

By definition, codependence is the pain in adulthood that comes from being wounded in childhood and leads to a high probability of relationship problems and compulsive behavior. The wounded, codependent child feels left out, unimportant, worthless. Gradually, he disconnects from his own needs and feelings and abandons himself in favor of obsession with others (to his own detriment). He is more oriented to the reality of others than of his own reality. One expert calls codependence "the abandonment of self."

Feelings of pain, shame, inadequacy, and rejection associated with lack of nurture in childhood prepare the adolescent to seek good feelings from sources outside himself.

- *Outside Sources Where Adolescents Seek Love*
    1. The right drug
    2. The right job
    3. A prestigious education
    4. Nice clothes
    5. Desirable friends
    6. A devoted spouse or lover
    7. More money
    8. The right hairstyle
    9. An effective diet
    10. A perfect body image

Obviously, when anyone looks outside himself for identity, meaning, or whatever he feels he is missing, there is in the substance or activity to which he looks, addictive potential. And the more effectively his "drug of choice" alters his feelings, the more addictive it is. People get addicted to relationships, to achievement, to work, to food, etc. They become involved with these substances and activities in an attempt to satisfy their unmet emotional needs.

But it doesn't work, for two reasons: (1) addictive behavior has negative consequences, and (2) the addict or codependent's needs are insatiable. As they say in Narcotics Anonymous, "One (drink or drug) is too many, and a thousand are never enough."

Codependence is the social/emotional/spiritual pathology that occurs when children grow up in a family system characterized by high stress and low nurturance.

- *Four Categories of Candidates for Codependence*
    1. Anyone currently in close relationships with an addict or alcoholic.
    2. Anyone with an addictive parent or grandparent — including all addictive disorders ranging from chemical dependence to workaholism, compulsive overspending, sexaholism, and child abuse.
    3. Anyone suffering significant childhood loss due to causes other than addiction — death, divorce, physical or emotional deprivation.
    4. Anyone from an emotionally out-of-touch or rigid, repressive family background.

Codependence may go unnoticed in a family system until physical illness or depression sets in and the codependent is forced to face his condition. Frequently, the problem is not recognized until one or more of the children manifest symptoms such as drug addiction, alcoholism, or sexual acting our and the family is forced to seek help. Seeking help is painful, but not shameful! It's normal to have problems and okay to seek help!

Available treatments include outpatient therapy, intensive inpatient care, and twelve-step programs. The prognosis for recovery is excellent if issues are faced and addressed therapeutically. The likelihood of recycling the disease into the next generation is also diminished.

☞   **Also see:** Alcohol; At-risk Behavior; The Bridge; Tobacco.

Codependency, continued

• Communicating

Good communication skills are essential for <u>youth ministry</u> leaders to effectively share purpose, objectives, information, and directions and for making a spiritual impact. Good communication also models necessary skills your youth will need in situations as diverse as asking for a date, delivering reports in school and being interviewed for a job.

• Five Secrets of Effective Communication

1. **Know your assignment.** Effective communication begins with knowing your assignment. You call balls and strikes at a baseball game differently than you lead a small group in <u>Bible study</u>.
2. **Know your audience.** Know their ages, their interests, and activities that took place during the week that may have raised questions, challenged them or made them happy.
3. **First impressions.** Dress appropriately for the situation (don't show up to do a <u>worship</u> at a school picnic in your best <u>Sabbath</u> outfit). Be on time. Be prepared. Don't be too nervous!
4. **Tell stories.** Illustrate your communication with plenty of easy-to-understand stories. Many people learn better from the illustrations than they do from the rest of your presentation.
5. **Stick to a time-limit.** The old wisdom is true: it's better for people to wish you would have said more than for them to wish you had said less.

In his book, *Back to the Heart of Youth Work* (Victor Books, revised, 1994), Dewey Bertolini suggests ways to communicate a personal touch. Among his suggestions are the following:

• Communicating a Personal Touch

1. Greet every young person at every meeting.
2. Phone or send an occasional note just to say hello.
3. Be the first to acknowledge a birthday.
4. Open your home for special events (New Year's Day, Super Bowls, etc.)
5. Send notes of congratulations and thanks.
6. Answer all mail and return all phone calls.
7. If you have an office which kids frequent, properly arrange it so that it communicates "welcome."

Communicating

Community

A community of faith is a group of people who share common spiritual understandings, beliefs, practices, experiences or commitments.

In a *Christian* community, all believers share the joyful experience of being children of God, created and redeemed by our Lord, Jesus Christ. "Our citizenship is in heaven," Paul assures us (Philippians 3:20); we are chosen and called to share in the riches of that glorious inheritance (Ephesians 1:18). Dietrich Bonhoeffer reminds us that Christian community springs *solely* from the biblical message of being justified by grace alone (*Life Together*, Harper & Row, 1954, 23).

Five Characteristics of Christian Community

1. **Inclusivity.** God's arms have been thrown wide open to receive His children. There is no room for an us-against-them mentality in the Christian community. See Romans 15:7; Galatians 3:28 and Colossians 3:11.
2. **Unity.** Being one before God and one in purpose on earth doesn't mean we all look alike or act alike or even like all the same things. Unity is not unison. We are united in our love for each other and in our desire to tell others about God's love. See 1 Corinthians 1:10; 12:25; Ephesians 4:3 and Colossians 3:14.
3. **Harmony.** Romans 12:16 and 1 Peter 3:8.
4. **Encouragement.** 1 Thessalonians 5:11.
5. **Compassion.** We care about people because we are cared for by our Heavenly Father. "Therefore, as God's chosen people, clothe yourselves with compassion" (Colossians 3:12). Also see Ephesians 4:32.

In a Christian youth ministry setting, community refers to belonging to a youth group that reflects the grace of God. Membership in such a group is never more important than during adolescence. Community must be intentional and constant, practical and tangible.

Community means spending time together, learning together, worshipping together, serving together, being enriched by each other's diversity and warmed by each other's affirmation. Community includes all the best that genuine Christian friendship can offer.

☞ **Also see:** Acceptance; Climate Issues.

Community

• Conference Youth Director

In the organizational structure of the Seventh-day Adventist Church, your *local church* is a member of a *local conference*, a geographical territory comprising a number of Adventist churches. (See: General Conference.)

Each conference employs administrators who oversee departments or ministries. In smaller conferences, one administrator may direct the activities of several departments. In larger conferences, certain departments may have a director and one or more associate directors.

Most conferences worldwide delegate the responsibilities for nurturing youth ministry professionals within the conference and for encouraging and enabling the lay leaders of youth ministry activities in local churches to a Conference Youth Director, the leader or administrator of the conference Youth Ministry Department. (See: AAYMP.)

It is the goal of Conference Youth Directors to empower local youth ministry. Here is how that empowerment generally takes place.

• Empowering Local Youth Ministry

1. By employing youth ministry professionals (such as youth pastors or chaplains) who will lead out in the youth ministry of a local church, and by encouraging the continuing professional growth of this employee.
2. By recruiting lay people and training them in the foundations and strategies of youth ministry in their local church.
3. By discovering and recommending excellent youth ministry resources, including people and ministries which provide resources and training.
4. By organizing youth ministry activities which are more efficiently done on a broader basis rather than by a local church. These activities might include summer camps, Pathfinder camporees, certain mission trips, youth congresses, etc.
5. By being an effective youth ministry advocate.

My Conference Youth Director:

_____   _____
Name   Phone Number

_____   _____
FAX   e-mail

• Confidentiality

"Can you keep a secret?"

We've been asking that question of our friends since we were little kids. The secrets usually dealt with relational things – becoming aware of the opposite sex, purchasing a Christmas present for a friend, trying to figure out whether or not to "tell on someone" for behaving badly, etc.

Confidentiality is the adult way of talking about keeping secrets. The word is much more sophisticated, but the "secrets" usually are still about relational dynamics.

• *Three Reasons to Honor Confidences*

1. **Youth Expect Confidentiality.** When kids open up to you and reveal their honest feelings, when they share with you their ups and downs, when they let you in on their experiences, they *assume* you'll keep the information to yourself. Your confidence is a matter of respect.

2. **Youth are Hurt by the Divulging of Confidences.** Betrayal; that's what it feels like when requested confidentiality is broken.

3. **Youth Build Trust on Confidence.** Trust in larger, more important issues is often built on confidences kept in smaller, more everyday matters.

There are, of course, some matters (such as physical or sexual abuse) in which even the reasonable *suspicion* of ill-treatment legally *requires* you (in most North American localities) to alert a child protective agency. Make sure your youth know that your love and concern for them, as well as your moral obligation to protect them, will lead you to obey such requirements.

☞ Also see: Counselling; Youth Leader.

Notes:

_____

_____

_____

_____

_____

Confidentiality

• Contemporary Christian Music

Contemporary (adj.) - marked by characteristics of the present period; modern.
Christian (adj.) - of or relating to Christianity; based on or conforming with Christianity.
Music (n.) - vocal, instrumental, or mechanical sounds having rhythm, melody, or harmony.

The debate continues to rage on the place of contemporary Christian music (CCM) in the church. Meanwhile, CCM continues to expand its already wide musical spectrum. It now includes pop, alternative rock, rap, and reggae on the one hand, and sometimes soft, sometimes rousing and rhythmic praise choruses and hymns for worship on the other. In some instances, even classic church hymns have been modernized by contemporary Christian writers and artists. As its name implies, CCM reflects the "modern" music styles and lyrics of today, making it suspect to many as an appropriate mode of sacred musical expression.

All Christian music originally was contemporary. Fanny Crosby, Isaac Watts, Charles Wesley, James White, Martin Luther and even Johann Sebastian Bach were the contemporary Christian musicians of their day. The psalms and hymns of the Scripture were contemporary to the people of Bible times because they were written during that period of history. In essence, CCM has always been part of church life.

• Six Principles For Evaluating and Using CCM

1. **Flexibility.** Who is the target group for the music we intend to use in ministry? (1 Corinthians 9:19-22)
2. **Excellence.** Does the music reflect diligent preparation and wholehearted devotion to excellence? (Colossians 3:23)
3. **Motivation.** Is the music from a "star" or a servant? (1 Peter 5:5)
4. **Credibility.** Is the music performed by a person or a group committed to being spiritually accountable before the church and before God? (Hebrews 13:17; 1 Timothy 3:2)
5. **Clarity.** Does the music clearly communicate the message of the Christian faith to its intended audience? (Colossians 4:3, 4)
6. **Sensitivity.** Does the use of this music reflect sensitivity toward an audience which may include individuals adversely affected by its style? (Romans 14:1-13)

• **More Great Advice:**

✔ Al Menconi, *Today's Music: The Window to Your Child's Soul* (Elgin, IL: David C. Cook, 1990).
✔ Steve Miller, *The Contemporary Christian Music Debate* (Wheaton, IL: Tyndale, 1993).
✔ Michael Tomlinson, "Contemporary Christian Music is *Christian* Music," *Ministry*, September, 1996.
✔ Stuart Tyner, "Thinking About Music," in *Shall We Dance* (Riverside, CA: Hancock Center, 1996).

• *Cornerstone Connections*

Cornerstone Connections is the <u>Sabbath School</u> lesson study material for the youth of the <u>Seventh-day Adventist</u> Church, age 15-18. The <u>General Conference</u> Sabbath School Department publishes *Cornerstone* in English and ten other languages, and prints over 65,000 copies of the quarterly four times a year.

Rather than merely a paraphrase of the adult Sabbath School <u>lesson study</u> material, *Cornerstone Connections*, which was first published in 1982, is the first effort by the Adventist Church to produce an entire four-year curriculum that focuses on the questions youth are asking and to demonstrate that practical Christian solutions exist for those questions. Both a student quarterly and a teaching guide are available.

Christianity is no less appealing today than it was in apostolic times when thousands were converted in a day. The problem is that we haven't captured the attention of young people or demonstrated Christianity's appeal. The attention of youth is distracted by a barrage of unchristian sights and sounds and feelings. *Cornerstone Connections* seeks to recapture that attention and then to allow the winning voice of Christ's message to speak in ways they will comprehend.

Cornerstone Connections
    12501 Old Columbia Pike
    Silver Spring, MD 20904
    Phone: (301) 680-6160
    FAX: (301) 680-6155
    CServe: 74617,1534

On the next two pages you'll find the *Cornerstone Connections* four-year curriculum plan, covering every Sabbath's lesson topic, quarter by quarter, week by week, until January, 2003. Use this lesson plan in advance of each quarter to plan your Sabbath School programming and to get acquainted with the topics your class will be studying.

Cornerstone Curriculum Plan

1st Quarter 1999: Success	2nd Quarter 1999: Gospel Dynamics	3rd Quarter 1999: Faith Challenges	4th Quarter 1999: Emotions/Life Skills
Cultural Views	God's Remedy for Sin	Secularism	Coping With Feelings
The Meaning of Success	Grace and the Law	Evolution	Depression
Identifying One's Gifts	Achieving Christian Wholeness	The Occult	Doubt
Making Use Of One's Potential	Assurance of Salvation	Cults	Fear of the Future
Setting Goals	Confession	Astrology	Joy
Biographies of Success	The Meaning Of Baptism	The New Age	Listening
Success Stories of the Bible	Christian Growth	Suffering	Empathy
Success In Adolescence	Making Everyday Decisions	Elitism	Serenity
Success and Self-Image	Witness as a Lifestyle Experience	Boredom	Faith
Effects of Peers on Success	Christian Praise	Leisure	Forgiveness
Substance Abuse and Success	Christian Thanksgiving	Fashion	Conscience
Choosing a Vocation	The Meaning of Discipleship	Entertainment	Feelings About Peers
Achieving Wisdom	Christian Character	Selfishness	Feelings About Family

1st Quarter 2000: Lifestyle	2nd Quarter 2000: Values	3rd Quarter 2000: World Issues	4th Quarter 2000: Christian Adventure
Stewardship of Time	Influence of Parents on Values	Responding to World Issues	Guilt in the Christian's Life
Stewardship of Talent	Influence of the Media on Values	Prejudice	Overcoming Bad Habits
Stewardship of Treasure	Church, School, and Values	Violence	Developing Good Habits
Stewardship of the Mind	Values and Decision-Making	Pornography	Developing Self-Discipline
Benefits of Christian Education	What to Base Decisions On	Hunger	Obedience
Financing a Christian Education	Defending One's Choices	AIDS	Sharing
Christian Friendships	Overcoming Dilemmas	Abortion	Responding to Discipline
Friendship and Communication	Values Clarification	Homosexuality	Being an Example for Others
Christian Ambition	Coping With Hypocrisy	Ecology	Responding to God's Call
Elements of Wellness	Trustworthiness	Freedom	Christian Responsibility
Diet	Ellen White's Role in the Church	The Rewards of Service	Overcoming Cultural Differences
Exercise	The Humanity of Ellen White	Giving to Others	Role of Women in God's Family
Substance Abuse and Health	The Spirit of Prophecy and Life	Christian Celebration	Overcoming Chemical Addictions
		The Christian Mission	

1st Quarter 2001: Life Challenges	2nd Quarter 2001: Self-Worth	3rd Quarter 2001: God With Us	4th Quarter 2001: In-But-Not-Of
Influences of Youth Culture	Individuality	Redemption From Sin	Making Choices in the World
Worldliness	Christian Self-Worth	The Sanctuary	The Abundant Christian Life
Hatred	Coping With Life's Changes	God's Word in the Christian's Life	Coping With Distractions
Doubt	Overcoming Feelings of Inferiority	God as King	Creativity and Routine
Stress	Self-Worth Through Belonging	God as Creator	Developing Christian Priorities
Christian Freedom	Friendship	Maintaining Christian Standards	Secular Music
Conformity and the Christian Life	Dating Relationships	The Sabbath	Religious Music
Conviction	Friendships With Non-Believers	Principles of Health	Symbols of God
True Love	Creativity	Principles of Stewardship	Religious Art
Trustworthiness and Love	Leadership	Overcoming Persecution	Poetry
The Role of Emotions in Love	Witnessing	Achieving Christian Unity	Stories
Premarital Sex	Education	Waiting for Jesus to Come	Case Studies
Christian Marriage	Wisdom	The New Earth	Movies

1st Quarter 2002: Identity Issues	2nd Quarter 2002: Personal Faith	3rd Quarter 2002: Bible Doctrines	4th Quarter 2002: Social Relations
Personal Identity	The Existence of God	The Early Christian Church	What Love Is
Christian Maturity	God's Interest in Us	The Inspiration of the Bible	What Love Is Not
Talents	Authority of the Bible	Applying the Bible to Life	Overcoming Loneliness
Identity in a Peer Group	The Bible as a Guide	How Sin Began	Biblical Principles for Dating
What is a Christian?	Bible Study Methods	Sin and the Earth's Creation	Proper Dating Behavior
Finding Meaning in Life	Why Pray?	Redemption From Sin	The Appropriate Age for Dating
Christian Decision-Making	Keys to Effective Prayer	Final Issues of Great Controversy	Appropriate Places for Dating
Relating to Rules	How Jesus Overcame Sin	Jesus' Final Triumph Over sin	Christian Intimacy
The Caring Christian Community	Victory Over Sin	The Importance of God's Law	Christian Marriage
God's Unconditional Acceptance	Claiming God's Promises	Sabbath-Keeping	Premarital Intimacy
The Meaning of Forgiveness	Why Jesus' Delay in Coming	The State of the Dead	Relating to Parents
Acceptance of Others	Jesus' Second Coming	Effective Witnessing	The Church as a Family
What is Worship?	The New Earth	Practicing the Christian Lifestyle	God's People

Cornerstone Curriculum Plan, continued

• Counselling

All of us have emotional difficulties at some times in our lives. And the fact is, those difficulties usually make us feel bad about ourselves. Confronting emotional problems requires *prompt action*, because the longer the problem lasts, the *more difficult* it is to treat properly.

When we are having strong emotional disturbances or unusual worries, it's very important to find a *competent* person to help. Sometimes the problem is not *too* complicated, as in the case of minor mood disorders, situational depressions, or light relational problems. The competent help in such cases can be provided by parents, a good friend, a teacher, or a pastor.

When things are more complex (as in clinical depressions, major mood disorders, mental illnesses, or serious marital conflicts), it's better to look for the professional help provided by specialized counselors, psychologists, or psychiatrists.

Don't hesitate to get help! Remember, getting help at the *beginning* of a problem is the first step to solving it!

• Four Things to Look for in a Counselor

1. **Warmth.** A good counselor is one who respects you and cares for your needs, who has a non-smothering concern for you regardless of your actions or attitudes.
2. **Genuineness.** A counselor can be effective only if he or she is "for real," – a sincere person who is open and avoids phoniness or the playing of some superior role.
3. **Empathy.** Having the ability to "feel with" is a must for a good counselor, so that he or she can understand your values, beliefs, inner feelings or fears, conflicts, and hurts.
4. **Christianity.** A *Christian* counselor will take into consideration your spiritual background and needs, focusing on aspects related not only to this present life, but considering eternity as well.

• Three Major Benefits of Counselling

1. Understanding that having personal problems is a common challenge, not something that's just affecting you. The Bible contains many examples of people facing the same situations

Counselling

you face. Its pages tell us about grief, discouragement, sadness, <u>violence</u>, anxiety, loneliness, doubt, abnormal sex, bitterness, poverty, greed, sickness, interpersonal tension, insecurity, worry, lack of faith, lack of hope, and a variety of other personal problems — sometimes seen in the lives of the greatest saints.

2. Counselling is a process that can help you to deal with your problems with the concurrence of a professional who will be able to assess the causes of your disturbances and lead you to their resolution.

3. A competent counselor can help you recognize hidden harmful attitudes, teach interpersonal skills and new behaviors, guide those who are making decisions or changing their lifestyles, or show how to mobilize one's inner resources to cope with a crisis.

One More Piece of Advice

Visit bookstore and look for books that deal specifically with the issues you're struggling with. There are many contemporary Christian authors who have been a blessing to people with problems, and you can benefit from their work, too.

Remember, though, that self-help never fully replaces the benefits of a competent professional's help.

Scriptures that Deal with Emotional Disturbances

Anxiety:	Philippians 4:6
Depression:	Psalm 43:5
Fear:	Isaiah 40:1-11; Psalm 56:3-4
Guidance:	Psalm 32:8
Guilt:	1 John 1:9; Acts 24:16
Irritability:	Galatians 5:22-23
Lack of confidence:	Hebrews 10:35-36
Lust:	Job 31:1
Self-control:	Titus 2: 1-15
Worry:	Matthew 6:34

Counselling, continued

CQ – Collegiate Quarterly (left margin, vertical)

• *CQ – Collegiate Quarterly*

Since 1979, *CQ* has been the <u>Sabbath School</u> lesson quarterly for <u>young adults</u>, age 18 through 35. It is prepared by the <u>General Conference</u> Sabbath School Department. World circulation is approaching 60,000, in English, Spanish, Finnish, Portuguese and Italian editions.

CQ is based on the conviction that the Word of God offers transforming power and that group study is one important way to tap into that power. *CQ's* purpose is to provide <u>Seventh-day Adventist</u> young adults with a resource for devotional study on mutual topics, which can then be discussed each week in Sabbath School. Many who use the adult quarterly find that because *CQ* deals with the same topics as those of the adult quarterly it enriches <u>lesson study</u> and <u>discussion</u>.

More than 200 individuals contribute to *CQ* each year, with writers selected from *CQ's* reading audience itself. The wide variety of the content reflects the cosmopolitan diversity of the contributors from around the world as they respond creatively and individually to the subject and draw on their own personal experiences.

• *Seven Weekly Features of CQ*

1. **Daily reading segments.**
2. **Introduction.** Captures the reader's attention and focuses on the week's theme.
3. **Logos.** Guides the direct, substantive study of the Bible passage for the week.
4. **Testimony.** Presents the perspective of <u>Ellen White</u> writings on the lesson theme for the week.
5. **Evidence.** Places the week's lesson in a historical, scientific, philosophical, or theological perspective.
6. **How-To.** Explores the practical, everyday aspects of the lesson.
7. **Opinion.** Provides closure of the week's lesson through a personal viewpoint.

CQ

12501 Old Columbia Pike
Silver Spring, MD 20904
Phone: (301) 680-6160
FAX: (301) 680-6155
Editor's CServe: 74617,1534

• Critical Thinking Skills

A <u>community</u> functions not only to make its members feel accepted, but also to challenge their thinking. In an active faith community, people feel free to explore their faith, to ask tough questions, and to evaluate traditions. Questioners don't fear reprisal or exclusion because they are seeking truth. In fact, a caring faith community understands that making our faith our own is a necessary step in the <u>faith maturity</u> process.

As your <u>youth group</u> discusses Christianity's response to the challenging issues of our day, encourage each member to ask specific questions that help clarify the issue and lead to truth-filled conclusions.

You can further this process by encouraging the development of what are known as critical thinking skills. Apply these skills frequently.

- • *Essential Critical Thinking Skills*
  1. **Defining the Issue**
     - • Identify central points
     - • Compare distinctive attributes
     - • Determine relevant information
     - • Ask clarifying questions
  2. **Understanding the Issue**
     - • Distinguish fact from opinion
     - • Check context and consistency
     - • Identify unstated assumptions
     - • Recognize cliches and stereotypes
     - • Recognize bias and propaganda
     - • Recognize value orientations
  3. **Drawing Conclusions**
     - • Determine data adequacy
     - • Predict probable consequences

Notes:

_____

_____

_____

_____

_____

_____

• Criticism, How to Deal With

No matter how great a <u>youth ministry</u> program you have going, you *are* going to get criticized. Sometimes it comes from right out of the blue. Sometimes it seems like someone is sticking a loaded gun in your ribs. Usually it comes when you least need to hear it, like right after a big youth weekend when you're exhausted, or when you think you're finally making some progress with the kids.

• Three Ways to Deal With Criticism

1. **Separate fact from fiction.**

   And use the facts to make changes.

   When a parent says "How come you never have any sports activities that my son, Brad, would enjoy?", bite your tongue. Refrain from defensively listing the rollerblading afternoon last July, the football every Fall Sunday, or the upcoming Basketball night. Ask your self if you need to implement more sports into your planning. Find out what your kids are wanting more of.

   And don't forget to put Brad on your activity planning committee!

2. **Ask for advice, before it's offered.**

   You hear that Mrs. Smith doesn't think your youth program is meeting her kid's needs. Don't wait for her to bring this up at the Church Board Meeting. Go talk to her. Find out what she feels are the weak areas and ask her for her ideas on improving.

   You're stumped on how to get Jon involved. Don't wait for his parents to complain that he never is included. Ask them for suggestions on how to spark his interest and make him a team member. Get Jon's input, too.

3. **Recruit!** You don't have to have all the answers.

   You're at your wit's end with Jill, a sullen and sarcastic youth who will not participate in any part of your Sabbath School programs. When Jill's mom complains that "Jill hates Sabbath School, and you need to make it better," ask for her help. It will give her a bird's-eye view of your planning and your efforts, as well as her daughter's attitude.

Criticism

Curriculum

In its broadest application, curriculum is the sum of all learning influences and interactions experienced by the learner in the local learning environment.

- ## The Physical Side of Curriculum
  1. The arrangement of the furniture in the room.
  2. The temperature and ventilation of the room.
  3. The color of paint on the walls.
  4. The attractiveness of the room.
  5. The nutritional state of the learner.

- ## The Interpersonal Side of Curriculum
  1. The size of the learning group.
  2. The friendliness of the youth leaders.
  3. The teaching methods utilized. (See: Active Learning)
  4. The learning styles of the learners.

Each of these influences and interactions is important to learning and must be a part of an effective strategy for youth ministry. A youth leader must be aware of, and strive to utilize to the best advantage, all the elements of the curriculum, not just curriculum materials.

- **Curriculum Materials** - the resources utilized in the local learning environment which communicate a given curriculum plan.

- **Curriculum Plan** - a structure, framework or design, which organizes all the subject matters and activities of a selected religious education endeavor. Such a structure guides the teachers and leaders in the process of communicating those subjects and activities to the learner. (See: Cornerstone Curriculum Plan.)

- **Local Learning Environment** – the place where the curriculum plan is put into action, where the learner interacts with, and is influenced by the curriculum. For youth ministry in local church settings, this environment includes the youth Sabbath School room and the other places where the youth group meets for social as well as Sabbath activities, including the home of the youth leader.

• Dancing

Adventists *don't* dance!

For decades now, that's been the sum of the dance discussion between most older and younger Adventist Christians. But the issue hasn't gone away, the questions haven't stopped being asked, and the definition hasn't held up. Today, many Adventists take part in national dances, many married Adventists dance romantically, many high school and college-aged Adventists dance regularly, and some Adventist academies sponsor "folk dancing" socials and fund-raisers.

Adventists *do* dance!

It's confusing. Especially for parents and youth leaders who hold to the prior <u>standard</u> yet want to relate positively to a generation forging their own definition of what it means to be an Adventist.

• *Three Discussion Questions About Dancing*

1. What's right about dancing? (You'll get answers such as "good exercise," "stress control," and "being with Adventist friends,"!)
2. What's wrong with dancing? (The answers usually center on three things: the atmosphere of the place where we dance; the music; and the overt sexual temptations.)
3. What activities can you plan and take part in that include the benefits of #1 without involving the negative aspects of #2?

In the 27 biblical references to "dance," "dances," "dancing," and "danced," the following principles can be discovered and applied to our lives (from, *Shall We Dance: Rediscovering Christ-Centered Principles*, published in 1996 by the <u>Hancock Center for Youth and Family Ministry</u>).

• *Five Biblical Principles of Dance*

1. Dance is an acceptable component of <u>worship</u>. Psalm 149:3 and 150:4.
2. Dance is an appropriate expression of <u>community</u> joy. Judges 11:34; 1 Samuel 18:6; Luke 7:32 and 15:25.
3. Dance should praise no other god but God. Exodus 32:19.
4. Dance should not promote inappropriate sexual arousal. 1 Corinthians 10:7, 8; Matthew 14:6; and Numbers 25:3.
5. Appropriate dance is dance in which God is invited as a witness and participant. 1 Corinthians 10:31 and Romans 14:23.

Dancing

• Dating

Dating wasn't always complicated.

When it was time for Isaac's first date, his father, Abraham, sent his chief servant to the old country to find the right girl. The servant prayed about his responsibilities, found Rebekah, brought her back to Isaac, and the two of them lived happily ever after (see Genesis 24).

When Samson found the girl of his dreams he simply said to his parents, "Go get her for me!" They did, and… well, that's another story (see Judges 14).

Today it seems that dating is on every teenager's mind from the time he or she enters junior high until the day of their wedding. (Then, of course, it's conventional wisdom that all dating stops! Husbands and wives don't really date, do they?)

So if you want to get a good <u>discussion</u> started, bring up the subject of dating. Here are a few questions to help focus the topic. Get lots of input from the members of your <u>youth group</u>, vote on the best answers, fill in the blanks and produce your own guidebook to the mystical, mystifying world of dating.

• What's the Purpose of Dating?

1. To find the type of person you'll eventually want to marry.
2. To become the type of person someone else will eventually want to marry.
3. _____
4. _____
5. _____

• What's Proper Dating Etiquette?

1. Make the other person comfortable. Be courteous.
2. Keep the conversations going. Talk about their interests.
3. _____
4. _____
5. _____

Dating, continued

- ## What Should You Do (or Not Do) on a First Date?

  1. Don't *overdo* it. If a guy shows up at his date's house in a limo, with two dozen red roses and two front row seats to the hottest ticket in town, he's overdoing it. Start slowly.

  2. Stay in a group. The most difficult thing on a first date tends to be conversing. The more people talking, the better.

  3. _____

  4. _____

  5. _____

- ## Make a List of Good Group Dates

  1. **Zany Scavenger Hunts.** Get everyone together and make up the items you want to collect. Be creative! Do a Poloroid hunt where you don't bring back items, just *pictures* of the items. Or send people to a variety of stores to buy things they wouldn't normally buy (false teeth adhesive, plumbing fixtures, etc.). Or make it an activity scavenger hunt; video one of the group members crossing a street (at the crosswalk, of course) on a tricycle, or slam-dunking a basketball.

  2. **Theme Parties.** Build a group date around a theme, such as the fifties, stars, sports or holidays. Invite lots of people to help plan the party. Prepare food that lends to the theme. Dress appropriately. Listen to music, play games or watch videos that fit the theme

  3. _____
     _____

  4. _____
     _____

  5. _____
     _____

• Day Camp

A day camp is a daily activity program usually aimed at children, usually held during the summer months, and usually staffed by the youth and young adults of your church. It's summer camp without the cabins, Vacation Bible School without the felts, with field-trips and outdoor activities thrown in. Fees are usually charged for the daily program, with extra activities carrying an extra price.

Many children remember that their first exposure to the Adventist church was a fun, enjoyable summer day camp experience.

• *Ten Commandments for Successful Day Camps*

1. Find a great staff. Advertise with your high school and college students in January when the summer camps are doing the same. Figure that you want one staff member per six children. A spirit-led staff is the most important key for success.

2. Calculate your finances in advance. Estimate how many children you'll have, their fees, and the amount of funding you can get from the local conference, union conference, and school. Take that number and compare it with your expenses. Hire staff according to your income.

3. Select your activities and commit them to a daily schedule. Rafting, rock climbing, water-skiing, swimming, miniature golf, cave exploring, beach trips, cycling, and bowling are just a few of the hot ones.

4. Take your schedule and commit it to a day camp brochure. In addition to the events, include registration and permission forms, prices, and other information.

5. Advertise. Send out several thousand brochures to school children, homes near your church, and church members. Also advertise in the newspaper. Some of it is free.

6. Develop a transportation plan. Hire a driver and rent a bus.

7. Invest emotionally in your staff. Develop them through a staff training week and continue with parties and rewards.

8. Ready your facility with user-friendly atmosphere.

9. Develop a spiritual strategy. What commitment do we want the children to make and how will we get there?

10. Pray.

Day Camp

• Death and Dying Issues

Death has been an unhappy part of the human experience ever since the day God revealed to Adam and Eve that their estrangement from Him would result in dying. "You will *surely* die," God told them, no doubt with tears in His voice (Genesis 2:17).

Dying was not a part of the original, Divine plan for God's created family. But with the interruption of that plan by Lucifer's rebellion and Adam's and Eve's fall, dying became *the distinguishing feature* of every Earthbound species, separating us all from every other animate creature in God's perfect universe.

Today we are so accustomed to death that we speak of people as dying of "natural causes." By this unfortunate phrase we mean the dying that occurs through the aging process. It wasn't always so. Fresh from the Creator's hand, with powerful immunities coursing through their bloodstreams, the inhabitants of the antediluvian period lived for centuries, some thriving for almost a thousand years! Now we speak of people in their *70s* as old, and virtually no one survives into their 80s and 90s without a serious diminishing of physical and mental activity.

This slow death by "natural causes" may be to teenagers the most incongruous of all the ways we die. Bursting with optimism, blessed with an abundance of energy and eager to experience whatever their future holds, youth are notoriously shortsighted when it comes to lifespan. Topics such as exercise, nutrition, obesity, serum cholesterol levels, dangers of smoking, hypertension, and preventative medicine usually have a much greater impact on an older crowd.

Which is not to say that death and dying issues don't impact teens. More and more youth are exposed each day to the tragic loss of life among teenagers due to *preventable* causes: violence, substance abuse, disease, alcohol-related accidents, AIDS, suicide, etc. The great majority of teenagers in North America have been touched by the death of classmates, friends or family members.

• *What's Behind the Fear of Death?*

1. **Pain.** Does it hurt to die?
2. **Finality.** The premature interruption of life's activities.
3. **Fear of the unknown.** What happens after we die?
4. **Guilt.** Could I have done something to prevent the death?
5. **Worry.** When and how will I die?

Experts who study death and dying issues have identified certain emotional stages through which a grieving person goes after suffering the loss of a loved one or friend, or even after finding out that someone close has a terminal condition. People seldom move smoothly from one stage to the next. We may experience several stages at the same time, move back and forth between stages, or skip stages. The healing process is different for everyone, and there is no timetable.

The stages of this "grieving process" usually include the following:

- *The Grieving Process*
  1. **Denial.** The initial sense of shock over the loss or potential loss causes many people to doubt, or refuse to believe, the reality of death.
  2. **Anger.** It is common to question the "fairness" or "justice" of death, even to blame God for abandoning His children. We feel cheated and often take out our anger on others.
  3. Depression. When the reality of the loss sets in, many experience despair, isolation and withdrawal. This stage may be the most difficult and longest-lasting of the stages.
  4. **Loneliness.** The closer the grieving person was to the one who is dying or has died, the more keenly that person feels the loss, and the stronger the feeling of loneliness.
  5. **Acceptance.** Though we don't forget the loss, ultimately we accept and deal with the reality of the situation and move on.

- *Five Ways to Help a Grieving Person*
  1. **Listen.** Let the grieving person talk openly and honestly. Be attentive and show interest. (See: Listening Skills.)
  2. **Talk About the Loss.** Don't hide your feelings. Talk about the person who is dying or who has died. Remember the good times, the laughter, the friendship.
  3. **Don't Talk Too Much.** Sometimes just *being* there is the support the grieving person most needs. Be sensitive. Crying together may be more important than talking.
  4. **Avoid Euphemisms.** Phrases such as "gone away" or "passing on" often raise more questions. Be honest about dying.
  5. **Be Patient.** It takes time to heal.

Sources: The Bereaved Families of Ontario, Canada; The Metropolitan Life Insurance Company; The National Center for Health Statistics; The Project on Death in America.

Death and Dying Issues, continued

• Depression

Depression is a very real and common illness, affecting, at any one time, as many as ten percent of the population. Sometimes, like other illnesses, depression just happens. Other times, depression follows traumatic events such as a <u>divorce</u> or death in the family, loss of a job, a move to a new city, or an unhappy home life. Depression can also be brought on by everyday occurrences like disagreements with people you love or even a lack of exercise. Often there's a link between depression and getting into trouble: trouble with <u>alcohol</u>, street drugs, or sex; trouble with school or bad grades; problems with family or friends.

• *Nine Signs of Depression*

1. You feel sad a lot, and the feeling doesn't go away.
2. You feel guilty; you have no confidence in your self.
3. Life seems meaningless, and you don't think anything good is ever going to happen again. You feel empty and hopeless.
4. You lose interest in ordinary pleasures like <u>music</u>, sports, friends, or having fun. You really want to be left alone most of the time.
5. It's hard to make up your mind. It's hard to concentrate.
6. You get angry or irritated often. You're so touchy that you lose control for no particular reason. You overreact.
7. There's often a change in sleeping and eating habits.
8. You feel restless or tired most of the time.
9. You think about death a lot, or about <u>suicide</u>.

A *depressive disorder* is a "whole-body" illness, involving your body, mood, and thoughts. It happens when someone moves from *being depressed* to *suffering from depression*.

A depressive disorder is not a passing blue mood. Nor is it a sign of personal weakness or a condition that can be willed or wished away. People with a depressive illness cannot merely "pull themselves together" and get better. Without treatment, symptoms can last for weeks, months, or even years. Fortunately, recovery is the rule, not the exception. The right kind of treatment can help over 80% of those who suffer from depression.

A complete physical and psychological diagnostic evaluation is an important first-step in dealing with depression. Check the Yellow Pages under "mental health," "social services," "suicide prevention," "hospi-

Depression

tals," or "physicians" for phone numbers and addresses of people and places that will make a referral to, or provide, diagnostic and treatment services.

- *Five Ways to Help Someone Who's Depressed*
  1. **Get appropriate diagnosis and treatment.** This may involve encouraging the individual to stay with treatment until symptoms begin to abate (several weeks), or to seek different treatment if no improvement occurs. On occasion, it may require making an appointment and accompanying the depressed person to the doctor. It may also mean monitoring whether the depressed person is taking medication.
  2. **Offer emotional support.** This involves understanding, patience, affection, and encouragement. Engage the depressed person in conversation and listen carefully. Do not disparage the feelings they express, but point out realities and offer hope. Do not ignore remarks about suicide. Always report them.
  3. **Be a friend.** Invite the depressed person for walks, outings, and other activities. Be gently insistent if your invitation is refused. Encourage participation in some activities that once gave pleasure, such as hobbies, sports, religious or cultural activities, but do not push the depressed person to undertake too much too soon. The depressed person needs diversion and company, but not too many demands.
  4. **Be patient.** Don't accuse the depressed person of faking illness or laziness, or expect him or her "to snap out of it." Eventually, with treatment, most depressed people do get better. Keep that in mind, and keep reassuring the depressed person that, with time and help, he or she will feel better.
  5. **Point to Jesus.** As you have opportunity, help the depressed person realize how much he or she is loved and accepted by Jesus and by their local community of faith, how persistent and victorious is God's grace, and how absolutely nothing that happens in this world can ever separate us from God's enduring love (Romans 8:31-39; 2 Corinthians 4:7, 8).

Sources: Agency for Health Care Policy and Research; National Institute of Mental Health; The Depression/Awareness, Recognition and Treatment Program; The U.S. Department of Health and Human Services.

☞ **Also see:** At-risk Behavior; Climate Issues; Counselling; Death and Dying Issues.

Depression, continued

• Dialogue

College and University Dialogue is an international journal of faith, thought, and action published by the General Conference Committee on Adventist Ministry to College and University Students (AMiCUS) in cooperation with the world Divisions of the Seventh-day Adventist Church. It was launched in 1989 as part of an interdepartmental nurture and outreach program involving Adventist Chaplaincy Ministries, the Education Department, and the Youth Ministry Department.

The journal is addressed to Seventh-day Adventists attending non-Adventist colleges and universities and also to Adventist teachers, chaplains, and young professionals around the world.

• Dialogue's Four Purposes

1. To nurture an intelligent, living faith.
2. To deepen the readers' commitment to Christ, the Bible, and Adventist Global Mission.
3. To articulate biblical responses to contemporary issues in the arts, humanities, philosophy, religion and the sciences.
4. To offer practical models of Christian service and outreach.

Dialogue is published three times a year in four parallel editions in English, French, Portuguese, and Spanish. Its combined circulation stands at almost 30,000 copies per issue. Copies of the journal are provided free to full-time Adventist college and university students who request it. *Dialogue* is also available through paid subscriptions, at $12.00 per year.

Dialogue
12501 Old Columbia Pike
Silver Spring, MD 20904-6600
Phone: (301) 680-5060
FAX: (301) 622-9627
Subscriptions: 110173.1405@CompuServe.com

Dialogue

Discipline

Everyone shows up early. Everyone brings their Bible. Everyone sings, volunteers to take part, asks insightful questions and gives great answers. Everyone's courteous and spiritual.

Sound familiar? It should! All youth leaders *dream* of the perfect youth group. But most of us are still trying to get there. And along the way, we have need for disciplinary skills. Here are a few suggestions.

Your Part in Discipline

1. **Build relationships.** They learn about spiritual things by your *example* more than your *instruction*. Be their friend. Listen as much as you talk. Know what's happening in their world.

2. **Remember what you can't do.** You're not their *parent*. You can't spank them or cut their allowance or send them to bed without any supper. You're not their *principal*. You can't flunk them or make them stay inside during recess or expel them. You're not their *warden*. It shouldn't be punishment to be with you.

3. **Be consistent.** If it's okay to laugh one Sabbath, but not the next, you're asking for trouble. If you're friendly one week and grumpy the next, you're the problem. If you lecture for a month and then ask for discussion, you're going to be disappointed.

4. **Maintain your sense of humor.** Smile. Laugh at appropriate attempts at being funny. Enjoy your ministry.

5. **Establish a high standard of program excellence.** Most discipline problems arise from boredom, lack of involvement, poor climate issues, narrow teaching styles, and irrelevancy.

6. **Make it easy to obey.** Invite the youth to join you in making the rules, setting the limits and establishing the acceptable standards of behavior. Limits should be few and reasonable.

7. **The goal is self-government.** Remember that the purpose of discipline is the formation of skills whereby the individual makes good decisions without extrinsic motivation. Measure all your discipline by this standard. (See: Ellen White, *Education*, 287.)

8. **Never discipline in anger.** Stop what you're doing. Cool off. Speak to the individual privately. Work it out quietly.

9. **Always discipline in grace.** Demonstrate your eagerness to forgive and forget. Be patient. Show favor to the undeserving.

☞ **Also See**: Evaluating; Faith Development Theory; Learning Styles; Understanding Teens.

Discipline

• Discussion

In most conversations with teens, especially in teaching situations (such as Sabbath School lesson study), the rule is that discussion is better than lecture. Discussion helps you hear the concerns of the person or group with whom you're talking. And discussion helps keep the subject focused, encouraging you to speak to real needs.

- ### The Three Best Ways to Kill a Discussion:
  1. **Lecture for twenty minutes**, then ask the kids, "Now, do you have any questions?"
  2. **Look for one, and only one, right answer** – "What one word best describes the character of God?" "Gracious." "No." "Righteous." "NO." "Merciful." "NO!!" "Love." "That's it!"
  3. **Belittle an answer you don't agree with** – "Who's your favorite Bible character?" "Joseph." "Oh, come on, you've been saying, 'Joseph' ever since you were a little kid. Why don't you grow up and choose a better character?"

- ### The Three Best Ways to Get a Discussion Going:
  1. **Begin with a question.** Don't wait for someone to ask. Make the question easy to answer. Appreciate the answer you receive.
  2. **Ask questions to specific people.** Don't expect volunteers.
  3. **Divide your youth into small groups.** Give an assignment that can be worked on together. Appoint a spokesperson for each group. ("The person with the longest hair will be the spokesperson this time.") Establish a time limit and hold to it (three minutes or five minutes, depending on the assignment). Pay attention to the answers.

More Great Advice:
✔ Ken Davis, *How To Speak To Youth* (Loveland, CO: Group, 1986);
✔ David Lynn, *High School Talk Sheets* (Grand Rapids, MI: Zondervan, 1987);
✔ David Lynn and Mike Yaconelli, *Amazing Tension Getters* (Grand Rapids, MI: Zondervan, 1981, 1985, and 1988);
✔ Edward N. McNulty, *Controversial Topics for Youth Groups* (Loveland, CO: Group, 1988);
✔ Stephen Parolini, *Controversial Discussion Starters* (Loveland, CO: Group, 1986).

☞ **Also See:** Active Learning; Boredom; Climate Issues; Involvement; Learning Styles.

Discussion

• Distancing

Distancing happens whenever you fail to take responsibility for your own behavior, or when you attribute your actions to someone else, like your church or your parents.

Distancing happens when someone asks you, "Why aren't you coming to the dance on Friday night?" and you answer by saying, "*My church* observes Sabbath from sundown Friday night to sundown Saturday night."

Distancing is the stance you take when someone offers you an alcoholic beverage and you say, "*My parents* don't want me to drink."

Distancing usually takes place for one of two reasons: because you feel you don't know enough about your beliefs or standards to really own them. Or because you're embarrassed about the positions you take, but you do it to please Mom, or so you won't let down the church, or even because you think God expects it of you, even though you don't know why.

– Taken from, *Walking On the Edge* (Lincoln, NE: AdventSource, 1997),17.

The members of your youth group are in that time of their lives when they begin to make their faith their own, when they begin to make decisions for themselves. It's an absolutely essential process through which all of us must go in order for our faith to mature. Effective youth leaders do all they can to encourage sincere questioning and to eliminate distancing.

• *Five Questions to Penetrate Distancing*

1. If you were responsible for making your own decisions, what would you do about it?
2. How would you explain that position to your best friend?
3. Is there a Bible story about someone who took a similar position to the one you're taking?
4. What would the benefits be of everyone in school taking the same position?
5. Are you interested in knowing the reasons behind such a position?

☞ **Also See**: Adolescence; Attachment; Climate Issues; Faith Development; Faith Maturity.

- # Diversity

In the Christian context, diversity is about accepting, respecting and valuing all people irrespective of their differences: age, culture, abilities, economic status, education, ethnicity/race, gender, social sphere or whatever the difference might be.

Respecting diversity, even celebrating it, results in an inclusive ministry model and leads to compassionate relationships with others. Managing diversity well can result in a wonderful, productive unity.

A diversified ministry endeavors to utilize the gifts and talents of all members to challenge and empower people to accept Christ regardless of the social barriers. Diversity is more than political correctness, it is a divine imperative.

- ## Seven Bible Passages on Diversity
  1. Acts 10 and 11 – Peter learns to be tolerant.
  2. Romans 12:10-21 – Live in harmony with one another.
  3. 1 Corinthians 12:21-27 – Have equal concern for each other.
  4. Galatians 3:28 – We are all one in Jesus.
  5. Colossians 3:11-15 – Perfect unity in Christ's people.
  6. Titus 3:1-3 – Hatred enslaves us.
  7. 1 John 3:11-23 – We should love one another.

- ## Five Ways to Bring Diversity to Youth Leadership
  1. **Be a lifelong learner.** Take a course or workshop in meeting the challenges of diversity. Encourage others to do the same. Read the latest books and reports on the issue.
  2. **Meet with other youth leaders** to discuss diversity. Ask what they are doing to build unity and to combat racism and other stereotyping.
  3. **Actively recruit** individuals for youth leadership positions from the cross-section of church members. Encourage diversity in elections to all church offices.
  4. **Use a variety of techniques and activities** to deliver information. Different people have different learning styles.
  5. Be sure that all your communication is **gender-inclusive and sensitive** to diverse groups.

Diversity

- *Seven Programming Ideas to Celebrate Diversity*

  1. Celebrate diversity annually with an event that highlights the personal and corporate spiritual benefits of diversity in Christian unity.

  2. Provide opportunities for youth to examine and study their own cultures. Create a forum for them to report on their findings (a <u>Sabbath School</u>/pot luck combination always works well). Use national dress, music, art forms, food, and language to highlight the culture.

  3. Divide your members randomly whenever you divide into <u>small groups</u> for youth activities.

  4. Be sure that program participants represent the diversity in your membership.

  5. Have your youth report on the accessibility of your church to the physically challenged. Blindfold them, cover their ears or let them use a wheelchair to do their research.

  6. Meet with a <u>youth group</u> from another culture.

  7. Go on a <u>mission trip</u>. Watch for things you can learn.

In January, 1990, the members of the North American Division Materials Development and Marketing Committee voted to adopt certain resolutions to further the goal of breaking down "the walls of alienation and division by actively promoting healing and mutual respect between the gender, racial, ethnic, socioeconomic, and age groups within the <u>Seventh-day Adventist</u> Church in North America."

To ensure that these attitudes of acceptance and understanding will be obvious in the Division's products and services, and to correctly portray the actual proportional representations of each group in the North American church rather than the percentages in the nations comprising the North American Division, the committee voted to recommend only those <u>resources</u> which met the following high standards:

1. **Racial and Ethnic Diversity**. We will insist that all materials that come before us remove inadvertent racial or ethnic bias and we will actively seek the input and advice of minority members to achieve this goal. We will strive to remain conscious of the changing circumstances of minority communities within the North American Church, and will require that accurate, proportional representations of these minority communities be portrayed in approved materials. We accept the challenge to editorial timetables that this patient, balanced appraisal will

Diversity, continued

Diversity, continued

require, for we affirm that fair and equal presentation of the church's many racial and ethnic groups is of immense value to the mission of the church.

2. **Equality of Men and Women**. We will insist that all material brought before us for recommendation present a balanced, biblical understanding of the full equality of men and women in the sight of God and in the life and witness of the church. We will not recommend materials which by role stereotyping and gender references suggest limitations on the full participation of women in the life of the church. We will adopt gender inclusive language in our own communications as a committee, and will insist on the same in all materials under our purview.

3. **Socioeconomic Diversity**. We will sensitize ourselves as committee members to the socioeconomic diversity of the Seventh-day Adventist Church in North America. We will resist the tendency to generalize about the church in the middle-class or middle-income language, and will encourage material producers to present a variety of portrayals of Adventist life from all socioeconomic groups. We will also resist the equation of race with socioeconomic status, and will encourage material producers to give positive portrayals of each group within the church.

4. **The Contribution of all Age-Groups**. We will actively encourage the production of materials that positively portray the abilities and contributions of persons of all ages to the church, especially including children, youth, and senior citizens. We will promote materials that feature the full inclusion of all age groups in church decision-making, service, leadership and witness.

- *Three Discussion Starters for Exploring Diversity*
  1. **Acknowledge the reality of prejudice.** What world events drew your attention to prejudice this week? Discuss current events in the light of the need for diversity.
  2. How would you respond to an act of discrimination? Where do we encounter such acts (racial or sexual jokes, for example)? **What would you say** to defuse the tension caused by such an act?
  3. **Tell the stories of discrimination.** Invite people who have been the objects of prejudice to tell their stories to your group. Be ready to ask sensitive questions.

• Divorce

It's a simple fact that divorce is affecting more and more of our church families today. Without making judgments and accusations, youth workers will need to minister to kids who are affected by the breakup of the family. In a world that cares little about their pain, what better place to find healing than in their church youth group! You can provide the encouragement and support that will help them survive and maintain a faith relationship with Jesus.

• Five Common Needs of Kids Experiencing Divorce
1. A healthy outlet for their anger
2. The need to be accepted, a place to belong
3. A relief from guilty feelings
4. The need to feel "normal"
5. Good role models

There are three things you can do to help in this painful time.

1. **Reassure kids that they are loved**. Divorce almost always produces anger towards a parent, God, or somebody else. Help them work through their feelings. Encourage openness through your faithful friendship and total acceptance. Assure them that it is normal to feel anger, and allow them to process the emotion. Pray with and for the young person, taking every opportunity to show them that you care.

2. **Affirm the kids worth and value**. Children of divorce tend to assume part of the blame for the failure of the relationship. This unhealthy guilt can cripple self-esteem, and cause some to withdraw emotionally. You can reassure the young person that they are not to blame for their parents' decision. And assure them that nothing can change their great worth to you. Encourage forgiveness of both parents.

3. **Provide a safe place for kids to hurt**. Ironically, church may be one of the places where kids of divorce may feel the least comfortable. Let's change that by making our churches and youth groups "real."

We can present a clear, true picture of a God who cares. We can accept painful behaviors and learn to handle them in godly ways. We can provide security in times of loss. We can help other kids provide a support network to care for kids in crises, and ultimately have kids who have been healed help others in the healing process.

Divorce

• Doctrines

A doctrine is a statement of belief, an idea or opinion that is held and presented as absolute truth.

The term "Christian doctrine" refers in general to what the Christian church believes and teaches, to those ideas most Christians hold in common. Doctrine can also refer to the *distinctive* beliefs and teachings of a particular denomination.

The Seventh-day Adventist Church first published a list of doctrines held by the church in 1872. The document explained the biblical background of 25 propositions and was referred to as a "synopsis of our faith." In 1889, the list was expanded to 28 statements and was included in the publication of the denomination's *Yearbook* (a listing of all institutions and workers) for that year.

During the early part of the 20th century, a committee of theologians produced another summary of the doctrines of the Adventist Church. This statement of 22 "principal features" of our faith was the official statement of Adventist doctrine from 1931 until 1980, and was the basis for the book, *Seventh-day Adventists Answer Questions On Doctrines*, published in 1957.

At the General Conference Session held in Dallas, Texas in 1980, delegates approved a list of 27 "fundamental beliefs" which are held and proclaimed by Seventh-day Adventists around the world. (See: *Seventh-day Adventists Believe... A Biblical Exposition of 27 Fundamental Doctrines*, published by the Ministerial Association of the General Conference in 1988.)

• 27 Fundamental Beliefs of Seventh-day Adventists

1. The Word of God
2. The Trinity
3. God the Father
4. God the Son
5. God the Holy Spirit
6. Creation
7. The Nature of Man
8. The Great Controversy
9. The Life, Death, and Resurrection of Christ
10. The Experience of Salvation
11. The Church
12. The Remnant and Its Mission

13. Unity in the Body of Christ
14. Baptism
15. The Lord's Supper
16. Spiritual Gifts and Ministries
17. The Gift of Prophecy (See: Ellen White.)
18. The Law of God
19. The Sabbath
20. Stewardship
21. Christian Behavior
22. Marriage and the Family
23. Christ's Ministry in the Heavenly Sanctuary
24. The Second Coming of Christ
25. Death and Resurrection
26. The Millennium and the End of Sin
27. The New Earth

- ## Jesus Is the Truth
  "I am the way and the truth and the life." Jesus, John 14:6.

- ## One Great Central Truth
  "There is one great central truth to be kept ever before the mind in the searching of the Scriptures — Christ and Him crucified. Every other truth is invested with influence and power corresponding to its relation to this theme." Ellen White, MS 31, 1890.

- ## The Truth at the Center
  "The sacrifice of Christ as an atonement for sin is the great truth around which all other truths cluster. In order to be rightly understood and appreciated, every truth in the Word of God, from Genesis to Revelation, must be studied in the light that streams from the cross of Calvary." Ellen White, *Gospel Workers*, 315.

- ## More to Be Discovered
  "Every doctrine, every belief, must reveal the love of our Lord. Here is a Person with an unconditional love and commitment unparalleled in human history. Recognizing that He who is the incarnation of truth is infinite, we humbly confess that there is still much truth to be discovered." *Seventh-day Adventists Believe...*, vii.

Doctrines, continued

• **Drama**

Drama is the telling of a story, the illustration of an idea, or the presentation of a concept through means which involve acting, such as plays, skits, pantomime, dramatic reading, puppets, clowns, role plays, and improvising.

Dramatization is an extremely effective means of education. Those who take part learn by being involved. Those who observe frequently discover insights and obtain knowledge that less interesting forms of education fail to effectively convey. As a means of *religious* education, especially in youth ministry, drama can be a powerful tool in the hands of creative youth leaders.

We are advised, however, that leading a Christian drama group is not for the faint of heart. Acting often reveals feelings and emotions that lie hidden just below the surface. Remember, in your setting drama is about *ministry*. Always be ready to stop what you're doing and explore the spiritual implications of your dramatic situation.

• *Starting a Drama Ministry*

1. **Recruit.** This is usually the easiest part. Just tell the kids how much fun they'll be having, even when they're making fools of themselves in front of their classmates and friends or acting out embarrassing situations in front of total strangers.

2. **Audition.** Set times when you can evaluate the people who want to be part of your ministry. Do group action activities. This is helpful in "breaking the ice" and setting everyone at ease. Examples are as plentiful as your imagination (e.g., ask your group to act out swimming through a pool of jello). Encourage your actors to relax and enjoy the process.

3. **Explore.** Read through a script. Find a good skit with plenty of parts. Ask for dramatic interpretation. Change emotions on the lines in the script. Your "cast" will grow through the exercise, and you'll be discovering their talents at the same time.

4. **Rehearse.** Establish a regular rehearsal schedule. Keep practicing. The better you know your parts, the more ministry can take place.

5. **Pray.** Always begin and end with prayer. It might not make the experience crisis free, but it sure will make a difference during a crisis.

Drama

- **Seven Excellent Christian Drama Sources:**

Covenant Players
    Post Office Box 2900
    Oxnard, CA 93034-2900
    Phone: (805) 486-7155
    FAX: (805) 486-2725

Samuel French, Inc.
    7623 Sunset Blvd.
    Hollywood, CA 90046
    Phone: (213) 876-0570
    FAX: (213) 876-6822

Group Publishing
    Post Office Box 4881
    Loveland, CO 8539
    Phone: (970) 669-3836
    FAX: (970) 669-3269

The Lamb's Players
    Post Office Box 18229
    Coronado, CA 92178
    Phone: (619) 437-6050
    FAX: (619) 437-6053

Lillenas
    Post Office Box 419527
    Kansas City, MO 64141
    Phone: (816) 931-1900
    FAX: (816) 753-4071

Willow Creek Resources
    Post Office Box 668
    Holmes, PA 19064-0668
    Phone: (800) 876-7335
    FAX: (610) 532-9001

Youth Specialties
    1224 Greenfield Drive
    El Cajon, CA 92021
    Phone: (619) 440-2333
    FAX: (619) 440-4939

Notes:

_____
_____
_____
_____

_____
_____
_____
_____

_____
_____
_____
_____

_____
_____
_____
_____

_____
_____
_____
_____

_____
_____
_____
_____

_____
_____
_____
_____

Drama, continued

• Eating Disorders

Eating disorders are serious emotional challenges that can have life-threatening consequences. These disorders occur when eating habits, weight management practices and attitudes about weight and body shape result in loss of self-control, obsession, anxiety, guilt, alienation from self and others, and physiological imbalances. The most common eating disorders are anorexia nervosa, bulimia nervosa and compulsive overeating.

People suffering from anorexia develop an irrational fear of body fat and weight gain and exhibit a fierce determination to become thinner. Bulimia is characterized by cycles of binge-eating, during which the person consumes a huge amount of food, and purging, often induced by vomiting. Compulsive overeaters engage in periods of gorging or continuous eating, frequently followed by attempts at dieting.

• Six Warning Signs of Eating Disorders
1. A sudden increase or decrease in weight.
2. Abnormal eating habits.
3. An intense preoccupation with weight and body image.
4. Compulsive or excessive exercising.
5. Self-induced vomiting, abuse of laxatives, diet pills or diuretics.
6. Feelings of isolation, depression or irritability.

• Three Things Not to Say
1. "What's the matter with you? You look sick!"
2. "Why don't you just eat?"
3. "Why are you doing this to me?"

• Helping Prevent Eating Disorders
1. Celebrate the wonder of God's creative genius. "I am fearfully and wonderfully made" (Psalm 139:14).
2. Examine society's overemphasis on beauty and body shape.
3. Resist the media's distortion of what is attractive.
4. Demonstrate the value of excellent nutrition.
5. Balance sensible eating with sensible exercise.
6. Build self-acceptance by non-judgmental acceptance.
7. Don't try to solve the challenge alone; seek professional help.

Eating Disorders

• Effectiveness Factors

Emerging from the _Valuegenesis_ study are 41 characteristics of families, congregations, and schools that are associated with both a deep, maturing faith and a commitment to the Seventh-day Adventist Church. We refer to these characteristics as _Effectiveness Factors_.

Young people who experience these Effectiveness Factors display greater faith maturity and/or deeper denominational loyalty. As each of the factors increases, the faith maturity and/or denominational loyalty of the person increases.

• 20 Family Effectiveness Factors

Family Practices
1. Engages in family worship
2. Family worship is interesting and meaningful
3. Engages in projects to help other people (See: Service)

Mother
4. Mother is religious
5. Mother is comfortable talking about her faith
6. Mother talks about her faith with child
7. Mother and child talk together about faith

Father
8. Father is religious
9. Father is comfortable talking about his faith
10. Father talks about his faith with child
11. Father and child talk together about faith

Support
12. Parent/child communication is frequent and positive
13. Family life is experienced as loving, caring, and supportive
14. Parents help child with school work

Control
15. Family enforces substance abuse standards
16. Family enforces Adventist "way of life" standards
17. Family enforces Adventist "popular culture" standards
18. Parents punish wrong behavior
19. Parents have strong standards against alcohol use by child
20. Parents set limits on use of time

Effectiveness Factors

Effectiveness Factors, continued

Analysis: Although all 20 Family Effectiveness Factors show a positive impact, the least impact is made by factors within the control theme. The strongest Family Effectiveness Factor is the quality of family worship. It is in the family context that standards enforcement plays a positive role, whereas such control is not particularly associated with the effectiveness of congregations or schools.

Finally, the power of parents sharing their own faith experiences is evident. Such sharing is particularly important to youth, because it both models a dynamic faith and also gives opportunity to reflect on and expand one's own religious understandings. – From *Valuegenesis, Report 1*, pages 17, 18

- *12 Congregational Effectiveness Factors*

Congregational Climate
1. Emphasizes learning, discussion, question-asking, and independent thinking
2. Feels friendly and hospitable
3. Youth frequently experience support and concern from adults
4. Youth frequently experience support and concern from peers

Religious Education Programming
5. Sabbath School and other church youth programs are viewed as interesting
6. Sabbath School and other church youth programs are thought-provoking
7. Emphasizes drug and alcohol education
8. Emphasizes sexuality education
9. Emphasizes involving youth in helping the poor and hungry
10. Emphasizes the teaching of Adventist standards
11. Involves youth in intergenerational programs and events
12. Religious educators are experienced as warm, caring and supportive

Analysis: Looking across the 12 Congregational Effectiveness Factors, we see that several themes predominate. Clearly, one is warmth and support. A second theme has to do with intellectual challenge. A third theme has to do with relevance to the adolescent experience, as evidenced by life-related topics such as drugs and sexuality. – From *Valuegenesis, Report 1*, pages 20, 21

- *9 School Effectiveness Factors*

Religious Programming and Faith Talk
1. Religious education program is of high quality
2. Students frequently talk to teachers at school about God and faith

Characteristics of Teachers
3. Caring and supportive
4. Competent

School Climate
5. School spirit is high
6. Discipline is fair
7. Students have a voice in school policy
8. Teachers refrain from "putting down" students
9. School enforces Adventist "way of life" standards

Analysis: Although each of the School Effectiveness Factors is important, the most powerful of the nine is the quality of the school religious education program.

A dominant theme in the nine School Effectiveness Factors is the affective nature, or "climate," of schools. Effectiveness is associated with a supportive, encouraging, open community marked by school spirit, treating students with respect, fair discipline, and teachers who care.

This kind of warm and supporting climate stands in contrast to a climate premised more on strict enforcement, authority and obedience. Such emphases on strictness were also measured in the study, but they do not appear to be associated with the development of faith maturity or denominational loyalty.

Only one of the nine school effectiveness factors relates to such an emphasis, namely, enforcement of Adventist "way of life" standards. It functions to promote denominational loyalty but not faith maturity. Strictness of enforcement of standards concerning Adventist "popular culture" standards is not related to either faith maturity or denominational loyalty. Strictness of standards concerning substance abuse is also unrelated.

It can be said with surety that there is no evidence that increasing the strictness with which the "popular culture" or substance abuse standards are enforced would have a benefit for either faith maturity or loyalty to Adventism. – From *Valuegenesis, Report 1*, pages 22, 23

Effectiveness Factors, continued

• Evaluating

"If it can't be evaluated, it didn't happen!" This adage stresses the importance of proper evaluation of all <u>youth ministry</u> activities. No program worth doing is beyond some type of evaluation. Here are some helpful hints about building a system of evaluation.

- ### • *Why evaluate?*
  1. **To describe** what has happened.
  2. **To discover** what intended outcomes have actually occurred.
  3. **To identify** where your ideas, programs, and activities are working, and where they are weak or where they fail.
  4. **To determine** the importance of the things you evaluate.

- ### • *Steps in Doing Evaluation*
  1. **Describe.** Discuss the event, program or activity you want to evaluate. Be sure everyone is talking about the same thing.
  2. **Measure.** Rank items from important to not important, or most effective to least effective. Get true and false responses. Use multiple choice answers. Create continuums.
  3. **Assess.** After you get the responses from your research, take time to analyze the information you've been given.
  4. **Evaluate.** Make a decision as to what took place and if it was good or not, and whether or not it should be continued.

- ### • *Five Types of Evaluation*
  1. Individual Interviews
  2. Quizzes and Questionnaires
  3. Personal Letters and Responses
  4. Telephone Surveys
  5. Voting

- ### • *What Can be Evaluated?*
  <u>Sabbath School</u> programming; teacher's or leader's effectiveness; behaviors; the environment, facilities and equipment; <u>curriculum</u> materials including lesson or program content; effectiveness of planning; knowledge; feelings; etc.

Evaluating

• Faith Development

In the spiritual dimension of each individual's life, "God is experienced in different types of expressions of faith through the cycle of life. Consequently, faith takes on a different meaning and emphasis during various times in life." [1] We refer to this spiritual growth as faith development.

Within faith development theories, faith experiences, stages or situations are proposed as categories which "can aid in both describing the faith experience that is seen in the growing person as well as providing some sort of focus and basis for nurture and ministry." [2]

"The promise of faith development theory is that by understanding the dynamics of the human dimension of faithing we can better disarm the blocks to authentic faith and assist others to grow." [3]

Understanding developing faith is particularly important for youth ministry leaders. Expressing faith in language teens understand, giving them a frame of reference, is a crucial step for faith development.

• Seven Faith Development Questions
1. How is faith seen?
2. How is religious experience known?
3. How do we enrich the faith experience?
4. What does this experience do for people at various ages?
5. What is the experience of faith like at various age levels?
6. How do you develop a faith experience?
7. How do individuals grow toward a certainty in God and know the vision God has for them in a personal way? [4]

• Five Characteristics of Teenage Faith
1. Religious experience must make sense in the present.
2. Faith must be freely chosen, without coercion.
3. There is a searching, questioning, committing and examining of one's faith.
4. There is a rapid change and reordering of the worldview.
5. Faith now becomes a verb. [5]

1   V. Bailey Gillespie, *The Experience of Faith* (Birmingham, AL: Religious Education Press, 1988), 75.
2   *Ibid*, 76
3   Gary L. Chamberlain, *Fostering Faith* (Mahwah, NJ: Paulist Press, 1988), 19.
4   Gillespie, *The Experience of Faith*, 66, 67
5   *Ibid*, 125-149.

Faith Development

• Faith Maturity

Utilizing a pioneering way of assessing the spiritual experience, the _Valuegenesis_ research identified the goal that all Christian youth ministry has for its youth. _Valuegenesis_ called this goal "faith maturity," and referred to it as "a process, not a product," in which our faith becomes increasingly evident in our "priorities, dispositions and behaviors."

Faith maturity is a vibrant, life-transforming faith marked by both a deep, personal relationship with a loving God and a consistent commitment to serving others.

• The Four Core Dimensions of Faith Maturity

1. Grace. Discovering the depths of God's love and experiencing the peace that comes form accepting His salvation.
2. Worship. Responding to the grace of God with all our lives, and exploring the riches of praise.
3. Community. Experiencing the joy of active involvement in a family of faith which models God's grace.
4. Service. Revealing the grace of God through a consistent commitment to ministering to the needs of others.

The gifts God gives us are to prepare His people _"for works of service, so that the body of Christ may be built up until we all reach unity in the faith and in the knowledge of the Son of God and become mature, attaining to the whole measure of the fullness of Christ. Then we will no longer be infants, tossed back and forth by the waves, and blown here and there by every wind of teaching and by the cunning and craftiness of men in their deceitful scheming. Instead, speaking the truth in love, we will in all things grow up into him who is the Head, that is, Christ."_ Ephesians 4:11-15.

Notes:

_____

_____

_____

_____

_____

_____

Faith Maturity

Family Worship

Family worship is the time a family sets aside, on a daily or weekly basis, at home, away from organized religious occasions, for seeking God together. This faith-building time may include such traditional worship elements as prayer, music and Bible study. It may also include such things as devotional reading, drama, games and service projects.

While family worship should be "the most interesting and enjoyable exercise of the home life,"[1] and "the sweetest and most helpful" time of the day,[2] most Adventist youth come from homes that do not have family worship with any regularity. *Valuegenesis* research indicates that a little more than a quarter of our youth *never* have family worship, and that another 40% have worship only a couple of times a month. Unfortunately, among those who *do* have family worship, a significant number find the activity to be boring and meaningless.

One of the best things you as a youth leader can do for your youth is to assist their families in establishing meaningful family worship practices. Here are a few clues about where to begin.

Five Principles of Successful Family Worship

1. **Establish a regular time.** Don't try to have worship when everyone is hungry. Or when favorite TV programs are starting. Or after the kids have begun working on their homework. Agree on a regular time when all of you can relax for a few moments without feeling the distraction of other pressures.

2. **Keep it short.** Length of time doesn't equal better religion. Ten minutes of participation is better than 30 minutes of lecture.

3. **Make it real.** Discover significant events in the lives of the kids. Ask questions that easily can be answered from their perspective. Discuss topics that have real impact on their lives.

4. **Vary the content and format.** Don't do the same thing night after night. Take part in a service project on Sunday. Read a continuing story on Mondays and Tuesdays. Explore the Bible together on Wednesdays. Play a Bible game on Thursdays. Etc.

5. **Involve everyone.** Don't lecture. Don't always be the one to read and pray. Don't even take all the responsibility for planning. Help eveyone discover the joy of participation.

1　Ellen White, *Child Guidance*, 521.
2　Ellen White, *Messages to Young People*, 341.

Family Worship

Federations

A Federation is a group of local Adventist Youth Societies – bound together by common goals, aspirations and needs – cooperating, communicating and coordinating activities.

Common Federation Activities

1. **Coordination.** The Federation serves the conference Youth Ministries office by communicating conference goals and emphases to local youth groups and by communicating the mood of sectional youth to the conference youth director.
2. **Sharing.** Federations become laboratories for new youth ministry ideas and methods.
3. **Leadership Development.** Federations provide opportunities for expanded leadership development beyond the local church level.
4. **Community.** Interchurch activities enhance peer fellowship. The sense of community belonging and worth greatly assists individuals in their struggles and challenges.
5. **Programming.** Federations assist in the development of relevant programs for youth groups in local churches.

The Federation concept emerged in different parts of the original Allegheny Conference territory almost simultaneously. In the northern New Jersey metroplex, pastors and lay people pioneered the idea of youth societies united. In Virginia and Ohio, others envisioned a strong federated youth movement.

Soon the fledgling organization began to grow and develop. Conference youth leaders added their expertise, supported by young adults. As the concept spread in the Regional Conferences, hundreds of youth were mobilized and trained for leadership and projects flourished.

Seven Federation Projects

1. On-the-street Rap Squads
2. Subway Stop Ministry
3. Evangelistic Tent Crusades
4. Bible Bowls
5. Park, Mall and Street Meetings
6. Better Living and Temperance Parades
7. Conference-wide Congresses, Retreats and Conventions

• FTC (For the Cause)

For the Cause (FTC) is a quarterly youth leadership <u>newsletter</u> published by the Florida Conference Youth/<u>Young Adult</u> Department. It is mailed to all youth and young adult leaders and <u>Sabbath School</u> teachers in the Florida Conference, as well as to all pastors and associates.

It is the prayer of the publishers of *FTC* that through the newsletter <u>youth leaders</u> will be encouraged to connect with one another (by <u>shared</u> <u>experiences</u>, insights, photos, etc.); connect with youth (by use of creative ministry ideas, <u>resources</u>, insight into facts and lives of young people); and connect with God (through inspirational messages and stories of touched lives). Call (407) 644-5000 for more information.

• Regularly Occurring FTC Elements

1. **Savvy Suggestions.** Tips for leaders.
2. **Check It Out.** Descriptions and reviews of latest resources available through the Youth Department's resource library.
3. **Just the Facts.** News items, factoids, latest information and statistics of what's going on in the <u>youth culture</u> around us.
4. **It's Your Call.** This is a section for questions about various youth-related issues. The questions are presented to our readers for their response and feedback. This section allows for peer interaction, sharing of experiences and encouragement, and a fostering of connection among the churches.
5. **Coming Soon.** A calendar section, divided by regions and highlighting events and programs going on during the quarter.
6. **Conference Connection.** Reports and photos of the Conference-sponsored youth events.
7. **Ministry on the Edge.** Special highlight of an innovative, creative, daring ministry begun by a youth leader or young person.
8. **Hot ideas.** Ideas to incorporate in your socials, outreach, relationship building, etc. The Conference awards $100 to a youth group for original ideas that have been tried and work!!!
9. <u>**Campus Advent** Update</u>. Update information about what's happening in our secular campus ministries.
10. **One-on-One.** Inspirational/encouragement article for youth leaders from the Conference Youth Ministries Department.
11. **Visions in Action.** Wild, crazy and fun photos of youth, leaders and youth groups enjoying life in Christ.

• Fund Raising

When you have to raise the money yourself to meet your own youth ministry <u>budget</u>, here are a few things to keep in mind.

• Four Secrets of Fund Raising

1. **The Personal Touch.** Most people respond better to face-to-face, personal requests for donations than to mass-mailings or telephone appeals.

2. **Targeted Requests.** People seem to prefer giving money to specific projects rather than to general operating funds. Be ready to summarize three or four projects you'd like to accomplish. Know how much each project will cost.

3. **Planned Giving.** You probably will find people more interested in giving on a regular, monthly basis than in giving a single, large donation. Apparently it's easier to say, "I'll give you $50 a month," than "I'll give you $500."

4. **Showing Appreciation.** Be sure to follow a donation with a thank-you letter. Don't create a form letter; write a personal, to-the-point note expressing your gratitude.

• Ten Fund Raising Ideas

1. **Holiday Greetings.** Create a group of special holiday activities to invite donations to your <u>youth ministry</u>. Here are a few examples:

   a. At the beginning of the new year, put together family resolutions boxes (devotional books, healthy recipes and mixes, exercise wear, etc.). Sell the boxes at a price that will return a good profit to you. Let people know that they're not only starting their year off right, but they're also helping the youth ministry budget get healthy.

   b. Bake Valentine's cookies, muffins and cakes, purchase gourmet hot drink mixes, fruit and small boxes of chocolates, and arrange them in baskets, finished with colorful wrapping and bows. Sell them to your church members as ready-made Valentine's Day celebrations.

   c. Plan other activities for other holiday or seasonal celebrations, including Mother's Day and Father's Day, the end of the school year, Thanksgiving, etc.

Fund Raising

2. **Harvest Auction**. Dedicate a Saturday night in the Fall to raising money for the youth ministry budget. Invite church members to create items to donate to the fund-raiser, including such things as cakes, cookies, pies and fudge, handmade toys, quilts, knitted sweaters, art work, etc. Start talking about the event early in the year so people have plenty of time to create items. Auction the items to the highest bidders, always reminding the audience that all the money goes to ministry to the youth of the church.

3. **Odd Jobs**. Put together teams of youth to do work that most of us dislike doing (chopping wood, washing windows, raking leaves, cleaning out the garage, etc.), then turn the work into fun social events. Hold a one-hour odd job blitz with as many kids as you can get together, charge a $25 fee for the work, and have a great time working together. Try to do four projects on a Sunday and raise $100 for your budget. (Of course, it would be acceptable if people wanted to pay you more, or if they wanted to also provide refreshments for the kids.)

4. **After-School Tutoring**. Organize a tutoring program for elementary students, especially ones who go home every day to empty houses. Hold the tutoring sessions at school or at the church. Have members of your youth group help the kids with their homework. Invite church members to donate money on behalf of the tutoring program.

5. **Softball Marathon**. Solicit donations for a specified amount per inning of softball played in one game (for example, $1 an inning). Draft all the kids in your youth group, start early in the morning on a Sunday and try to play 25 innings. During the game, have soft drinks and peanuts available to sell to all the spectators who come to watch.

6. **Provide Transportation**. Enlist a few of your older youth (or their parents) to establish a regular transportation service for kids needing to be taken to or from school, for seniors who need to be brought to church, or for school field trips. Try to find a van or station wagon to use, charge $2 per round trip, and pick up five or six people at a time.

7. **Internet Research**. Have your teens form a research company that will pursue topics on the Internet for high school students writing a paper, pastors needing background material for sermons, or families planning a vacation. Charge a flat fee

Fund Raising, continued

($10, for example), do the research, and print a good collection of articles to deliver.

8. **Disaster Preparedness**. Collect all the necessary items to create a disaster preparedness kit (flashlights, batteries, water, flares, blankets, etc.). See if you can get companies in your community to donate items (be sure to fully explain your project). Hold a kit preparation party, then exchange the kits for donations to your budget.

9. **Family Worship Stories**. Collect fun worship stories, make multiple copies and give them to members of a family worship team. One night a week (in exchange for a donation, of course), have team members go to the homes of various church members and read the stories for worship.

10. **Video Greetings**. Organize teams of your youth to video holiday, birthday or just friendly greetings to send to friends and family members. Video five minutes of a family's greetings, put the video in a mailer, address it and then deliver or mail the package. The charge for the video greeting is a donation to the youth ministry budget.

• **More Great Advice**:
✔ David and Kathy Lynn, *Great Fundraising Ideas for Youth Groups* (Grand Rapids, MI: Youth Specialties/Zondervan, 1993);

Write more fund raising ideas here:

_____

_____

_____

_____

_____

_____

_____

_____

_____

_____

_____

_____

_____

_____

_____

Fund Raising, continued

• Games

There are tons of great game books available for youth ministry leaders. You can find them in any good Christian book store or order them directly from the publisher. Here are ten of the best.

• Ten Great Books on Games
1. Nelson E. Copeland, Jr., *Great Games for City Kids* (Grand Rapids, MI: Youth Specialties/Zondervan, 1991).
2. Jeff Hopper, Steve Torrey, Rod Yonkers, *Adventure Games* (Grand Rapids, MI: Youth Specialties/Zondervan, 1990).
3. Tom Finley, *Good Clean Fun* (Grand Rapids, MI: Youth Specialties/Zondervan, 1986).
4. Tom Finley, *Good Clean Fun, Volume 2* (Grand Rapids, MI: Youth Specialties/Zondervan, 1988).
5. *Great Group Games for Youth Ministry* (Loveland, CO: Group Publishing, 1994).
6. *Have-a-Blast Games* (Loveland, CO: Group Publishing, 1991).
7. *Quick Crowdbreakers and Games for Youth Groups* (Loveland, CO: Group Publishing, 1988).
8. Wayne Rice and Mike Yaconelli, *Play It! Great Games for Groups* (Grand Rapids, MI: Youth Specialties/Zondervan, 1986).
9. Wayne Rice and Mike Yaconelli, *Play It Again! More Great Games for Groups* (Grand Rapids, MI: Youth Specialties/Zondervan, 1993).
10. Wayne Rice and Mike Yaconelli, *Holiday Ideas for Youth Groups* (Grand Rapids, MI: Youth Specialties/Zondervan, 1989).

More Resources for Games:

_____
_____
_____
_____
_____
_____
_____
_____
_____
_____

Games

Gangs

A gang is a group of individuals which forms an allegiance for a common purpose, usually including engaging in unlawful, violent or criminal activity. Gangs involve all races and socioeconomic levels.

Gangs are predominantly territory oriented. Each gang has its own turf and graffiti marks its boundaries. Anyone not belonging in the area, especially if they appear to be from a rival gang, is subject to attack.

Why Youth Join Gangs

1. The excitement of gang activity
2. _Peer pressure_
3. Financial benefit
4. The lure of a "family"
5. A lack of realization of the hazards involved

Gang membership extracts a terrible toll from the lives of members and their families, as well as the communities in which gangs operate. Vandalism lessens property values and drives away local business. Bystanders often become the innocent victims of violence. Formal education is usually discarded by gang members. Extensive police records limit future employment opportunities. Family members live in constant fear that their loved ones will be killed.

What We Can Do About Gangs

1. **Become Aware.** Learn about gang activity in your neighborhood. Discover what the police are doing to combat gangs.
2. **Cooperate With the Experts.** Direct interaction is best left to experts trained to handle dangerous situations.
3. **Neighborhood Involvement.** A gang's power grows by fear. Neighborhoods that unite in a spirit of cooperation toward stopping crime and violence will greatly hamper a gang's efforts.
4. **Provide Alternatives.** Especially for the younger members of the community, churches can provide activities that keep them busy, help them focus on positive goals, and keep them out of the direct influence of street gangs.
5. **Serve the Community.** Christlike _service_, for the people and with the people of a community, helps to head off the problems upon which gangs feed.

Gangs

• Gender Protocol for Youth Leaders

Outside of the immediate family, no adults are in closer, more frequent, more emotionally-charged contact with young people than are <u>youth leaders</u>. Effective <u>youth ministry</u> *begins* with strong, personal relationships. And while we wouldn't have it any other way, sometimes in those relationships, boundaries which appropriately *separate* adults and adolescents unfortunately are crossed.

Youth leaders feel genuine love and affection for "their" kids. During <u>adolescence</u> energy abounds with enthusiasm and excitement. Personal spiritual growth often involves long, intense, one-on-one discussions. Appreciation for spiritual maturity and leadership can be confused with romantic feelings. Warmth can be mistaken for intimacy.

And before you know it, situations develop which threaten marriages, cause long-term emotional damage, divide churches, and even end up in court.

How much better to be aware of problems before they occur, to remember to act in accordance with the Christian's high calling, and to constantly treat others with respect, dignity and honor (See Romans 12:10).

• *Five Gender Protocols for Youth Ministry*

1. **Be an Equal Opportunity Encourager.** Don't reserve your verbal or physical expressions of encouragement for just the girls or just the boys. Treat all your youth with equal affection and appreciation. Hug their parents, too.

2. **Stay Out in the Open.** Be public with your affection. Hug your kids openly, in front of everyone. But avoid physical contact in individual counselling and in one-on-one situations. (In fact, it's a good idea to always keep your door open, or to have another person present, when you're in those one-on-one experiences.)

3. **Stay in Your Place.** Greetings should be warm and affectionate. Hugs are reassuring and comforting. But pats and pinches on the bottom are unwelcome, embarrassing and confusing. A kiss on the cheek, under certain circumstances, may be perfectly acceptable. A kiss on the lips is almost certainly to cause questions and accusations.

4. **Draw the Line.** Be actively involved in good humor. But draw the

line on any humor which involves sexuality. Sexual teasing, "dirty" jokes, remarks or gestures, or comments about body parts, are never appropriate (even when you're a guy and you're just with the other guys, or you're a girl and you're just with the other girls). "There should not be even a hint of sexual immorality," Paul counsels us in Ephesians 5:3, 4.

5. **Watch What You Watch.** Sometimes inappropriate behavior comes into our lives through the media we choose to entertain us. Popular magazines, television, movies and music all present interpersonal behavior from a different worldview from the Christian's. Be careful about your sources.

• Gender Protocol and Inclusion

Appropriate gender protocol also has to do with being inclusive. Be sure that your youth council, your youth group officers, and your programming includes both guys and girls, and that the roles you assign members of your youth group reveal your inclusivity.

For example, don't always ask girls to pray in Sabbath School, and guys to take up the offering. Or, in preparing for social activities, don't always ask the girls to do the cooking and the guys to set up the tables. Become conscious of any stereotyping behavior and eliminate it.

• Gender Protocol and Bible Study

Another area in which you can demonstrate your inclusiveness is in reading Bible passages. Obviously Bible versions are *technically correct* when they translate the original languages into masculine pronouns. But it does *no injustice* to the spirit of a passage to utilize gender-inclusive language.

For example, look at this correct translation of 1 Corinthians 14:3: "Everyone who prophesies speaks to men for their strengthening, encouragement and comfort." It would certainly be appropriate to read: "Everyone who prophesies speaks to us all for our strengthening, encouragement and comfort."

Here's another example: "You are all sons of God," (Galatians 3:26) can appropriately be read: "You are all children of God."

Don't exclude the young women in your youth group when you direct them to the Bible.

☞ Also See: Diversity; Sexuality Issues.

Gender Protocol, continued

• General Conference

In the organizational structure of the <u>Seventh-day Adventist</u> Church, your *local church* is a member of a *local conference*, a geographical territory comprising a number of Adventist churches (e.g., the Alberta Conference, the Bermuda Conference, the Carolina Conference, the Southeastern California Conference, etc.).

Local conferences are members of larger geographical areas known as *union conferences* (the North Pacific Union, the Atlantic Union, Mid-America Union, the Southwestern Union, etc.). Today there are 58 local conferences in nine unions in North America.

Union conferences belong to *divisions* (the North American Division, the South Pacific Division, the Inter-American Division, etc.). The Adventist Church currently is divided into thirteen world divisions.

All the divisions in the Church are part of the *General Conference* (or the "GC," as it is affectionately called).

Each administrative unit is more than a geographical territory. Each of the entities has an office building, elected and appointed officers, directors and staff, financial responsibilities, statements of mission, constitutions and bylaws, and delegated levels of coordination and authority throughout its territory.

The General Conference is the largest administrative unit in the Seventh-day Adventist Church. General Conference officers serve as the final decision-making body for matters which affect the denomination as a whole and its world membership. The GC building, located in Silver Spring, Maryland, is the world headquarters for the Church.

Every five years the General Conference holds a meeting to elect officers and discuss items of current importance to the Church. Up to 2,000 appointed and elected delegates attend these *General Conference Sessions* from churches, local conferences, union conferences and divisions around the world. In 1995 the GC Session was held in Utrecht in the Netherlands. The Session in the year 2,000 will be held in Toronto, Canada. The 2005 Session is scheduled for St. Louis, Missouri.

The General Conference of Seventh-day Adventists
    12501 Old Columbia Pike
    Silver Spring, MD 20904-6600
    Phone: (301) 680-6000
    FAX: (301) 680-6090
    http://www.adventist.org

General Conference

• Generations

Within a family it's easy to define generations. There are the grand-parents and the parents and the kids – three generations. It's also easy to see the differences: what TV programs each generation likes to watch, what music they enjoy listening to, how they dress, even how they wear their hair!

Defining the characteristics of a *nation's* generations is much more difficult. According to *American Demographics* magazine (May 1993), there is no universally accepted formula for setting the boundaries of an age-defined generation, or what is known as an "age cohort." How-ever, there is a general consensus for several groupings, and those are listed below.

Ministry is most successful when it takes into consideration the char-acteristics of the generation to which the ministry is directed. For ex-ample, members of a generation will more likely respond to <u>worship</u> services when you utilize targeted <u>music</u>, appropriate teaching styles and illustrations which come from the generation's <u>shared experiences</u>.

• *Seven Generations*
1. The GI Generation. Born before 1930.
2. The Depression Generation. Born between 1930 and 1939.
3. War Babies. Born between 1940 and 1945.
4. <u>Baby Boomers</u>. Born between 1946 and 1964.
5. Baby Busters (or <u>Generation X</u>). Born between 1965 and 1976.
6. Baby Boomlet. Born between 1977 and 1995.
7. Echo Bust. Born from 1996 on.

Notes:
_____
_____
_____
_____
_____
_____
_____
_____
_____

Generations

• Generation X

Almost 50 million Americans were born between 1965 and 1980, following the huge generation of <u>Baby Boomers</u> (72 million born after the Second World War until 1964). These 50 million (and millions of others around the world who are adopting their attitudes and lifestyles) have been called Baby Busters, Slackers, the 13th Generation and Generation X.

This generation of <u>young adults,</u> now in their early twenties to early thirties, full of frustration, brimming with ability, requires an understanding, targeted approach if ministry to them is to be successful.

• *Five Gen X Characteristics*

1. They are the most racially diverse generation in history.
2. They have never known a time without <u>television</u>.
3. They are our first computer generation, completely comfortable and at home with computers, the Internet, e-mail, programming, etc.
4. They don't like labels. Douglass Coupland wrote in *Generation X* (the novel that gave birth to the generation's title), "I am not a target market." An article on the generation in *Forbes* was titled, "Don't Call Me a Slacker."
5. This is the first generation in a long, long time that is not inheriting a world superior to that of their parents, and many harbor resentment because of that fact. As they look at the state of the world they see an endless succession of disasters: the economy, national debt, <u>AIDS</u>, the environment, <u>violence</u>, <u>divorce</u>, <u>suicide</u>, teen pregnancy, mindless television programming. They tend to feel unwanted and alienated. They feel alone. They feel abandoned.

In their book, *Inside the Soul of a New Generation* (Grand Rapids, MI; Zondervan, 1996), Tim Celek and Dieter Zander point out the major differences between Generation Xers and Baby Boomers.

• *Boomers vs. Xers*

1. **Product vs. Process.** Results matter most to Boomers. Busters value relationships over results. The process by which you accomplish something counts as much as the product.

Generation X, continued

2. **Live to Work vs. Work to Live.** Boomers see work as a fulfilling end in itself. They tend to live lifestyles of luxury, especially compared to their parents. For Xers, job prospects remain limited, regardless of how much schooling they have. They are more inclined to put family first (what they missed as a child) and to work to live.

3. **Individual vs. Team.** Boomers stressed the maverick mentality and autonomy. Their heroes are people like Donald Trump, Ivan Boesky, Lee Iacocca and Michael Milken. Boomers tended to do their own thing. They've been called "the Me Generation." Xers are rediscovering the importance of a team approach. They socialize in groups. *Friends* has been their favorite TV program. They're more of a "We generation."

4. **Active vs. Reactive.** Boomers are among the most active (some would say "hyperactive") generation ever. Xers, determined to find their own identity, tend to do the opposite of Boomers. If the image of Boomers was well-groomed and proper, the image of Xers probably includes disheveled clothes, goatees and multiple piercings. If Boomers thought they could change the world, Xers are more cynical and pessimistic.

Celek and Zander point out four dynamics that must characterize our ministry to Gen Xers.

- *Four Crucial Dynamics of Ministry to Gen Xers*
  1. **It Must Be Real.** We must be authentic, sincere, sensitive, vulnerable, transparent, and willing to admit personal flaws as opposed to arrogant, guarded, perfect, and conscious of perpetuating an image.
  2. **It Must Be Rousing.** We can't rely on "matters as usual." Many Xers are ready to leave the church. They're tired of the same old order of service, the same old songs, the same old presentations; more than that, they're *fed up* with routine.
  3. **It Must Be Relevant.** This is a very practical generation. What we talk about has to connect with their lives. They may be more interested in the Bible's position on environmental issues or on racism or on business principles than they are in what it has to say about the state of the dead.
  4. **It Must Be Relational.** Xers need <u>community</u>.

• Gente Joven

Gente Joven is a magazine for local church Hispanic youth leaders in the North American Division of the Seventh-day Adventist Church. It includes a variety of ideas, programs, activities, and events that help the youth leader to better minister to the needs of the Hispanic Adventist youth. *Gente Joven* has in mind the Hispanic Adventist youth residing in North America in its urban bilingual-bicultural context.

Gente Joven started in 1986 as a Florida Conference Youth Ministries Resource Newsletter for Youth Leaders in Hispanic Churches. As other Hispanic churches heard about the resource, they requested subscriptions for use in their youth ministry. In 1995, *Gente Joven* became the official Hispanic Youth Ministries Resource Magazine of the North American Division Youth Ministry Department.

Gente Joven is published 4 times a year. The cost of the subscription is currently $20 a year. You can subscribe to *Gente Joven* through your local Adventist Book Center, or by contacting the Pacific Press at the numbers listed below.

Gente Joven
   Subscription Department
   Pacific Press Publishing Association
   PO Box 5353
   Nampa, ID 83653
   Phone: 1-800-545-2449

Notes:

_____

_____

_____

_____

_____

_____

_____

_____

_____

Gente Joven

• Giraffe News

Giraffe News is a 32-page publication of the <u>Center for Youth Evangelism</u>. Affiliated with the North American Division Department of Youth Ministries, as well as the various youth resource centers throughout the NAD, *Giraffe News* serves as the official voice of the <u>Association of Adventist Youth Ministry Professionals</u>.

The editorial staff of *Giraffe News* is committed to its task of encouraging youth leaders to more effectively "stick their necks out for youth and young adults."

To subscribe to *Giraffe News*, contact the Center for Youth Evangelism.

• Four Promises from Giraffe News

1. We will listen to young people, and to the leaders who work with them.
2. We will continue to speak to the wider Seventh-day Adventist Church in relation to what we hear and to share what we have learned.
3. We will attempt to provide youth ministry resources that will enable youth leaders to more effectively minister.
4. We will strive to remember that our church must be the place where these young people can find a future that is bright with hope as they experience a church community that welcomes them in grace and faith.

Giraffe News
Center for Youth Evangelism
8903 South US 31
Berrien Springs, MI 49103-0904
Phone: (616) 471-9881 or (800) Youth.2.U (968-8428)
FAX: (616) 471-9883
e-mail: cye@andrews.edu
http: //www.andrews.edu/CYE

Giraffe News

• Giraffe Society

The Giraffe Society is a grass-roots service network of Seventh-day Adventists from all walks of life: parents, pastors, educators, administrators, lay people, church officers, youth and young adults.

Recognizing that surveys such as *Valuegenesis* reveal that our church's youth and young adults are on the endangered species list, the Society is committed to enhancing the lives of Adventist youth and young adults through its effort, communication, money, and presence.

Toward this aim, the Society's members state that they will risk standing up and sticking their necks out against any form of negligence or mistreatment of youth and young adults.

The Society puts it this way: "We desire that youth and young adults know, in an experiential way, that the gospel of Jesus Christ is serious and fun, ever-constant and ever-adapting, challenging and restful, combative and gentle. We will involve them in every area of ministry possible, and will exult in discovering new avenues for their involvement."

• *Benefits of Giraffe Society Membership*
1. Be a member of a pro-active youth ministry organization.
2. Be introduced to the very best youth ministry resources and programs currently available.
3. Be part of a network of people who passionately care about youth ministry.
4. Receive a Giraffe Society membership pin and certificate.
5. Receive a one year subscription to the Giraffe News leadership publication.
6. Receive discounts on Giraffe clothing and Giraffe Society items.

For more information, or to become a member of the Giraffe Society, contact the Center for Youth Evangelism at the numbers below.

Giraffe Society
   Center for Youth Evangelism
   8903 South US 31
   Berrien Springs, MI 49103-0904
   Phone: (616) 471-9881 or (800) Youth.2.U (968-8428)
   FAX: (616) 471-9883
   e-mail: cye@andrews.edu
   http://www.andrews.edu/CYE

• Giraffe University

Giraffe University, NAD's youth leadership training initiative, enables and equips local Seventh-day Adventist youth leaders to effectively lead young people to Christ and to evangelize their community.
In Giraffe University, you will:
A. Establish a foundation for youth ministry that you can build on.
B. Capture the vision for excellence in youth ministry.
C. Be renewed as you connect with God and friends in worship.
D. Be trained by some of the best Adventist youth leaders in North America.
E. Be networked to a national youth ministry movement.
F. Take home cutting-edge resources and tons of usable information.

• Three Steps to Hosting a Giraffe University

1. Contact your conference youth director or the Center for Youth Evangelism to find out when the next Giraffe University will be held in your area.
2. Ask for a registration or host information packet.
3. Get ready to "stick your neck out" at a powerful youth ministry training event.

Giraffe University
Center for Youth Evangelism
PO Box C
8903 South US 31
Berrien Springs, MI 49103-0904
Phone: (616) 471-9881 or (800) Youth.2.U (968-8428)
FAX: (616) 471-9883
e-mail: cye@andrews.edu
http://www.andrews.edu/CYE

Giraffe University

• Gospel

"Gospel" is the word Christians use to refer to the story of the life, death and resurrection of <u>Jesus</u>, the good news of the salvation that is ours because of God's gracious gift to us of His Son (Romans 1:16). "The gospel about Jesus Christ," (Mark 1:1; Acts 8:35) is the gospel of our salvation (Ephesians 1:13), the gospel by which we are saved (1 Corinthians 15:2), the everlasting gospel we are to tell to every nation, tribe, language and people of the world (Acts 20:24; Revelation 14:6) before the end of time (Matthew 24:14).

The gospel was preached before Abraham's day (Galatians 3:8) and by the Old Testament prophets (Romans 1:2). It was preached by Jesus (Luke 20:1), by His disciples (Luke 9:6; Acts 8:25), and by the evangelists of the first century church (Acts 8:40; 16:10; 1 Corinthians 1:17).

"The gospel of Christ is from beginning to end the gospel of saving <u>grace</u>."[1]

"The message of the gospel of His grace was to be given to the church in clear and distinct lines, that the world should no longer say that <u>Seventh-day Adventists</u> talk the law, the law, but do not teach or believe Christ."[2]

"No grace, no gospel," said James Moffatt in his book *Grace in the New Testament.*[3]

"The substance and the essence of the true gospel are the doctrine of God's grace. If you take away the grace of God from the gospel, you have extracted from it its very lifeblood, and there is nothing left worth preaching, worth believing, worth contending for. Grace is the soul and the music of the gospel; without it, the gospel is silent."[4]

• *Five Reasons Why Teens Need the Gospel*

1. All of us have sinned and all of us are made right with God the same way — through Jesus. Romans 3:23.
2. God's kindness leads us to repentance. Romans 2:4.
3. The gospel keeps us from being afraid of God. Luke 2:10.
4. Good news makes us healthy! Proverbs 15:30.
5. The gospel defines our mission and purpose in life. Isaiah 61:1 and Mark 16:15.

1　Ellen White, *Evangelism*, 552.
2　Ellen White, *Testimonies to Ministers*, 92.
3　James Moffatt, *Grace in the New Testament*. (London: Hodder and Stoughton, 1931), xv.
4　Charles Spurgeon, *Grace Triumphant* (Grand Rapids, MI: Baker Book House, 1964), 99.

Gospel

• **Grace**

Early in the Bible story, we hear sadness in the voice of God as He acknowledges how great human wickedness on the earth had become. God concluded that every inclination of the thoughts of human hearts was "only evil all the time." It grieved God that He had created humans, and "His heart was filled with pain," (Genesis 3:5, 6).

Over the next several thousand years the conclusion about humanity would remain the same. "There is no one who does good, not even one" David would record in Psalm 14 . "All have sinned and fall short of the glory of God," Paul would add (Romans 3:23).

In letters to the early Christian churches, Paul described fallen humanity in the bleakest of terms: "powerless," "ungodly," "sinners," "God's enemies," "dead in transgressions," "disobedient," "by nature object of God's wrath," (see Romans 5:6-10 and Ephesians 2:1-3).

• *How Can We Be Saved?*

But throughout the centuries, many people would feel the pain in God's heart, recognize their own estrangement from God and desire reconciliation with the Infinite. They would ask the question, "How then can we be saved?" (See Acts 16:30; Luke 10:25 and 18:18.)

Seventh-day Adventists believe that only *perfect obedience* to all God's commands – and perfect means *never* sinning, not just *stopping* sinning – only perfection *merits* salvation. Only a perfect grade point average on all the courses in our life experience, only a 1.000 lifetime batting average, makes us *worthy* of salvation. No failures. No strikeouts.

Ellen White puts it this way in *Steps to Christ*, page 62: "The condition of eternal life is now just what it always has been, – just what it was in Paradise before the fall of our first parents, – perfect obedience to the law of God, perfect righteousness. If eternal life were granted on any condition short of this, then the happiness of the whole universe would be imperiled. The way would be open for sin, with all its train of woe and misery to be immortalized."

And just to be sure none of us get the wrong idea, God gave us the Ten Commandments (Exodus 20). Here is a description of what a perfect person would look like. Here is what a perfect, sinless society would be. Here is an illustration of what *all* our actions would be like if *all* of us loved God with *all* of our hearts *all* of the time.

But, all of us *don't*, do we? The Ten Commandments remind us that we are *not* perfect, we *don't* love God all the time. We're *not* going to be saved by our actions. Not even by good things we sometimes do. Through the Law we become conscious of our sin (Romans 3:20).

So Adventists understand that the purpose of the Law is to lead us to Jesus. It shows us why we have to rely on Him for salvation, instead of on ourselves (Galatians 3:24). No wonder we're grateful for the Law – it points us to our Savior.

Listen to the rest of page 62 from *Steps to Christ*: "It was possible for Adam, before the fall, to form a righteous character by obedience to God's law. But he failed to do this, and because of his sin our natures are fallen, and we cannot make ourselves righteous. Since we are sinful, unholy, we cannot perfectly obey the holy law. We have no righteousness of our own with which to meet the claims of the law of God. But Christ has made a way of escape for us. He lived on earth amid trials and temptations such as we have to meet. He lived a sinless life. He died for us, and now He offers to take our sins and give us His righteousness. If you give yourself to Him, accept Him as your Saviour, then, sinful as your life may have been, for His sake you are accounted righteous. Christ's character stands in place of your character, and you are accepted before God just as if you had not sinned."

• Saved By Grace

Over and over again, the Bible says that salvation is ours because of the *grace* of God, freely given to us in Jesus.

"The grace of God that brings salvation has appeared to all," (Titus 2:11). "It is through the grace of our Lord Jesus that we are saved," (Acts 15:11). God has "saved us and called us to a holy life – not because of anything we have done but because of His own purpose and grace. This grace was given us in Christ Jesus before the beginning of time," (2 Timothy 1:9). We "are justified freely by His grace through the redemption that came by Christ Jesus," (Romans 3:24). "In Him we have redemption through His blood, the forgiveness of sins, in accordance with the riches of God's grace," (Ephesians 1:4-7).

"Grace" is the Bible's word for the magnificent, amazing quality of God that motivates Him to treat sinners with love and favor, to *give* us His righteousness in place of our unworthiness. Grace is God's loving answer to the accusations of tyrannical, arbitrary rule hurled at Him by Satan: "Let us then approach the throne of grace with confidence, so that we may receive mercy and find grace," (Hebrews 4:16).

Grace, continued

"Grace is an attribute of God shown to undeserving human beings. We did not seek after it, but it was sent in search of us... Our need is the qualification which gives us the assurance that we shall receive this gift."[1]

• Grace in Youth Ministry

You see why the issue of grace is fundamental to youth ministry; no one needs acceptance, inclusion, forgiveness and love more than teens do. At the very time in their development when they most are in need of the assurance of their acceptance, the grace of God wraps around them like the hug of the welcoming father in the parable of the Prodigal Son (Luke 15:20).

The language of grace is just what the teenager needs to hear: "patience," "security," "chosen," "adopted," "included," "forgiven," "marked in Him with a seal, the promised Holy Spirit, who is a deposit guaranteeing our inheritance," (1 Timothy 1:15-17; Hebrews 6:19, 20; Ephesians 1:4-14).

Does grace mean that God approves of everything teenagers do? Of course not! God does not approve of the sin by which *any of us* inflict ourselves and others with pain. He is not pleased when we decide to fight Him. But His desire for us to "go and sin no more," is always preceded by the gracious assurance, "neither do I condemn you," (John 8:3-11).

"God did not send His Son into the world to condemn the world, but to save the world through Him," (John 3:17). "I did not come to judge the world, but to save it," (John 12:47).

Grace is the reason we are not afraid of God. "Since we have been justified through faith, we have peace with God through our Lord Jesus Christ" (Romans 5:1).

His grace is the means of our salvation: "Because of His great love for us, God, who is rich in mercy, made us alive with Christ even when we were dead in transgressions – it is by grace you have been saved" (Ephesians 2:4,5).

"Grace is not something God Himself gives us, it is the way God gives us Himself."[2]

1   Ellen White, *God's Amazing Grace*, 10.
2   Robert Brown, *The Spirit of Protestantism* (NY, NY: Oxford University Press, 1961), 55.

Grace, continued

A Grace Orientation

A grace orientation is a perspective on the Christian experience which comes from the belief that our place in God's kingdom is assured because of God's great love for us, not because of our good works (See Romans 3:20-24 and Ephesians 2:4-9).

The Gospel of Grace

Long before we were born, in fact even before the creation of the world (Ephesians 1:4), God chose us, adopted us as His children (Ephesians 1:5), and set in motion the plan to redeem us (Ephesians 1:7). In accordance with this lavish, unmerited favor (Ephesians 1:8) which He has freely given to us (Ephesians 1:6), God has forgiven our sins (Colossians 1:14), qualified us to share in the inheritance of the saints in the kingdom of light (Colossians 1:12), rescued us from the dominion of darkness (Colossians 1:13), brought us into the kingdom of Jesus (Colossians 1:13), and guaranteed our eternal inheritance (Ephesians 1:14). "It is by grace you have been saved," (Ephesians 2:5, 8).

We call this good news the gospel of our salvation (Ephesians 1:13). In its rightful place the gospel of grace is the center of all our theology, it pervades all our worship, is reflected in all of our relationships with other Christians within our community, and motivates all our service to others. Christians live and move and have their being within a grace orientation (Acts 17:28).

A Works Orientation

By contrast, a *works* orientation is the belief that our place in God's kingdom is awarded to us, either in whole or in part, in exchange for, or in reward for, or because of, our obedience, our proper behavior, our correct belief, the strength of our faith, the merits of our Christian life, our acceptance of Christ's offer of grace, or *anything* else, other than the wholly undeserved favor of God, manifested to us in Jesus.

A Grace Orientation in Youth Ministry

The establishment of a grace orientation in the hearts of our youth is the foundation of all successful youth ministry.

- ## Group

An independent, interdenominational publisher, Group specializes (and excels!) in <u>resources</u> that encourage and support children, junior high and youth ministries. From Group headquarters in Loveland, Colorado, almost 200 employees representing a wide spectrum of Christian denominations work together to create innovative magazines, books, curriculum materials, videos, music, camps and training events.

- ### Four of Our Favorite Group Resources

1. **Group Magazine.** Most <u>youth minstry</u> people agree that this is the single best youth ministry magazine being published for <u>youth leaders</u> today. Contents include articles on youth ministry issues, <u>programming</u> ideas, current events, <u>drama</u>, <u>service</u> ideas, hands-on help, and lots and lots of ads for youth ministry <u>resources</u> and services. Call 1-800-877-6143.

2. **Group's Active Bible** <u>Curriculum</u>. Four-week studies for Junior and Senior High students. Over 60 topics to choose from. Active learning applied to issues faced by today's teens. Uses <u>games</u>, simulations, role-plays, and skits to drive home important Bible truths. Complete teacher's guide, handout masters, publicity helps and bonus ideas. Call 1-800-447-1070.

3. **Group Videos.** Hot Talk-starters. Real-life issues which demand Christian responses. Easy to use. Four topics per video. Leader's Guide. Photocopiable handouts. Call 1-800-447-1070.

4. **National Youth and Children's Ministry Convention.** Group's once a year, high-powered event for youth, children's, and family ministry workers. Practical training at over 70 workshops, plus hands-on learning labs, panel discussions, great speakers, comedy and music. For complete information, schedule and location, call 1-800-774-3838.

Group Publishing, Inc.
  1515 Cascade Avenue
  Loveland, CO 80538
  Phone: (970) 669-3836
  FAX: (970) 669-3269
  http://www.grouppublishing.com/about.html
  E-Mail: info@grouppublishing.com

Group

• •

• Guitar

For a <u>youth pastor</u>, a guitar can be an invaluable asset to ministry, an effective tool in communicating the <u>gospel</u>. Its portability makes it more practical than a keyboard, less intimidating than drums, and the fact that it can be played without electricity is an added benefit.

• Guidelines for Finding a Guitar

1. **Price.** Remember, you get what you pay for. For $200 you're getting a bottom of the line guitar, and if you take your instrument seriously you'll be looking for a replacement within a few months. In order to find an instrument with electronics (under the saddle pickups, on board EQ), you'll probably need to plan on spending about $400 to $600.

   If a new guitar is out of your price range, check pawn shops and music stores that sell on consignment. A used guitar can be a great deal, but shop with someone who knows guitars.

2. **Quality of Sound.** Become familiar with terms such as a "warm" sound, a "bright" sound, a "thinline" guitar (guitar with very shallow sides), "intonation," and "pickups."

3. **Company Reputation.** The most reliable name in acoustic guitars is Martin. Other good names include Gibson, Yamaha, Washburn, Taylor, Alvarez, and Guild.

4. **Nylon or Steel?** Unless you plan on playing a lot of classical music, buy a steel stringed guitar. Nylon strings produce a wonderful, rich tone, but don't have the intensity or the volume that you normally look for. Extra volume will come in handy some day at the beach, or during a noisy session at <u>summer camp</u>

• Becoming a Better Player

1. **Get a Teacher.** Don't be too proud, you're never too old to learn.

2. **Get in a Group.** Play often with as many people as you can. Everyone who is better than you has something to offer. And don't be afraid to learn from your youth who play.

3. **Practice.** We have a responsibility to do every aspect of ministry well. Take time during the day to practice. Put it into your schedule. You're not wasting time learning this important skill.

4. **Dedicate.** Finally, give your instrument to the service of God. It's a vital part of youth ministry today.

Guitar

The Hancock Center for Youth and Family Ministry

In response to the need to renew professional and volunteer youth ministry in the Seventh-day Adventist Church, and to support and expand the educational endeavors of conference and union youth ministry departments, a research and resource center for youth ministry was established on the campus of La Sierra University on May 23, 1991.

The Center is named for Elder John H. Hancock, whose lifetime of youth ministry began in the Southeastern California Conference in 1946 and continued until his retirement as General Conference Youth Director in 1980. During his tenure as youth leader for the church, Elder Hancock was influential in organizing Pathfinder clubs throughout the world. He was also the moving force behind the creation of the student missions program, an experience which continues to have a major impact on the spiritual formation of the youth in the Adventist church.

Three Hancock Center Activities

1. **Conducting research** to provide a deeper understanding of youth and youth ministry. (See Valuegenesis.)
2. **Creating resources** to maximize the youth ministry of pastors, teachers, parents and layworkers. (Have you read the following great youth ministry resources?)
   a. *Shall We Dance: Rediscovering Christ-centered Standards*
   b. *Summer Ministries* – Hundreds of ministry activities for small, medium and large churches.
   c. *Walking On the Edge* – Thirteen Interactive Bible Studies for Seventh-day Adventist Students in Public High School
3. **Providing training** to establish and enrich youth ministry in the local church. This training includes:
   a. The Three:20 Zone – local workshops and seminars
   b. A youth ministry masters degree from the School of Religion at La Sierra University.

Three Ways to Quickly Reach the Hancock Center

1. **By phone** at (800) 785-HCYM or (909) 785-2091
2. **By fax** at (909) 785-2199
3. **On the Internet** at www.lasierra.edu/hcym

• Hancock Center Symposium

Once each year the Hancock Center for Youth and Family Ministry hosts a symposium on the campus of La Sierra University dedicated to exploring a specific ministry topic.

In 1994 the discussion was on the great need for youth to be involved in urban ministry. A successful inner city project, known as Urban Embrace, grew out of this symposium, and today continues its operation in Los Angeles.

Since that initial symposium, topics at the annual gathering have included youth ministry structure, ministry to Generation X, the spirituality of youth and youth leaders, adolescent sexuality and contemporary worship.

For the dates and topics of this year's Hancock Center Symposium, contact the Center at (800) 785-HCYM.

- ### • The Twofold Purpose of the Hancock Symposiums

  1. **Staying in Touch.** The Hancock Center is committed to maintaining contact with contemporary youth and young adults, to understanding their Christian journeys, and to helping meet their spiritual needs through publications and training. Each symposium assists the Center in knowing how to strategically plan for new directions.

     Through each symposium, the Center also becomes acquainted with two important segments of youth ministry:
     a. specialists who can become involved in training events and contribute to Hancock Center resources, and
     b. successful ministries which can be used as models for other ministries.

  2. **Encouragement.** Each symposium also serves as an encouragement to people active in the specific ministries discussed. Professionals hear of work being done by other professionals in their same field. Lay leaders from local churches realize they are not alone in their efforts. Ministerial students are given an exposure to dynamic and effective ministries to which they, too, can devote their lives.

     Ideas are shared. Resources are introduced. New approaches are explained. Success stories build enthusiasm and keep the vision clear.

Hancock Center Symposium

• Home Study International

Home Study International (HSI), also known as Griggs University, is a global <u>Seventh-day Adventist</u> educational institution, with a mission to provide educationally sound, values-based, guided independent study and distance education programs. Educational offerings include preschool, elementary, secondary, and higher education courses. These courses respond to learner needs in the context of a lifetime learning experience and are available to all who can benefit from them.

Since its founding in 1909 by educator and visionary Frederick Griggs, 300,000 students have studied with the program. The student body currently represents over 500 countries. HSI employs 51 part-time faculty members. In addition, 11 full-time nonteaching professionals provide assistance to students and teachers.

- *HSI "Teachers On Paper" (Each course study guide)*
  1. All learning objectives
  2. Instructional sections
  3. Reading assignments
  4. Supplemental information
  5. Self-diagnostic tools
  6. Lessons

The student also receives a full set of supplies including a textbook and sometimes cassettes, lab equipment, and reading supplements. Experienced teachers are assigned to each course to provide positive, individual interaction with students.

HSI is fully accredited by the Distance Education and Training Council and approved by the Maryland State Department of Education. It is also a member of the International Council for Distance Education and is affiliated with Columbia Union College.

For more information, include tuition prices, or to request a free information catalog, contact HSI at the following numbers:

Home Study International
  PO Box 4437
  Silver Spring, MD 20914-4437
  Phone: (301) 680-6570 or 800-782-GROW
  Fax: (301) 680-5157
  http://www.griggs.edu

(vertical text, left margin) Home Study International

Inner-City Ministry

Most churches achieve little in inner-city ministry for two reasons. First, urban ministry demands the sort of creativity that takes us into territory where *traditional* evangelism methods don't work.

And second, churches generally express themselves in middle-class terms. This wouldn't be a problem if we all enjoyed roughly the same level of education and economic ease. But we don't! Inevitably, many people we talk to barely understand what we say — *only the things we do make sense.* That's what inner-city ministry is all about.

Three Sources for Inner-City Ministry Ideas

1. Tony Campolo's book *Ideas For Social Action* (Grand Rapids, MI: Youth Specialties/Zondervan, 1983, 1991) describes ways churches can impact their community.
2. One section of *Summer Ministries* (by Stuart Tyner, V. Bailey Gillespie and David Wood, Lincoln, NE: AdventSource, 1997) gives dozens of inner-city ministry ideas.
3. Contact the chaplain at your nearest Adventist college. Many campus ministry programs involve urban outreach activities, including soup kitchens, health clinics and other services.

Translate every idea into manageable tasks for your youth group. Get advice from local welfare organizations. Brainstorm with others involved in inner-city ministry. Talk to potential sponsors.

Five Possible Inner-City Projects

1. **Rescue Centers.** A place for teenage runaways and dropouts.
2. **Green Machines.** Adopt a park. Turn a ramshackle corner of town into a paradise. Plant trees. Landscape. Beautify.
3. **Habitat for Humanity.** Building new homes for the homeless.
4. **Brush Days.** Gather a team of cleaners, painters, menders, and gardeners and redo a house in a day.
5. Urban Embrace. See the entry in this book for a wonderful, on-going project idea your entire church will get excited about.

• **More Great Advice:**
✔ Monte Sahlin, et.al., *Ministries of Compassion* (NAD Church Resources Consortium, 1994).
✔ Steve Fiffer and Sharon Sloan Fiffer, *50 Ways to Help Your Community* (NY, NY: Doubleday, 1994).

• Insight; Insight Out

Insight is a 16-page, weekly magazine, published since 1970 for <u>Seventh-day Adventist</u> teens by the Review & Herald Publishing Association. The previous Adventist magazine for teens was called *The Youth's Instructor* and was published from 1852 to 1969.

Insight's mission is to speak to Adventist teenagers with editorials, true dramatic stories of personal <u>faith development</u>, readers' letters and questions, reviews of <u>contemporary Christian music</u>, devotionals, advice columns, and profiles of church youth groups.

The second week of each month, *Insight* becomes *Insight Out*. *Insight Out* is the outreach issue of *Insight*. All weekly subscribers receive the issue. Separate subscriptions to *Insight Out* issue may be purchased.

Insight Out is different from the other weekly issues because it contains no direct reference to Adventism or its institutions, uses no Adventist jargon and includes no stories based on distinctly Adventist cultural practices. The exceptions are stories that present Adventist distinctives for an evangelistic purpose. The objective is to draw teens of all faiths (or no faith at all) into an awareness of God and the <u>gospel</u>.

• *Insight's Writing Contest*

1. Each year *Insight* holds a writing contest for young people 21 years of age or under.
2. Winning entries will be awarded cash prizes and will be published in *Insight*.
3. For full information, contest deadlines, categories of entries and current amount of cash awards, contact the *Insight* office and ask about this year's *Insight* Writing Contest.

Insight wants to put a teen from your <u>youth group</u> on its cover!

Insight covers are dedicated to showcasing Adventist teenagers who are contributing to their community, school, church, family, and friends and are nominated for outstanding service or leadership.

Nominations for individual teens or groups of young people (ages 14-19) come from local church <u>youth leaders</u>. You can nominate SDA teens who have done such things as:

a. led out in a campus or community spiritual activity or event, such as <u>Sabbath School</u> programs, dramas and skits, weeks of prayer, <u>mission trips</u> or community <u>service</u> projects;

b. used their talents or skills to benefit the spirituality of others; or

c. begun or accomplished an unusual activity that helps develop their own or someone else's spiritual experience.

Call or write to *Insight* with your nominations. Include you name, title, and daytime phone number, the name of the teen you're nominating, the reason for your nomination, and a phone number where *Insight* can contact the nominee.

- *Five Insight-ful Places to Start Discussions*

1. **In Stories.** At least one story each week, and sometimes more, raises more questions than it answers. Have your teens read the story and discuss. Or pull questions from the basic scenario of the story. Check frequently on the content of the weekly "So I Said..." story. It almost always ends with an arguable opinion or a controversial point of view.

2. **In Q&A Columns.** You can use the Reader Question in the biweekly "Qs From U" column as a starting point. Or take the more personal "Ask Anything" questions and challenge your teens to provide answers.

3. **In Karl Haffner's Column.** Pastor Karl Haffner's "Walk the Talk" column is related to, but distinct from, the week's Sabbath School lesson topic. He includes a quiz in some columns, and asks provocative questions in others.

4. **In Music Reviews.** At least once a quarter, bring up the subject of music choices. Look for analytical comments in *Insight's* recent reviews ("Sound Affects"), and draw your teens into discussing their choices in Christian and/or secular music.

5. **In Youth Group Profiles.** One youth group is featured each month to highlight special activities in which they have been involved. Check what others are doing for service and fun. Activities include 30-hour Famine, Vacation from Noise, and involvement in local church projects.

Insight
Review and Herald Publishing Association
55 West Oak Ridge Drive
Hagerstown, MD 21740-7301
Phone: (301) 791-7000, ext. 729
FAX: (301) 790-9734
http://www.rhpa.org

Insight, Insight Out, continued

• Involvement

There are two people sitting in your youth room during Sabbath School. One sits on the back row, feet up on the chair in front of him, hands behind his head, looking out of the window, thinking about what he's going to be doing tonight. The other one is on the front row, waiting her part in the program. In the meantime, she's paying attention to what's going on, answering questions, and looking forward to the scheduled youth activity for the afternoon.

Now's here's the question: which one of these two young people is likely to be a church member ten years from now? Why?

All other things being equal, the one programming factor that predisposes kids for long-term church membership is *involvement*. Kids who are not involved don't stay involved.

• Places To Involve Your Youth

1. **Planning.** How many kids do you have on your youth council? How many are working on planning the Sabbath School and AYS programs? How many are putting together ideas for social activities? Or service projects? Use as many of your youth as you can, in as many committees as you have activities.

2. **Preparing.** Once the creative work is done, there's still a lot to do. Someone has to ask people to take part. Someone has to purchase supplies. Someone has to make all the contacts.

3. **Presenting.** Many of your youth have up-front skills. They enjoy doing the jobs that others shy away from: welcoming people, introducing the program, leading music, giving special music, reading the scripture passages, taking part in skits, etc. Find as many opportunities as you can to involve these kids.

4. **Behind the Scenes.** There are also kids who don't like to be up-front who would be happy to take part in activities that keep them off center stage: creating bulletins for your programs, working on the newsletter, creating costumes for drama presentations, etc. Look for these jobs as well and match them up with your behind the scenes kids.

5. **Evaluating.** Frequently ask your youth for their opinion on how things are going. Give them plenty of chances to evaluate your programs, your projects and your overall ministry. Respect their opinions and make appropriate changes.

Involvement

Jesus

Some say he is no more than a great story, a myth, a figment of the fertile imagination of religious zealots who needed a founding father.

Some say he was just a minor rabble-rouser, a caustic rebel whose confrontation with hypocritical religious authorities of the day ultimately led to his execution as a criminal.

Others call him an exorcist, a miracle-worker, who mesmerized his followers and made them believe he was more than a common man.

Still others say he was simply a great Jewish teacher – Jesus, son of Joseph, born in Bethlehem 2,000 years ago during the Roman occupation of Palestine.

Some refer to Jesus primarily as the successful human founder of one of the world's great religions, who, along with Buddha and Mohammed, encouraged millions of people around the world to live a life of spirituality, compassion and good works, and to hold high moral standards in an increasingly wicked world.

But Christians insist He was more.

The record of the life and teachings of Jesus, contained in just four books of the New Testament, has accomplished its purpose: "These are written," one of His disciples tells us, "that you may believe that Jesus is the Christ, the Son of God, and that by believing you may have life in His name" (John 20:31).

Before the Beginning

The Bible teaches us that Jesus existed long before the day the angels announced to the shepherds of Bethlehem that they would find the newborn Messiah wrapped in swaddling clothes and lying in a manger (Luke 2:8-20). Before the creation of the world (Colossians 1:15-17), before the beginning of time (Micah 5:2), Jesus already existed, co-eternal with God, whom Jesus would call the Father (John 1:1-14). Jesus is worshipped, by human beings and the inhabitants of heaven alike, as the Creator of our world (Revelation 4:1-11).

The Long-Awaited Messiah

In the earliest communications between the Creator and His earthbound creatures we hear the promise of an end to sin and suffering, of the coming of a Messiah to save His people (Genesis 3:15; 22:18). Isaiah tells us, in words we can never forget that "He was pierced for our

Jesus, continued

transgressions, He was crushed for our iniquities; the punishment that brought us peace was upon Him, and by His wounds we are healed" (Isaiah 53:5). Jesus is the supreme demonstration of the active, consuming love of God, given to us by the Father so that by believing in Him we might have eternal life (John 3:16). Salvation belongs to Jesus, the Lamb who was slain (Revelation 7:10).

The Conquering King of Kings

But the life and ministry of Jesus does not end with His death on earth. By the power of the Source of all life, Jesus was raised from His earthly grave to be reunited in heaven with His Father (Hebrews 1:3). There He continues to minister in our behalf, providing His needful human children with confidence, mercy and grace (Hebrews 4:14-16) until the day when He returns to earth as King of Kings and Lord of Lords (Revelation 19:16) to claim His ransomed people and take us to our eternal home. "And so we will be with the Lord forever" (1 Thessalonians 4:17).

In all the dynamics of youth ministry keep Jesus at the very center. A Christian youth ministry with anything else at the core will eventually become only creative programming and busy social activities.

- **Three Ways to Center Your Ministry on Jesus**
  1. For every activity ask, "Where is Christ in this? How is He glorified?" Don't proceed until you've found the answer.
  2. Begin and end all activities by inviting Christ to be central and thanking Him for His presence with you.
  3. Build into your youth ministry year an intentional focus on the qualities which characterized Christ's ministry.
     a. Jesus loved to worship His heavenly Father— youth ministry leads young people in meaningful worship.
     b. Jesus listened to people's problems and challenges— youth ministry has a counselling component.
     c. Jesus enjoyed being out of doors and attending social activities— youth ministry includes a social aspect.
     d. Jesus was involved in helping others— youth ministry has a service focus.
     e. Jesus trained and nurtured His disciples— youth ministry succeeds when new disciples are formed.

• Junior High Ministry

In his probing look at ministry directed toward early <u>adolescents</u>, *Junior High Ministry*, Revised Edition (Grand Rapids, MI: Zondervan, 1987), Wayne Rice, describes nine key characteristics which make this essential ministry successful.

• *Nine Keys to Successful Junior High Ministry*

1. <u>Diversity</u>. Provide different types of programs each week. Consider the developmental stages and learning styles of the kids.
2. **Self-Exploration and Definition**. Junior highers need opportunities to explore and understand their emerging personalities and their new worlds. "They need adventure."
3. **Meaningful Participation**. Give them more and more responsibility in areas that correspond to their interests, skills and abilities. They need to feel they are making a contribution that is important and appreciated.
4. **Positive Interaction with Peers and Adults**. Build <u>community</u>. Give encouragement freely and often. Use <u>discussion</u> instead of lecture in your lesson studies.
5. **Physical Activity**. Don't expect them to sit still for an hour and a half, and then get angry when they wiggle. Their attention span is relatively short. Divide activities into short segments. Change the pace. Keep them active.
6. **Competence and Achievement.** Junior highers want to do something well. They want to show you their competencies. Giving them the opportunity often involves risk. Stay close to them. Applaud their successes. Help them learn from mistakes.
7. **Structure and Clear Limits**. Make your rules simple, clear and easy to follow. Invite them to help set the rules. Freedom within limitations is the key concept. (See: <u>Discipline</u>.)
8. **Fun**. Adolescents learn from positive, pleasant experiences (don't we all!). Fun for them is the opposite of <u>boredom</u>: involved, meaningful times build around interesting topics. Rice points out that fun doesn't always mean *funny*. It's not that kids have to rolling in the aisles with laughter. Just that they need to be enjoying themselves if we expect them to learn.
9. **Family-oriented**. Include the <u>parents</u>. Use family stories in your <u>newsletter</u>. Ask the kids to interview adults and report back to the youth group. Explore family topics.

• Leading Music

Success in leading a group of young people in singing is no accident. It takes careful thought as to the setting, clear understanding of your role as a leader, wise choice of <u>music</u>, and an understanding of group dynamics. Rather than allowing music to be used as "filler" until the *real* meeting or activity begins, music should create an atmosphere and prepare participants for what will follow.

In order for this to happen, the group must feel confident in their song leader. They must feel secure with each other and their environment. And they must feel comfortable with the music.

- ### • *Five Flaws that Spell Failure for Song Leaders*
  1. Being unfamiliar with the song.
  2. Not making the lyrics available to everyone in the group (or the music for the musicians).
  3. Being out of tune or out of sync with the other musicians.
  4. Leading as a soloist rather than as a part of the group.
  5. "Putting down" people when they don't sing.

- ### • *Three Steps to Success as a Song Leader*
  1. **Prepare yourself** by:
     a. knowing well the songs you intend to lead or teach.
     b. having enough songbooks for everyone, or using an overhead.
     c. setting the key at the right pitch (not too high or low).
     d. realizing that your music is an offering of praise to God.
  2. **Prepare your setting** by:
     a. keeping the group together.
     b. having an appropriate sound system or good acoustics.
     c. determining what mood or atmosphere you're trying to create by the songs, tempo, and the sequence you select.
  3. **Prepare your group** by:
     a. getting their attention with a familiar or favorite song.
     b. teaching them songs they aren't familiar with.
     c. keeping track of songs you sing (don't overuse songs).
     d. genuinely affirming them for their participation.

- More Great Advice about Leading Music:
- ✔ Gary Lindblad, "How to Be a Better Song Leader" *Group*, November/December, 1986.
- ✔ Bob Stromberg, "Get Kids to Sing," video tape (Loveland, CO: <u>Group</u> Publishing, 1991).

Leading Music

• Learning Styles

The manner, technique or environmental conditions under which individuals learn, including the physical, social, and emotional way in which instruction is delivered, can be referred to as a learning style. We learn best when the *teaching* style matches our *learning* style.

Youth ministry leaders, especially those involved in teaching situations (whether in classrooms or as Sabbath School lesson teachers) will want to provide activities which adequately meet the needs of all learning styles and which answer the types of questions asked in each style. (Also see: Multiple Intelligences.)

• Four Learning Styles
   a. Innovative learners — Why should I learn this?
   b. Analytic learners — What should I learn?
   c. Common sense learners — How does it work?
   d. Dynamic learners — What if the information is applied differently?

• Another View of Learning Orientations
   a. Auditory learners — Do you *hear* what I'm *saying*?
   b. Visual learners — Do you *see* the point *clearly*?
   c. Tactile/Kinesthetic learners — Can you *grasp* the meaning?

• An Exercise in Learning Styles
   Search each of the Bible passages below for clues as to the writer's learning orientation. Which type of words (auditory, visual or tactile/kinesthetic) predominate?

   Then observe how John, in the passage in 1 John 1, attempts to involve all the learners in his audience.
   a. Auditory Orientation. Luke 2:16-20.
   b. Visual Orientation. John 20:1-8.
   c. Tactile/Kinesthetic Orientation. Ephesians 3:14-19.
   d. Multiple Orientations. 1 John 1:1.

•   **More Great Discussion on Learning Styles:**
✔   Linda Campbell, *Teaching & Learning Through Multiple Intelligences* (Needham Heights, MA: Simon & Schuster, 1996).
✔   Howard Gardner, *Frames of Mind: The Theory of Multiple Intelligences*, (New York, NY: Basic Books, 1983).

Learning Styles

• Lesson Study

Traditionally, the study of the Sabbath School lesson has been a large part of the youth <u>Sabbath School</u> time. The lesson curriculum plan for youth in the Seventh-day Adventist church is known as <u>*Cornerstone Connections*</u>. The lessons deal with issues and challenges that are important to high-school aged youth. The lesson material is delivered in a Sabbath School lesson quarterly, which is ordered by your church secretary from the General Conference on a form known as the Standing Periodical Order form. Each individual in your youth group should receive a quarterly.

- • *Five Essential Elements in Successful Lesson Studies:*
  1. **The Preparation Strategy**. Be prepared. Study your lesson ahead of time. Take the time to find the best stories to tell to illustrate your points.
  2. **The Incarnation Principle**. <u>Jesus</u> dwelt among us; "moved into our neighborhood" is the way the *Message Bible* puts it. Know what's happening in the lives of your kids. Begin the lesson discussion by talking about their challenges and opportunities. Use illustrations from their world.
  3. **The <u>Discussion</u> Imperative**. Don't lecture! Involve your youth from the very first minute of the lesson study time. Ask a lot of questions. Comment on their answers.
  4. **The Personal Application**. This is not a history lesson. It's a spiritual focus that must become real in the lives of your learners. Help them make a personal application.
  5. **The Lesson Study's Center**. All authentic Christian study leads to Jesus. Make Jesus the reason for our beliefs, the motivation for all our behavior, the theme of every study.

☞   Also see: Active Learning; Discussion; Learning Styles; Small Groups.

Lesson Study Notes:

_____

_____

_____

_____

_____

- ## *Listen*

Listen is a 32-page monthly magazine which communicates <u>Seventh-day Adventist</u> temperance principles to secular <u>teens</u> and <u>young adults</u> in a way that emphasizes positive alternatives and lifestyle choices.

Consistent with its upbeat image, *Listen* magazine features nationally known role model personalities. Additionally, *Listen* makes sure that every issue includes a story giving real life situations with either the positive or negative results of the choice. You'll also find drug-education facts, life-skills, how-to articles, and ultimate activities including sports and hobbies.

In communicating temperance principles, *Listen's* overall approach emphasizes moral choices and life skills. Rather than dwell on the negative *Listen* attempts to broaden a young person's horizons to see that a life without drugs is ultimately more fulfilling and productive.

Many *Listen* magazines are used in public high schools across North America. Because of this *Listen* is careful to present spiritual <u>values</u> in a way that is acceptable in the secular environment, and as a consequence is non-preachy, and will lead a questioning young person to higher values. *Listen* is an ideal outreach magazine for communities in general, as well as being a necessary publication for our own Adventist young people as they grapple with the realities of an increasingly secular and dangerous world.

Listen is sold by direct subscription, as well as bulk sales to schools. The current circulation for *Listen* magazine is 30,000. You can contact *Listen* at any of the following numbers.

Listen
Editor
Review and Herald Publishing Association
55 West Oak Ridge Drive
Hagerstown, MD 21740
Phone: (301) 745-3888
CompuServe: 74617,3102

• Listening Skills

Why do any of us need instruction in listening? After all, it's one of the earliest capabilities we acquire, you never have to take a class in school on how to listen, and, in fact, the problem really seems to be that there's way too much to listen to!

Actually, those are the very reasons we need to think more seriously about listening. We do so much of it, we just assume it takes place. We ignore the skills we could improve and consequently we don't listen very well. And we have so many distractions, we tend to listen poorly to almost everything.

But when a teenager comes to you for spiritual help, or to pour out his or her heart about family challenges, or to find understanding on the really tough issues of life, you better be prepared to listen. Here are a few skills to work on for the sake of your youth.

• Four Listening Skills

1. **Minimize distractions.** Stop whatever else you're doing. Turn of the TV. Hang up the telephone. Close the book you're reading. Turn away from your computer. Focus your attention on the person who's talking to you.

2. **Make eye contact.** Look directly into the eyes of the person to whom you're listening. Don't be distracted by his or her gestures, a strong accent or style of speech, or what he or she is wearing. Nod your head to provide feedback.

3. **Clarify.** Be sure you understand what the person is talking about. Ask intelligent, reflective questions: "Do I understand you correctly to be saying that...?" "Are you implying that...?" "What do you mean by that?"

4. **Stay on track.** Don't wander. Don't digress or change the subject if the conversation is going well. Try to deal with one thing at a time.

Notes:

_____

_____

_____

_____

Listening Skills

• Magabooks

Over 1,500 teens and young adults are currently selling Magabooks (books formatted in large magazine style) door-to-door in cities and towns across North America. Magabooks include special editions of *Christ's Object Lessons, Great Controversy, Steps to Christ, Ministry of Healing*, vegetarian cookbooks, Arthur Maxwell's story books, *Listen* magazines, *Bible Readings for the Home* and others.

Most students who participate in structured Magabook programs for 8 or 10 weeks in the summer earn between $2,000 and $5,000. Nearly all North American Adventist colleges and universities support students participating in Magabooks with an additional scholarship. Magabook programs provide transportation, team leaders, orientation and training.

• Six Parts of Magabook Training
1. Spiritual motivation for gospel literature sales
2. Money and time management
3. Temperament analysis
4. Canvass techniques
5. Team building
6. Public speaking

Acceptance into a Magabook program is similar to the process for working at a conference summer camp, including filling out an application, supplying references, and interviewing with the Magabook director. Call your Union Conference office for the name, address, and phone number of the Magabook director closest to you. Though most Unions have a Magabook program, there is no centralized Magabook director or office at this time.

For those unable to join an organized Magabook program, Magabooks can be purchased for individual sales from the Review and Herald or the Pacific Press Publishing Association.

Magabooks

Marketing

Marketing is the process by which an organization communicates its message, offers its services or sells its product to potential customers. The goal of marketing is to convince the consumer that the message is correct, the service is desirable, or the product is superior so that the consumer will accept the message, utilize the service or buy the product.

Within the context of the church, marketing asks several key questions: who are the people we are trying to reach? What specific needs do those people have? How can we best minister to those people? How can we best demonstrate the Incarnation of Jesus in their lives?

Many people are hesitant to employ *marketing* vocabulary or strategies in *ministry*. They prefer concepts such as "witnessing," "evangelism," "outreach," "mission," and "spreading the truth," to terms that suggest selling or turning religion into a business. And, of course, *none of us* wants to be involved in religious commercialism. However, the understanding of effective marketing strategies really is just another tool we can use to sharpen our ministry, to best meet the needs of the people we seek to serve, and to more successfully communicate the message of the gospel.

One Adventist pastor explains the process like this: "In church work, marketing is ministry itself. Don't think of it as a means to communicate an event so they can hear the gospel. Think of it as presenting the gospel itself. With this in mind, you will not be just another Madison Avenue entrepreneur. You will be a minister."

For effective youth ministry to occur, the youth leader must take advantage of all the avenues of communication, blend those dynamics into a strategy for success, and carry out that strategy efficiently.

Remember that the key with marketing your youth ministry is trust. If the parents and students know that you are reasonably sane, then you've already done your best marketing and the rest is easy.

Six Marketing Activities

1. Research. Don't make youth ministry decisions in an information vacuum. Find out as much as you can about the members and potential members of your youth group (your specific consumers). How old are they? Where do they live? Where do they go to school? How do they feel about your church? What in-

volvement have they had in your church's youth ministry? (Also see: <u>Evaluating</u> and <u>*Valuegenesis*</u>.)

2. **Recruiting.** No single marketing activity is more important to <u>building your youth group</u> than the face-to-face interaction between you and prospective members.

   How intentional are you in recruiting new members? Where do you meet potential members? What questions do potential members ask you about your youth ministry program? How do you use present members to recruit new members? What activities do you schedule throughout the year specifically to attract new members?

3. **Resonating.** Marketing also includes a broad realm of activity we refer to as *resonating*, the building of meaningful, lasting relationships with individuals who have an immediate, direct influence on those kids we seek to recruit.

   Who are those influential people in your <u>community</u>? Student leaders. The faculty and staff at school. Alumni of your youth group. Parents and grandparents. Make a list of all the influential people who need to resonate with the goals and activities of your program and begin to contact them.

4. **Public Relations.** Here is where you tell the story of your ministry to a wide audience. How familiar are your church members with your youth group activities? How does your community learn about the <u>service</u> projects in which your group is involved? (Also see: <u>Newsletters</u> and <u>Press Releases</u>.)

5. **Events.** Every time you hold a Saturday night party, take part in a short-term <u>mission trip</u> or host a Bible Bowl competition, you are marketing your youth group. What do your social functions say about your youth ministry goals? What do your <u>worship</u> programs reveal about your <u>philosophy of youth ministry</u>?

6. **Advertising.** Where and how do you announce your programs? Do you use posters, bulletin announcements, post cards, telephone calls, ads in your newsletter? Do you have a youth group home page on the <u>world wide web</u>?

   How about having some of your students video events and use the video in promotion of upcoming activities. Play the video in church or in the church lobby on continuous play.

Marketing, continued

Master Calendar

If you're new to <u>youth ministry</u>, there are two things you have to know: first of all, it's the most rewarding ministry in the world. Secondly, you're about to run out of time!

There's never enough time for youth ministry! There's just not enough hours in the day to plan all the things you want to do, organize all the things that need to be in order, and do all the things you know would make an impact. Throw in visiting, <u>counselling</u>, publishing a <u>newsletter</u>, putting on a <u>youth church</u>, leading a <u>mission trip</u>, and playing a late-night basketball game with the kids. (And don't forget your own family and all their needs!) Sometimes it seems <u>burnout</u> is more likely to happen than meeting your youth ministry goals!

Youth ministry professionals everywhere will tell you the importance of establishing a master calendar, an ironclad list of events, programs and activities that becomes the official youth ministry calendar for your <u>youth group</u>. Here are a few tips on creating such a tool. Involve your youth group members and your <u>youth council</u> in the entire planning process.

- *Three Pre-Calendar Activities*
    1. **Collect Everybody's Calendars.** Start with your own church's calendar. Add the calendars for the local schools, the <u>summer camp</u>, the choir and band trips, the <u>Pathfinders</u>, etc.
    2. **Plan Personal Retreats.** You can't be an effective <u>youth leader</u> if you work every <u>Sabbath</u>, 52 weeks a year, year in and year out. Choose time right now, at the beginning of the master calendar planning process, for getting away. Reserve family birthdays, anniversaries, holiday celebrations and just quiet weekends, and don't double book! Guard these personal retreats jealously. Your ministry will benefit.
    3. **Highlight the Celebrations.** Make a note on your calendar of all the holidays, write in the birthdays of the kids in your youth group, and add any local traditions you want to remember.

- *Six Steps to a Master Calendar*
    1. **The Way Things Are.** What's happening in the current program that you want to keep doing? What activities do you want to do again? What things do you want to change?

2. **Where We Want to Go.** Where do you need to grow? What new priorities do you want to introduce? What new goals do you want to establish? How will your priorities be altered?

3. **What We're Going to Do.** What activities will help you meet your goals? What implications do your goals have on your pro-gramming? What new programs do you want to introduce? When would be a good time for a short-term mission trip?

4. **Who's In Charge?** Who will be responsible for each program and activity? (Be sure to spread the responsibility around. Don't ask too few people to accomplish too much. Establish teams to be in charge of social activities, worships, service projects, Sabbath School, etc.)

5. **The First Draft.** Publish your initial effort. Ask for input. Did we miss anything really important? Are we headed into any conflicts? Can parents and church members support your endeavors?

6. **The Finished Product.** Once you've evaluated the first draft input and incorporated everything you can, publish the master calendar. Without being unreasonable, do your best to hold to the calendar. Reevaluate and rework the calendar every year.

Calendar Notes:

_____

_____

_____

_____

_____

_____

_____

_____

_____

_____

_____

_____

_____

_____

_____

_____

Master Calendar, continued

• Mentoring

A *mentor* is a close, trusted and experienced counselor, guide or role model. *Mentoring* is a nurturing relationship that facilitates growth, such as that of a senior business partner helping a junior partner achieve professional success. The mentor challenges, motivates and encourages, sets performance standards, helps make connections and gives support.

In a <u>youth ministry</u> setting, this nurturing can be referred to as *faith-mentoring*; the purposeful connection between a <u>youth leader</u>, parent or another adult and an adolescent that inspires spiritual growth and enhances the discerning of God's active <u>grace</u> in our lives.

• Five Biblical Examples of Mentoring
1. Jethro and Moses
2. Moses and Joshua
3. Elijah and Elisha
4. Barnabas and Paul
5. Paul and Timothy

In her formative book, *Faith Matters: Faith-Mentoring in the Faith Community*, Sondra Higgins Matthaei defines a faith-mentor as "any person who becomes a vehicle for the expression of God's grace in the growth of other people." Such a process is enhanced by the intentionality of the interaction.

• Seven Areas Where Faith-Mentors Serve as Models
1. <u>Spirituality</u>. Demonstrating a growing relationship with God.
2. **Lifestyle**. Exhibiting high <u>standards</u> of behavior, passing on traditions, sharing attitudes, perspectives and a Christian <u>worldview</u>.
3. <u>Values</u>.
4. **Personal Faith Stories**. Sharing your own spiritual journey.
5. **Vocation**.
6. <u>Community</u>. Being a best friend, showing acceptance.
7. **Femininity/Masculinity**. Demonstrating what it means to be a Christian woman or man.

"As a living representative of God's grace, a faith mentor has experienced God's grace in her or his own life, and through grace-full living the mentor offers that grace to others. . .

Mentoring

"Faith mentors are called to embody God's love through their behavior, to help discern God's will in others' lives, and to share their talents and insights in self-giving love on behalf of others. Faith mentors witness by their very lives to the grace they have been given. Relationships at work, at school, on the street, and in the community all have the potential of being faith-mentoring relationships."

- ## Seven Characteristics of Faith Mentors
  1. Caring
  2. Accepting
  3. Challenging
  4. Discerning
  5. Dependable
  6. Shares knowledge and problem solving skills
  7. Grace orientation

- ## Five Challenges to Mentoring
  1. **A shortage of qualified or willing mentors.** Start with as many adults as you can interest and motivate. Use their testimonies, as well as endorsements from the mentored kids, to attract more adults.
  2. **Kids who don't want to participate.** Of course, not every member of your youth group will want to take part. Explain the program, invite everyone to participate, provide mentors for those who are interest to join if and when they're ready.
  3. **Youth-mentor mismatches.** Inevitably, you'll put a youth and an adult together who end up not getting along. If the relationship can't be salvaged, match both parties with new people.
  4. **Mentors who don't follow through.** Sometimes the job is bigger then people imagine. Sometimes family or job pressures increase. Help end the relationship positively and provide a new mentor for the youth.
  5. **Mentors who turn out to be untrustworthy, immoral or dangerous.** In the worst of all possible scenarios, something terrible may go wrong. Intervene immediately. Provide protection, counselling and long-term support. Be open about the problem with your youth group.
  - Adapted from Miles McPherson and Wayne Rice, "Replace Meetings with Mentors," in *Youthworker*, Fall, 1995, 28-36.

Mentoring, continued

• Mission Trips

The sun comes up over an unfamiliar body of water. It's already too warm. A dozen teenage boys begin to stir from their mats on a hard cement floor. Not too far away the girls are already getting ready for the day. The sounds from the village center are foreign and so different from the sounds of downtown, but are no less unmistakable morning sounds.

Now begins the fun part: the local breakfast specialties, the attempts at communicating in a totally unknown tongue, the bumpy ride to the construction site over dirt roads with deep, muddy ruts, the sounds from the nearby jungle, the regular cloudbursts of warm rain.

Why didn't we know of this joy long ago? How could so much hard work bring so much reward in such little time?

It's been said that nothing boosts the morale of a <u>youth group</u>, nothing builds <u>faith maturity</u>, and nothing promotes the Christian way better than mission experiences. Most of us can only afford short-term mission trips. But the impact remains high.

The testimony to the benefits of mission <u>service</u> are almost unanimously positive. You'll hear things like, "I know now why I'm a Christian," and, "For the first time in my life I'm proud to be an Adventist."

Young people, especially, discover in mission service a purpose for their life. Like nothing else, mission trips get kids' minds off of their own pedestrian challenges and temptations and on to the higher road of living for others.

• Do-It-Yourself Mission Trips

1. Lots of churches have contacts (through members who have been in the mission field or who have friends or relatives in the mission field) that can make mission service possible. You need to know three things:
   a. a site that is open to a short-term project,
   b. what the specific project will be, and
   c. how many people the site can support for the amount of time you can give.
2. You also need to make contact with someone who has done this sort of thing before. Ask your conference youth director for a recommendation. Then follow the good advice you receive and take the time to be fully prepared.

The best single resource for getting prepared for mission trips is *Maranatha Guide to Adventure, an Instructive Guide to Short-Term Missions* by Steve and Debbie Case. Published in 1994 by Maranatha Volunteers International, the resource includes such pre-trip items as a philosophy of short-term mission trips, everything you need to do to prepare for your trip, how to construct and raise a <u>budget</u>, a preparation time-line, and what to look for in a pre-trip visit.

In an "At the Project" section the guide explains how to get to your project, how to construct the work day on site, how to relate to the locals, and how to make the experience spiritually beneficial to your group.

Finally, the guide explains how to reenter your own culture successfully, how to report the experience to your church and others and how to keep the enthusiasm going.

The appendix to the manual includes sample application blanks, budget sheets, evaluation forms, materials lists and menus. It also gives you architectural plans for building a typical mission church, lists of things to take along, sample letters to appeal for donations, and much, much more.

Maranatha Guide to Adventure is available direct from Maranatha Volunteers International, 1600 Sacramento Inn Way, Suite 116, Sacramento, CA 95815. You can call Maranatha at (916) 920-1900. You'll get the 150-page manual, a 35-minute video tape and a 50-card card deck with instructions on how to use the cards, all for $49.95.

– Adapted from *Summer Ministries* (Lincoln, NE: <u>Advent*Source*</u>, 1997).

- *Seven Steps to a Successful Mission Trip*
  1. **Select Key Staff.** (See: <u>Resource People</u>.)
     a. Project Coordinator.
     b. Spiritual Leader.
     c. Construction Superintendent.
     d. Cook.
  2. **Define Your Trip.** What's the primary purpose?
  3. **Recruit Participants.** Skilled and unskilled.
  4. **Construct a Budget.** Be sure to include all the details, including transportation, housing, insurance, food, excursions and construction costs.
  5. **Raise the Funds.**
  6. **Conduct a Pre-trip Site Visit.**
  7. **Train Your Staff.**

Mission Trips, continued

• Movie Ratings

The Motion Picture Association of America (MPAA) voluntarily rates every movie that is produced in America. The ratings are based on a guide which describes certain behaviors, language or depictions. The MPAA describes the ratings as follows.

• G: General Audiences — All Ages Admitted

Some snippets of language may go beyond polite conversation but they are common everyday expressions. No stronger words are present in G-rated films. The violence is at a minimum. Nudity and sex scenes are not present; nor is there any drug use content.

• PG: Parental Guidance Suggested

The theme of a PG-rated film may itself call for parental guidance. There may be some profanity in these films. There may be some violence or brief nudity. But these elements are not deemed so intense as to require that parents be strongly cautioned beyond the suggestion of parental guidance. There is *no drug* use content in a PG-rated film.

• PG-13: Parents Strongly Cautioned

Any drug use content will initially require at least a PG-13 rating. If nudity is sexually oriented, the film will generally not be found in the PG-13 category. If violence is too rough or persistent, the film goes into the R rating. A film's single use of one of the harsher sexually derived words, though only as an expletive, shall initially require the Rating Board to issue the film at least a PG-13 rating. More than one such expletive must lead the Rating Board to issue a film an R rating, as must even one of these words used in a sexual context.

• R: Restricted

No one under 17 is admitted without an accompanying parent or adult guardian. An R-rated film may include hard language, or tough violence, or nudity within sensual scenes, or drug abuse or other elements, or a combination of some of the above, so that parents are counseled in advance to take this advisory rating very

Movie Ratings

seriously. Parents must find out more about an R-rated movie before they allow their teenagers to view it.

- ## NC-17: No children under 17 admitted

  The reasons for the application of an NC-17 rating can be violence or sex or aberrational behavior or drug abuse or any other elements which, when present, most parents would consider too strong and therefore off-limits for viewing by their children.

- ## Not Rated

  Not Rated generally means the movie was created before the rating system was in place.

- ## Unrated

  Unrated means the movie was not submitted to the MPAA for a rating (many foreign films are not), or that it was created for another medium, such as a cable movie network. Often unrated movies are movies which have restored violent or sexually explicit scenes which were cut to achieve an R rating.

- ## X: Adults Only

  The MPAA does not give X ratings; this is a self-generated, mostly promotional rating given to sexually explicit, adults-only movies.

Notes on Movies:

_____

_____

_____

_____

_____

_____

_____

_____

_____

_____

_____

Movie Ratings, continued

• Movies

There was a time when part of the *definition* of being a <u>Seventh-day Adventist</u> was that we didn't go to movies. Today, research reveals that more than 95 per cent of Adventist young people watch movies in theaters regularly, and rent movies to watch at home on their VCRs.

This striking change in behavior, as well as technological developments and cable movie networks (HBO, Cinemax, etc.), have forced us to focus our discussions about movies on the *content* of the movies we view instead of the *places* we view the movie.

For a full discussion of the movie issue, see "Thinking About Movies" in *Shall We Dance: Rediscovering Christ-centered Standards*, published in 1996 by the <u>Hancock Center for Youth and Family Ministry</u>.

• *Three Movie Choices*

1. **Watch Virtually Anything**. To accept this argument means to turn our back on biblical wisdom and good sense.
2. **Totally Eliminate Movies.** This means not only cutting out going to the theater, it also means not renting videos to watch at home, not watching movies on cable TV, not watching regularly scheduled network movies, and even refusing to see movies sponsored by your church or school.
3. **Be Discriminating** in What You See. This is the most difficult option. It means raising a high standard and sticking to it, regardless of what friends are watching on Saturday night. (Taken from *Shall We Dance, pages 354-357.*)

• *Four Principles for Discriminating Viewers*

1. Make choices that contribute to your long-range goals. Don't spend time in pursuits that lead you away from your established objectives, that encourage you to abandon those goals, or that lead you to adopt someone else's goals.
2. Never watch a movie unintentionally.
3. Check the ratings. When the Motion Picture Association of America rates a movie, there's a reason for the rating.
4. Get acquainted with the critics. Read reviews in newspapers and magazines that aren't published by the movie industry. Find one or two critics with whom you consistently agree. (Taken from *Shall We Dance, pages 358-362.*)

Movies

Multi-Cultural Youth Ministry

"What makes us all the same is that we all are different" - Edward James Olmos
"We need to understand each other in order to appreciate each other." - Delbert Baker

Ministry to youth is even more challenging in the diverse <u>community</u> of believers in which we live today. How can a <u>youth leader</u> in a multi-cultural setting effectively meet the needs of each individual in the <u>youth group</u>? How do you approach and shape your ministry in this type of environment? How do you make the entire youth group sensitive and thus defuse potential tensions? How do you build a true community of faith?

- ## Four Foundations of Multi-Cultural Ministry

  1. **Cultural awareness.** Culture is a way of life, a basic perspective, the underlying expectation for all aspects of behavior in a specific society.

     Naturally, different groups of people, different societies, have different perspectives, different expectations. In a multi-cultural setting, effective youth leaders *celebrate* those differences rather than allowing them to become *barriers*.

     Are you ready to break down the barriers and establish personal relationships? Do you understand the neighborhoods from which your youth come? Are you prepared to make each individual feel comfortable, to incorporate them into your "family," to show genuine interest, to learn their customs, traditions and perspectives? Are you even willing to learn their language, to at least greet them in their native tongue, as they are learning to fit in to your culture?

  2. **Common ground.** Get to the heart of the individual. In Christian settings our <u>diversity</u> is peripheral; what is *central* to Christians is central to us all. Come close to each other on common ground. While worship styles differ, the Person we worship is the same.

     In youth ministry there is more common ground to celebrate. All teens are on a similar journey. All teens have similar needs. Explore the similarities together and start your ministry there.

     One church has found that young people relate well with each other over food. Why not plan a multi-cultural pot luck?

Ask each youth group member to bring a national dish or a favorite family food. Talk about the ingredients, the flavorings, the festive occasions that so often include special meals. Make sure everyone samples *all* the fare! (By the way, it's okay not to like everything you taste. Just make sure the distaste is acknowledged as a matter of what we're used to. Don't allow any blanket judgements, such as, "Pakistani food is no good.")

3. **Participation.** Empowering different young people to work towards a common goal is one of the most rewarding aspects of multi-cultural ministry.

Invite your youth to talk about and demonstrate how things are done in their culture. Ask them for creative suggestions on how to incorporate their traditions into your program. Also explore together ways to welcome new members from other new cultures.

4. *Service.* Nothing takes us away from petty squabbles about differences better than working to meet the real needs of others. Nothing will help you build a community of faith better than serving others. Explore the possibilities of short-term mission trips, local community service projects, and ongoing outreach activities. Watch the differences melt away.

Always remember to respect each others views. Ask yourself the question, "How can I love others as God has loved me?"

☞   **Here's a Helpful New Resource:** *SAAAY* is the youth newsletter published quarterly by the African-American Youth Department of Southen California Conference of SDAs. You can get in touch with *SAAAY* at the following addresses: *SAAAY*, P.O. Box 969, Glendale, CA 91206-4107; phone (818) 730-1839; fax (818) 497-7099; Editor's e-mail - 73360.1324@compuserve.com.

Notes:

Multi-Cultural Ministry, continued

• Multiple Intelligences

Perhaps you've already experienced the optimum teaching moment. It's that instance when, for the very first time, a student understands something you've been trying to explain.

• *The Optimum Teaching Moment*
1. It happens when a child learns to tie his or her shoes.
2. It takes place in an elementary classroom when a first grader suddenly understands why 2+2=4.
3. It's that magic moment when a piano student moves from playing by memory to playing by heart.
4. It happens with members of your <u>youth group</u> each time someone grasps how exciting it is to have a friendship with <u>Jesus</u>.

At that precious moment of comprehension when the light comes on behind the eyes (many call this instance the "Aha!" phenomenon), there is a look on the face of the learner that is nothing short of heavenly. Once you've seen it happen, you realize that a genuine miracle has taken place, and you want it to happen over and over again.

• *Eureka! I Have Found It!*
We love to tell the famous story of the Greek mathematician, Archimedes (c. 298 BC - 212 BC), whose theorem on the weight of a body immersed in a liquid is known as Archimedes' Principle. The story insists that Archimedes made the discovery while taking a bath. Apparently the breakthrough moment of comprehension occurred just as Archimedes settled into his tub. He got so excited about his sudden insight that he bolted from the tub and ran naked through the streets yelling, "Eureka!" which means, "I have found it!".

Apocryphal or not, the story exactly describes the excitement of the optimum teaching moment.

Since 1983 more and more teachers have been experiencing this Eureka moment with their students through the application of a new educational theory about intelligence. First introduced by Howard Gardner in his book *Frames of Mind: The Theory of Multiple Intelligences* (New York, NY: Basic Books, 1983), the theory argues that intelligence is multifaceted, that there are many ways people learn. Gardner helps

Multiple Intellegences

us see that learning is enhanced when we approach a topic through "entry points," doors into a subject which he describes as specific cognitive strengths, abilities or "intelligences."

- **Eight Kinds of Smart**
  1. **Art Smart.** Spatial intelligence. The ability to comprehend shapes and images in three dimensions. Essential for artists, sculptors and architects. Also important to airplane pilots and navigators and to people who like to solve mazes!
  2. **Body Smart.** Kinesthetic intelligence. Physical coordination and dexterity. Using motor skills. Expressing oneself or learning through physical activities. Athletes utilize these abilities, as do people who like to work with their hands.
  3. **Interpersonal Smart.** Understanding and communicating with other people. It's an ability we all need, but it is essential to teachers, politicians and salespersons.
  4. **Intrapersonal Smart.** Having an understanding of yourself, knowing your goals and abilities. Being in touch with your own temperaments, intelligences, moods and emotions.
  5. **Logic/Math Smart.** Involves number and computing skills, classifying and sequencing and solving problems through logic. Scientist and mathematicians exhibit these skills.
  6. **Music Smart.** Especially evident in musicians, of course. Producing and remembering melodies, harmonies, rhythms and musical patterns.
  7. **Naturalist Smart.** Having the sensitivity to the natural world. The newest addition to Gardner's model is used in many of the sciences, and also by farmers, environmentalists and chefs.
  8. **Word Smart.** Linguistic intelligence. The capacity to use language to effectively communicate. Successful poets, writers, preachers and lawyers use this intelligence.

Teachers who utilize these entry points into the "core notions" of their subjects report significant improvement in learning, including increased independence and self direction, and the strengthening of both cooperative and leadership skills.

☞ **Also see:** Active Learning; Critical Thinking Skills; Discussion; Involvement; Lear ning Styles; and Shared Experiences.

Multiple Intellegences, continued

● **Music**

Music is intensely personal. The never-ending argument over music is perpetually fueled by the subjective nature of music appreciation. All of us are critics. We like the music we like.

Adult musical interests are influenced by our cultural background, the songs we enjoyed as kids, and the music preferred by our parents. We appreciate songs we've learned to appreciate.

But there are some who feel compelled to put a *spiritual* value on our musical preferences, and youthful music is most often at the bottom of the list. That's where the youth ministry battle usually begins.

As Christians, we certainly should apply high spiritual standards to all our activities, including our music. But we also must be quick to be tolerant. Let's not confuse spirituality with cultural conditioning.

While the clash between musical values is not exclusively a generational one, it is where most of the shouting is heard, The resulting conflict, as ancient as Jubal and as contemporary as tomorrow's latest release, must be settled over and over again by each generation through the application of timeless principles to current situations.

● *Three Pre-Discussion Commitments*

1. **Become Informed.** Don't get off to a bad start by talking to your youth group about rock stars who haven't had a hit song since your kids were born. This is a constantly changing scene and you need to be an up-to-date witness. Spend 20 minutes with MTV. Ask your kids what radio station you should tune in to. Watch the annual Grammy awards show on TV.
2. **Don't Impose Your Judgement.** You've probably already made up your mind. But don't force people to agree with you. Teens want to discuss the issues and make their own decisions. Help them learn how to make informed decisions.
3. **Evaluate All the Factors.** Be willing to look at all sides of the issue. Refuse to stereotype. Be ready to take the discussion category by category, artist by artist, song by song.

● *Five Components of Music to Evaluate*

1. **Intention.** What's the purpose of the music? What response is the composer attempting to elicit? How do the performers intend for us to react?

Sometimes the answers are easy. More difficult challenges arise in relation to music openly intended to be Christian music, but which compositionally cannot be distinguished from its secular counterpart (see <u>Contemporary Christian Music</u>). Perhaps Paul would advise us to be careful here and to separate style from spirituality. "It is not for you to judge someone else's servant," he has cautioned us (Romans 14:4, 10).

"It is on the intention that all depends," C. S. Lewis observed. Noel Paul Stookey (of Peter, Paul and Mary fame) expresses the same thought like this; "God hears music from the inside out." (Also see 1 Samuel 16:7.)

2. **Presence**. (See 1 John 4:1-3 and Philippians 1:15-18.) Before a band beings to play, you can easily observe the particular atmosphere that animates the audience. How are the guys and girls treating each other? What statement is being made by the prevailing fashion? Does the atmosphere rely heavily on drugs and alcohol? What do the lifestyles of the performers tell you about their influence? Be sure to consider presence in evaluating a Christian concert, too.

3. **Lyrics**. (Read Philippians 4:8.) What is the message of the song based on the lyrics? What does the song say about its topic? Is the message consistent with what you believe?

4. **Music**. (See 1 Samuel 16:23 and 2 Chronicles 20:13-22.) This arena of musical evaluation is the most difficult one. How do we fairly evaluate all the elements of the music itself — the melodies, harmonies, rhythms and dynamics? How can we separate personal preference from spiritual effect long enough to come to an accurate decision?

Exactly where to draw the line is an intensely personal decision. We can invite discussion on the topic, we can offer guidelines, we can encourage decisions. But in the end, each individual will base his or her decision on the personal impact of each piece of music.

5. **The Spiritual Dimension**. Above all, Christians remember that music, as all influences in our lives, has an impact on our Christian experience. As we make decisions on this subject, let's resolve to concentrate on the spiritual dimension and not to argue about musical styles and personal preferences.

- Adapted from, "Thinking About Music," in *Shall We Dance* (Riverside, CA: <u>Hancock Center for Youth and Family Ministry</u>, 1996), 104-141.

Music, continued

• National Black Youth Resource Center

The National Black Youth Resource Center (NBYRC) was established on the first of February, 1995 to preserve and enhance the Black <u>youth ministry</u> program in the North American Division, and to make that program relevant to the Black experience by providing training, creating <u>resources</u>, and conducting <u>research</u>, while establishing and coordinating a youth leadership network.

When the NBYRC idea was first conceived, the <u>Black Adventist Youth Directors' Association</u> (BAYDA - the official sponsors of the Resource Center) felt strongly that the NBYRC should be housed at Oakwood College. The Chaplain of the College, who also is a member of BAYDA, suggested that it could be housed in the Chaplain's office along with the Campus Ministries programs.

The Center functions at Oakwood as an on-campus resource provider for the Youth Ministries professional in local conferences and churches. The Center networks with other departments on campus (such as the Office of Student Affairs, Religion and Theology, English, Communications, and the Center of Academic Advancement) to provide services in conjunction with these other entities already in place in the academic and social life of Oakwood College.

Along with providing services, the Center collects data that is pertinent to fulfill the NBYRC's mission and purpose.

National Black Youth Resource Center
    Oakwood College
    Office of Spiritual Life
    Huntsville, Alabama 35896
    Phone: (205) 726-8426
    Fax: (205) 726-8141
    http: www.tagnet.org/nbyrc
    Email: nbyrc@hotmail.com

Notes:

_____

_____

_____

_____

_____

National Black Youth Resource Center

• Newsletters

Here's another wonderful way to keep in touch with your youth, to advertise <u>youth ministry</u> activities, and to highlight the importance of youth ministry – a regularly scheduled newsletter, full of information by, for and about the youth of your church.

- ### • Three Pre-Publication Considerations
  1. **Interest.** Who are the potential writers in your <u>youth group</u>? Is this important enough to raise money for regular printing and postage? Can the interest be sustained?
  2. **Schedule.** How much time are you going to be able to devote to this activity? Who will be able to find time to help? How often do you want to publish? Monthly? Quarterly?
  3. **Style.** Find newsletters that look good to you. Tear out pages of magazines that have the right feel. Look for design, layout, type, headlines, how pictures are used, etc. Have your youth agree on the best style for *their* newsletter.

- ### • Four Phases of Your Editorial Meeting
  1. **Make Evaluations.** Discuss the strengths and weaknesses of the last issue of your newsletter. Be sure to laud excellent reporting and creative writing.
  2. **Assign Articles.** What events are coming up? What columns should appear? What feature articles would be helpful? Decide who will write what. Talk about the type of article you want. Determine the length. Ask for short, descriptive sentences.
  3. **Establish Deadlines.** Create a reasonable deadline and enlist everyone's commitment to it.
  4. **Get to Work.** <u>Research</u> comes first. Then interviews for content, comments and opinions. Then a first draft (create, create, create, then edit). Deliver the written piece on a disk so that it doesn't have to be re-keyboarded.

- ### • Twelve Article Ideas for Your Newsletter
  1. **People.** Report birthdays, vacations and visits, graduations, promotions, milestones, baptisms. Hold interviews with interesting people in your church and/or <u>community</u>.

2. **How To.** Whatever topic your editorial team thinks should be covered: how to study your Bible; how to pass a test; how to share your faith; how to eat healthfully; how to ask someone for a date; etc.

3. **Special Events.** What celebrations, social activities or mission trips are coming up? When's the next <u>youth church</u> scheduled? Don't forget holiday parties, graduations, baptisms, etc.

4. **Regular Events.** Who's in charge of next month's <u>Sabbath School</u> programs? What are the AY program topics? Include items from your <u>master calendar</u>.

5. **Regular Columns.** A word from the chair of your <u>youth council</u>. Inspirational thoughts from your pastor. Questions and answers. What's hot and what's not. Reviews on <u>music</u>, <u>movies</u> magazines and books.

6. **Explanatory Articles.** Write about how Sabbath School is planned, how your <u>budget</u> is met, what <u>*Cornerstone Connections*</u> is planning to discuss this quarter, etc. Use entries from *The ABZs of Adventist Youth Ministry.*

7. **Financial News.** What financial needs are most pressing? What <u>fund raising</u> events are planned? Talk about scholarships, donations, work opportunities, etc.

8. **Recipes.** Favorite cookies. Creative <u>pizza</u> ideas. Holiday treats. Healthful snacks.

9. **Cartoons.** Most youth ministry magazines carry cartoons you can use. Find cartoons in <u>clip art</u> books. Or, better yet, create your own and personalize them.

10. **Quizzes, Puzzles, <u>Games</u>.**

11. **Excerpts and Reprints.** Find articles appropriate to your setting in *<u>Insight</u>, <u>Group</u>, <u>Adventist View</u>, <u>Listen</u>,* etc. Call for permission to reprint in your newsletter.

12. **Photo Essays.** Be humorous. Or get serious. Pick a topic. Ask for everyone to submit pictures with captions.

More Newsletter Ideas:

_____

_____

_____

_____

_____

_____

Newsletters, continued

North American Division Youth Ministry (vertical, left margin)

• North American Division Youth Ministry

North American Division Youth Ministries exists to empower those in each local setting who minister directly to <u>teens</u> and <u>young adults</u>.

Under the leading of the Holy Spirit, in anticipation of our Lord's soon return, in confidence of the power of the <u>gospel</u>, and as a committed team of <u>Seventh-day Adventist</u> professionals from diverse cultures and experiences, we desire to strengthen those who seek to nurture teens and young adults and to mobilize them in Christian <u>service</u>.

Holding these values, we make these commitments as goals in teen and young adult ministry:

• 1. Relational Ministry

We will establish a *relational* model of teen and young adult ministry, based on the gospel elements of a <u>grace orientation</u> and the clear calling to be joyful citizens of the heavenly kingdom.

• 2. Inclusive Ministry

We will establish an *inclusive* model of ministry which involves people in the planning and implementation of teen and young adult ministry regardless of race, color, language, gender, age or educational experience. (Also see: <u>Diversity</u>.)

• 3. Trained Ministry

We will establish a *trained* model of teen and young adult ministry in which those who minister to teens and young adults understand the specific purposes of <u>youth ministry</u>, the age-specific spiritual needs of youth, the most effective methods of youth ministry and the best <u>resources</u> available to accomplish youth ministry.

• 4. Professional Ministry

We will establish a *professional* model of teen and young adult ministry in which those who are employed by the church in teen and young adult ministry will sense their great value to the denomination, will have access to professional growth and career enhancement opportunities, and will take part in a creative and enriching network of ideas, recommendations and <u>evaluation</u>.

- **5. A Ministry of Service**
We will establish an *infrastructure of service opportunities* through a Youth Service Network in order to provide teens and young adults with the experience of encountering and sharing Jesus through a life of service. (Also see: YouthNet.)

In order to achieve the five goals of our mission statement, enabling teens and young adults and their leaders to accomplish ministry, we commit to the following initiatives.

- **A. The Adventist Youth Service Network**
  - *Empower* the experience of MISSIONARY and VOLUNTEER as a lifestyle among Adventist teens and young adults in North America
  - *Recruit* and train 10,000 Adventist teens and young adults in evangelism to local and global communities
  - *Establish* an infrastructure of service opportunities in North America amplifying the experience of North America as part of the mission field

- **B. Strengthen opportunities for youth to have group meetings on a regular basis.**
  - *Revive* the church AY meeting (See: Adventist Youth Society)
  - *Strengthen* the Youth Sabbath School
  - *Establish* area youth federations
  - *Enlarge* the online Forums for teens and young adults

- **C. Model Diversity in Youth Ministry**
  - *Host* a symposium on diversity with the goal of highlighting the power of cultural affirmation and inclusion in youth ministry
  - *Produce* a manual and brochures for application strategies and suggestions for youth leaders at all levels focusing on three key areas:
    - Information - Awareness building
    - Education - Curriculum
    - Modeling - Programming
  - *Produce* a book series on cultural affirmation and inclusion in youth ministry for publication

NAD Youth Ministry, continued

- D. Train 1000 local church youth leaders per year
  - *Equip* church youth leaders for ministry
  - *Provide* a certification process for those who choose to seek a specialization in church youth ministry
  - *Offer* two basic formats for training in the various settings of the North American Division

- E. Support the occurrence of large youth congresses
  - *Inspire* and recruit youth for service
  - *Enhance* a sense of a youth movement in North America
  - *Support* events in five areas of the North American Division

- F. Encourage the production of and the availability of current youth ministry products
  - *Produce* and encourage the production of a minimum of ten youth ministry resources each year
  - *Establish* a plan for evaluation of all products

- G. The Association of Adventist Youth Ministry Professionals
  - *Network* youth ministry professionals throughout the NAD
  - *Enhance* professional growth through educational in-service opportunities
  - *Identify* people who possess special gifts and recruit them to professional youth ministry service
  - *Advocate* the hiring of youth ministry professionals within church institutional staffs
  - *Promote* the spiritual growth, retention and involvement of teens and young adults in ministry

North American Division Teen and Young Adult Ministries
12501 Old Columbia Pike
Silver Spring, MD 20904-6600
Phone: (301) 680-6434
FAX: (301) 680-6464

• Pantomime Ministry

A pantomime is a dramatic presentation without words, using only actions and gestures. Pantomime ministry provides the opportunity to share messages on sensitive issues in a non-confrontational yet thought-provoking manner.

- • *Pantomime Ministry Is a Creative Way To:*
    a. witness to an unreached, seldom touched population segment.
    b. train and disciple youth in witnessing principles.
    c. demonstrate positive, Christian life-changing principles.
    d. establish positive recognition of <u>Seventh-day Adventists</u>.
    e. address issues such as the <u>gospel</u>, relationships, substance abuse, <u>AIDS</u>, <u>self-esteem</u>, <u>peer pressure</u>, choices and <u>values</u>, and the influence of media.

Pantomime ministry reaches people "where they are," at shopping malls, on city sidewalks, and in public high schools. (Permission to perform in public places is usually granted only if you promise not to focus on religious issues. However, the very presence of the team, the interaction with spectators, the presentation, and the content result in a very definite witness.)

Pantomime ministry has been demonstrated successfully by the group, "Inside Out," of Kelowna, British Columbia, with presentations on city streets in Western Canada. Street performances in popular areas have drawn television news crews and have provided exciting witnessing opportunities. The group also performs at churches, schools, community service centers, long-term care facilities, and nonprofit organizations.

An excellent source for professional training material for pantomime is:

Mimeistry Inc.
    1605 E. Elizabeth Road
    Pasadena, CA 91104
    Phone: (818) 398-2300
    FAX: (818) 398-2301
    E-mail: 74372.321@Compuserve.com

• Parents

Besides being the most important people in the lives of your youth, parents can also be your biggest supporters or your most stringent critics. Be sure to give parents the attention they need to be drawn into a strong supporting role for your ministry.

• Keeping Parents Involved

1. Hold a parent's night twice a year (early in the calendar year and early in the summer) when you discuss upcoming events, fix dates in your master calendar, talk about topics you'll be exploring (see: Cornerstone Connections), invite suggestions for improved ministry, and outline budget needs and plans.
2. Ask parents to host social activities at their homes. Don't tax the hospitality of the same people over and over again; instead, get six or eight different families to accept the responsibility, but just once or twice a year. Be sure to provide funds for food and drink for the evening, unless, of course, the family would like to contribute to your needy budget!
3. Invite parents to become youth group sponsors and have a ready list of activities for them: planning Sabbath Schools, vespers or AYS meetings; providing transportation; travelling with you on mission trips; contributing to a special fund for kids who can't quite pay their bill at school; etc.

In addition to impacting self-esteem issues, research continues to show highly significant relationships between parenting styles and a number of essential dimensions of faith development, including Christian commitment, an individual's view of God, denominational loyalty, denominational orthodoxy and acceptance of lifestyle standards. The most effective parenting style is one in which there is emotional warmth and affection and in which young people are free from an overprotective environment.

There is also a high, positive relationship between parents talking about their faith and the Christian commitment of their children. Perhaps the two most important things you can do for the members of your youth group is to help their parents know how to keep communicating about faith issues with their kids, and how to have meaningful, interesting family worship.

Parents

• Pathfinder Ministries

Pathfinders is a church sponsored club for boys and girls in the Seventh-day Adventist Church, patterned after the Boy and Girl Scout organization, with an added spiritual dimension. Club activities include worship, crafts, games, nature studies, field trips, marching, etc. Club members meet weekly, wear uniforms, and earn honors in over 200 areas, as diverse as dressmaking, auto mechanics, orchids and Indian lore. Official Pathfinder manuals guide club leaders and counselors in every aspect of the ministry.

Now a worldwide organization with thousands of volunteer leaders, and hundreds of thousands of members, Pathfindering had its beginnings in southern California in the early 1930s. John McKim, a Scoutmaster and a member of the Santa Ana SDA church, began a club for the junior youth of his church. The club met in a church member's home, and called themselves Pathfinders, after the nickname of John C. Fremont, pioneer explorer of early California and, in 1856, the first presidential candidate of the new Republican party.

Unfortunately, however, older members of the Santa Ana church were not happy with the new club. They thought that the club's activities were "bringing the world into the church." The church board voted that the club should be disbanded and threatened church discipline if the action were not taken immediately.

Official Pathfindering didn't recover from this early blow until the fall of 1946. Elder John Hancock had become youth director for the Southeastern California Conference. With the encouragement of the pastor of the Riverside church, Hancock established a club for 10-15 year old youth and called it a Pathfinder Club. He designed a sleeve emblem for the new club's uniform, purchased uniforms at Army Surplus stores, and arranged to meet in a school building. The Riverside group of about 15 boys and girls was the first conference-sponsored Pathfinder Club in the Adventist Church.

Other clubs soon followed. Lawrence Paulson established a club in Glendale and then 11 additional clubs across southern California. Between 1947 and 1950, the General Conference encouraged the development of the Pathfinder concept. In 1950, the entire Pathfinder program was adopted at the General Conference Session in San Francisco. The first General Conference world Pathfinder Director, L. A. Skinner, was elected that same year.

Pathfinder Ministries

Pathfinder Ministries, continued

- **Six Things You Should Know about Pathfinders**

  1. **They are growing.** From its small beginnings (15 kids in southern California) Pathfinders has grown to a worldwide organization. By the year 2,000, it is expected that there will be one million Pathfinders around the world.

  2. **They enjoy getting together.** Most local conferences organize local camporees, hold Pathfinder investitures, and sponsor Pathfinder fairs on a yearly basis. Call your conference youth director for information about the schedule and cost of activities. Also ask the director about the availability of training for Pathfinder leaders.

  3. **They are enthusiastic about camporees.** Unions and Divisions plan camporees every five years. Recent North American Division camporees have included the 1985 Colorado Camp Hale experience, the 1989 Friendship Camporee in Pennsylvania, and the 1994 Dare to Care Camporee in Colorado. In August 1999, 18,000 Pathfinders are expected to attend the Division-wide camporee, called Discover the Power, in Oshkosh, Wisconsin.

  4. **Supplies are readily available.** AdventSource, located in Lincoln, Nebraska, provides supplies for local clubs. You can reach them at (800) 328-0525.

  5. **Leadership remains committed.** The division leadership for Pathfinders is located in the North American Division Office.

Notes about your local Pathfinder club:

_____

_____

_____

_____

_____

_____

_____

_____

_____

_____

_____

_____

• Peer Counselling

Youth helping other youth – that's what peer counselling is all about. Studies continue to show that the most effective counsellors are other people from your same peer group. Students usually talk more readily, easily, and openly to other students. They also assume that other students share the same challenges as they do and therefore respond to those challenges the same way they can or should.

So, more and more, in high school and college settings, students are being trained with the necessary skills to genuinely help each other.

• Seven Skills for Peer Counsellors
1. Paying attention
2. Showing empathy
3. Summarizing
4. Asking appropriate questions
5. Being genuine
6. Being assertive
7. Knowing how to solve problems

Peer counsellors should be specifically trained for this service opportunity. The effectiveness of such programs usually depends on a variety of preparations, including giving adequate information about the counselling process, being observed and coached by a trained counsellor, and knowing when to refer to a professional.

• Seven Peer Counselling Situations
1. Providing school work tutoring
2. Training for leadership
3. Dealing with alcohol and drug use
4. Recognizing eating disorders
5. Coping with loss
6. Responding to thoughts of suicide
7. Considering ethical decisions

☞ **Also see:** Death and Dying Issues; Depression; Listening Skills; Mentoring; Sexuality Issues.

Peer counselling

Peer Pressure

All of us feel pressure to conform to the norms of our peer group. The pressures assault us in mass media messages and expensive, well-done advertising. They come at us through friends, social acquaintances and work associates. We even feel the pressure to be like others in our faith communities. The pressures cause us to want to act, talk, dress and appear like others we consider important and trend-setting.

Adolescents, however, are at an age when they are *particularly* susceptible to the influence of their peers. Often these pressures assert themselves in negative realms: challenging authority, taking part in <u>at-risk behaviors</u>, <u>distancing</u> from established beliefs and practices, especially religious <u>values</u>.

Peer pressure can also be positive. Friends are the most important influence in avoiding <u>alcohol</u>, <u>tobacco</u> and other drugs, and in choosing positive values over negative ones. High school students challenge others to excel in school work. Youth group members provide the strength for others to accept and value the spiritual life.

• Seven Strategies in Peer Pressure Challenges

1. **Accept peer pressure as normal.** It happens to all of us. It certainly is a factor in the growth of your youth.

2. **Identify positive and negative pressures.** Talk to your youth about the pressures they feel. Help them distinguish between good and bad influences. Discuss consequences.

3. **Build self-confidence.** Bad self-image continues to be the number one reason teens give in to pressure. Be a constant encourager. (See: <u>Self-esteem</u>.)

4. **Demonstrate how to say no.** Identify and demonstrate ways to respond appropriately and immediately to negative peer pressure.

5. **Avoid negative circumstances.** Discuss the situations and places where your youth feel most vulnerable to negative pressures. Talk about how to avoid those situations.

6. **Applaud positive pressure.** Draw attention to instances where one teen or group of teens positively influenced others. Appreciate these efforts loudly and frequently.

7. **Keep talking.** Peer pressure doesn't go away. Continue to discuss this powerful dynamic.

• Philosophy of Youth Ministry

Most of the time we don't think much about the philosophy behind our youth ministry. After all, our most pressing challenge is to get ready for Sabbath School, right? The youth will be there at 9:30 a.m. and we have only a few minutes left to prepare. We smile and call this a "pragmatic" approach to youth ministry – it's motivated by the job that needs to be done and its quality is often directly proportional to the time we have to work on it!

Even this approach to youth ministry, however, is a kind of philosophy. "The tyranny of the immediate forces many to neglect the weightier matters of youth ministry. Probably the most crucial issue in youth ministry is why there should be a youth ministry."[1]

• *Ten Elements of a Youth Ministry Philosophy*

1. What kind of a God do you serve? The picture you have of God will help you understand what motivates your ministry. We serve a God that seeks us. Our God understands and, by His grace, accepts us unconditionally. The biblical picture of God shows us that the God of the universe is personal, know-about-able, and standing up for us during these last important days of earth's history.

2. How does that God get in touch with us? This means we must think about the way God is revealed in this world. Is it immediate? How obvious is His revelation to us? We have to spend some time understanding the trustworthy and utterly reliable revelations of God. This answer will help you see the place of Bible study and devotional practices in your ministry.

3. How do youth learn? How does anyone know anything? Where do you fall in your understanding of the learning process. What are the higher learning skills that are needed to understand theology and religion? For example, is rote memory learning less useful than synthesis and analysis? Should restatement be incorporated in our learning about God, or should we only read things passively and then reflect on them? And, of course how do people learn anyway? (See: Learning Styles.)

4. What is ministry all about? Here studying the life of Jesus is most helpful. Is ministry servanthood, selfless giving to others? Is the purpose of ministry so that youth can grow and

Philosophy of Youth Ministry, continued

develop into all that God is calling them to be? Is ministry something that we do alone, or only with the power of the Holy Spirit? Are only certain people called to be ministers or servants?

5. How do adolescents grow? Does effective youth ministry treat adolescents as children or adults? Are there some areas of religious life that are especially meaningful to youth and young adults that are not important for older adults?

6. The outcomes of your ministry? Some time must be spent in visioning what you want to accomplish in six months or one year, or, for that matter, five years down the line. After deciding, you can transfer these outcomes into actual plans for ministry.

7. How should other leaders be involved in your ministry? How do you build a ministry team? What is important when you select youth and adult leaders? How should you train them and what role should the church play in assisting them to become competent leaders?

8. What kinds of programs are consistent with our mission and understanding of youth ministry? What you do is directly related to your philosophy of ministry. All theoretical ideas eventually must be translated into actual things that impact youth. Programming is no exception to this rule. What programs need to be developed and carried out that reinforce your philosophy?

9. What does your church think of youth ministry? All too often local congregations see youth ministry as an addendum to the church program. How vital to your church is your ministry? Here is a call to develop a personal, local mission statement which will focus your ministry into objective target areas.

10. How do you understand your own gifts for youth ministry? Vital to your philosophy is your own view of yourself. How well do you know your skills and gifts? In what areas do you need decisive help and in what ways can you carry the program on your own? And, what are the implications to this answer for your personal religious life?

These are the basic building blocks in a strong foundation for youth ministry in your local church. When you are finished answering these questions you are ready to begin to plan for local action.

[1]   John M. Dettoni, *Introduction to Youth Ministry* (Grand Rapids, MI: Zondervan, 1993), 17.

Pizza

Pizza is that wonderful, delicious, almost nutritious, not-too-expensive, Italian-American food voted "The One Meal I Couldn't Live Without" award by teenagers everywhere. Whether you eat it Chicago style or New York style, whether your favorite is the plain cheese variety from the frozen foods section of your local grocery store or you've discovered the gourmet delights of the California Pizza Kitchen, pizza is the number one food for teens.

Many people believe that pizza contains a secret ingredient that is indispensable to youth ministry success. Youth pastors report having observed an extra-large pizza turn a small, timid youth group into an enthusiastic crowd. Lay youth leaders tell us that if you'll combine a pizza with a root-beer float, you can make a noncooperative spirit disappear. And some people even say they have witnessed a teen politely offer the last piece of pizza to someone else, although such reports are as yet unconfirmed.

Three Ways to Enjoy Pizza

1. **Bring your own.** Next time you have a pizza feed ask every guy to bring a medium pizza (homemade, store-bought, or fresh from the best pizza place in town) and every girl to bring a two-liter bottle of soft drink and some ice cream. Watch to see what the favorite flavors are.

2. **Make your own.** Appoint a small group of your youth to do the shopping and have them get all the ingredients for good pizza, including tomato sauce and cheese, and all the toppings they think your group will enjoy; mushrooms, olives, onions, pineapple, etc. Use prepared pizza crusts, Boboli bread or sourdough English muffins for the crusts, and invite your youth to assemble their own mini-pizzas. Also have the supplies for the kids to mark or color tooth picks to use to identify their own pizzas.

3. **Just desserts.** Eat something else for the main course and prepare dessert pizzas for after the meal. Use a pie crust or cookie or pastry dough covered with sweetened cream cheese, then be creative and top with things like fruit, candy, granola, nuts and icing, and drizzle with warmed jam or jelly, or hot fudge.

Pizza

• Planning an Event

It usually starts in a brainstorm.
"Why don't we take our entire group to Mexico and build a church!"
"Let's plan a big pizza party for graduation night."
Or, "How about hosting a training convention?"
When it's your turn to plan an event, start here.

• Seven Steps to Planning an Event

1. **What's the point?** What are your goals for the event? Are they primarily spiritual, social or service oriented? Are you building your youth group? Or nurturing them? Or training them for a certain project? Be specific.

2. **Who's the target?** Are you aiming this event at your youth, at their parents, at the members of your congregation, or at potential new members?

3. **What's the duration?** How long should the event last? Is it an hour Sabbath School program? A Saturday night party? A weekend retreat? A week-long mission trip?

4. **Who's in charge?** The bigger the event, the more people you should delegate to be in charge of different elements: programming, inviting guest speakers, public relations and marketing, fundraising, scheduling, etc.

5. **What do we need?** A place to hold the event? Reservations? Guest speakers? A theme? Get input from your target and the people you place in charge.

6. **How much will it cost?** Estimate the cost of each element of the event. Start with the major factors: for your event will you need to budget for food, transportation, lodging? Try not to overlook any of the minor details, as well. Do you already have that money in your budget? Or will you need to raise the money before plans are set in concrete?

7. **When do we start?** First find a place on the master calendar. Then allow as much time as possible for planning, securing reservations and commitments where necessary, and obtaining supplies. The more advance time you give yourself, the less stress will be involved in the planning, and the more successful you are likely to be.

Planning an Event

• PlusLine

Youth ministry leaders in the Seventh-day Adventist Church are facing an information glut. New products and materials, denominational and otherwise, are multiplying at such a rapid rate that it's virtually impossible for active church members and pastors to keep up with it all. As a result, some are needlessly wasting precious time looking for resources, while others are redeveloping products which already exist.

It only makes sense that the church provide a way for its members and leaders to quickly find the information they need. Establishing a central clearing house where information can be stored will help facilitate church members and leaders alike. The PlusLine Ministry HelpDesk is just such a service – an idea whose time has come.

PlusLine provides online support to help people find the best tools to get their ministry jobs done. PlusLine pledges to take the hassle out of locating ministry-related information. If an item cannot be found in their files, consultants conduct personalized searches and strive to provide callers with their findings as quickly as possible.

• What PlusLine Can Do for You

1. Provide program ideas.
2. Find books and materials.
3. Put you in touch with other resource organizations.
4. Provide suggestions for special events.
5. Help you with phone numbers and addresses.
6. Register people for specific events.

PlusLine was started as a local experiment in the Pacific Union Conference in May of 1993. What started out as a trickle quickly mushroomed into a tidal wave of calls. The success of the project brought a recommendation from the nine union conference Church Ministries directors that PlusLine be expanded to serve the entire North American Division. This action was implemented on October 1, 1994. Union Conferences are personalizing the ministry with custom advertising to their local fields. The cost of operating PlusLine is shared by the NAD and its union conferences. PlusLine team members are located at the Pacific Union Church Resource Center in Westlake Village, California.

You can access PlusLine from anywhere in North America by calling 1-800-SDA-PLUS.

PlusLine

• **Prayer**

"Be faithful in prayer," Romans 12:12.
"Devote yourselves to prayer," Colossians 4:2.
"Pray continually," 1 Thessalonians 5:16-18.

In her classic book on Christian spirituality, *Steps to Christ*, Ellen White defines prayer in the most personal terms: "Prayer is the opening of the heart to God as to a friend."[1]

In the dialogue of faith between human beings and God, prayer is our turn to talk. We hear God's voice in the wonders of creation and the councils of His Word, in the whisperings of the Spirit and the encouraging words of others. In prayer we respond to God and open our innermost thoughts to Him. "Through nature and revelation, through His providence, and by the influence of His Spirit, God speaks to us. But these are not enough; we need also to pour out our hearts to Him."[2]

When we pray, we are accepting God's gracious invitation to come immediately into His welcoming presence. We are not to be afraid of censure or disapproval. We are not to worry about being rejected or made to stand in line (God doesn't put us on hold with a shallow assurance of getting back to us in the order our call was received). We are not to be nervous about saying the right words. Prayer is coming to God, just as we are, and saying exactly what's on our heart.

What can we talk to God about?

"Keep your wants, your joys, your sorrows, your cares, and your fears, before God. He who numbers the hairs of your head is not indifferent to the wants of His children. Take to Him everything that perplexes the mind. Nothing is too great for Him to bear, for He holds up worlds, He rules over all the affairs of the universe. Nothing that in any way concerns our peace is too small for Him to notice. There is no chapter in our experience too dark for Him to read; there is no perplexity too difficult for Him to unravel. No calamity can befall the least of His children, no anxiety harass the soul, no joy cheer, no sincere prayer escape the lips, of which our heavenly Father is unobservant, or in which He takes no immediate interest."[3]

Just speak to God from your heart. "The task is not preparing your heart for prayer, but speaking from your heart as it is. We can easily get this backward in the religious life, assuming that our primary spiritual assignment is to make ourselves presentable to God instead of presenting ourselves to God as we are."[4]

Prayer

- *Three Questions to Open a Discussion on Prayer*
  1. What can we learn from the following biblical prayers?
     a. David's Prayer ("Create in me a clean heart.") See Psalm 51.
     b. Jehoshaphat's Prayer ("We don't know what to do,") See the full story in 2 Chronicles 20.
     c. Daniel's Prayer ("We have sinned.) See Daniel 9.
     d. Jesus' Prayer ("Father, forgive them.") Luke 23:34

  2. Discuss the following important purposes of prayer. Make a list of prayer topics you would place in each category. What other purposes would you add?
     a. Praise (See the quotation below.)
     b. Confession
     c. Thanksgiving
     d. Petition

"Our devotional exercises should not consist wholly in asking and receiving. Let us not be always thinking of our wants, and never of the benefits we receive. We do not pray any too much, but we are too sparing of giving thanks. We are the constant recipients of God's mercies, and yet how little gratitude we express, how little we praise Him for what He has done for us."[5]

  3. If our focus is primarily on receiving "answers" to prayer, we probably think of prayer mostly as petition, as asking God for favors or blessings or miracles. We may not be incorporating the other aspects of prayer (praise, confession and thanksgiving) into our prayer life. Consider the following statement:

"Prayer isn't bending God's arms in order to get things, or talking God into things. God is already totally given… It's not that we pray and God answers; our praying is already God answering. Your desire to pray is God in your heart. Your reaching out to enter into dialogue with the Lord is already the answer of God. It is grace that makes us desire grace."[6]

1   Ellen White, *Steps to Christ*, 93.
2   *Ibid.*
3   *Ibid.*, 100.
4   James P. Carse, *The Silence of God; Meditations on Prayer* (New York, NY: Macmillan, 1985), 2.
5   Ellen White, *Ibid.*, 102, 103.
6   Richard Rohr, *Radical Grace* (Cincinnati, OH: St. Anthony Messenger Press, 1993), 172.

Prayer, continued

Press Releases

A press release is a concise written article or news story designed to get someone interested in your event, story or announcement. It contains the who, what, where, when, why and how, yet is brief, succinct and easy to read.

Here are four steps to writing a successful press release.

Step 1 – Audience and Objectives

Before you write your release, identify your audience and objectives. Decide what section of the newspaper your item fits into best, and contact the reporter in that section before you send the release to pitch the idea to him or her. This allows you to tell more information and adjust your release before you send it, and it gives the reporter a "heads up" on your story.

Step 2 – Writing the Release

When you write the release, have all your facts straight, and lead with the piece of information you think is most important or most attention-getting. Create a hook and a headline that is interesting or catchy so the reporter will keep reading. Use simple, clear language and always submit your release typed and double-spaced. Keep it to one page if at all possible. Include the name and phone number of the contact person at the top of the page.

Step 3 – Sending the Release and Following-Up

Mail or fax your release to the specific person you pitched it to. Follow-up with a phone call a day or two later, offering more information, interviews, etc., and to find out if your release has been passed to another section, then follow-up there. You may have to re-pitch your story to the new section, but don't be afraid to allow it to take a slightly different angle. That may just get your story published.

Step 4 – Relationships for the Future

Take time to build relationships with local reporters or editors. Call them and chat about issues they will be working on in the future. Pitch stories of upcoming events or on-going programs; sending them resource lists of experts among your pastoral or lay staff will help you become a valued source.

- *Ten Items That Could be Newsworthy*
    1. Events: celebrations, anniversaries, special observances
    2. Graduation
    3. Special lectures or classes
    4. Special groups visiting your church
    5. Youth groups on tour
    6. Youth receiving an award, credential, degree or honor
    7. Programs, such as <u>youth church</u>
    8. <u>Service</u> projects
    9. Short-term <u>mission trips</u>
    10. Completion of a long-term project

- *Example of a Good Press Release*

From: Julie Monroe (916) 987-6543

Twenty Teens Attack Old Home

Twenty members of the Sacramento Valley Seventh-day Adventist youth group early Sunday morning surrounded an old home in the Rancho Sierra district of Fair Oaks. Residents of the 800 block woke to unusual sounds as the teens came armed to remodel the home of 83-year-old Mildred Hackenbridge.

The youth group, under the leadership of Jim and Sylvia Christianson, chose the Hackenbridge home because of its classic style, the landscaping potential of the front yard, and, not in the least, because Mildred couldn't do the work herself.

"These kids are a lifesaver to me," reported Mildred to every passerby who stopped to observe the activity. "Look at the difference they're making! It's just a miracle!"

Neighbor Maria Salinger agreed. "I can't wait till I'm 83," Maria said. "Maybe the kids will come fix up my house then."

Press Releases

Printing Your Material

Okay, you'd like to produce an attractive, four-color, slick some-thing-or-other (announcement, poster, newsletter, whatever). Your old black and white printer won't deliver. Color copying at Kinkos is too costly for the quantities you're considering. Hand-coloring each copy is out of the question. Looks like you're going to have to work with a professional printer.

- *Five Times When You'll Have to Work with a Printer:*
  1. When the old dot-matrix printer at the church office finally quits working.
  2. When your newsletter has to go to absolutely everybody on your mailing list.
  3. When posters for a fund-raising event have to look extra-good.
  4. When invitations to a youth evangelism series have to be mass-produced.
  5. When your youth choir needs a program for a concert they're presenting at a dozen different churches.

- *Six Things to Know Before You Visit the Printer*
  1. **Specifications.** What's the exact product you need printed? "I want to print a four page, 8 1/2 X 11 newsletter in two colors." "I need an 11 X 17 four-color poster." "Can you print our youth group name on the back of #2 envelopes?"
  2. **Quantity.** How many copies of the product do you need? "I need 2,500 envelopes." "We want 150 posters."
  3. **Paper stock.** Take an example of the type of paper you want your project printed on. Heavy or lightweight? Plain or glossy? Smooth or textured?
  4. **Colors.** Take a sample. Your printer will help you determine the exact color by matching your sample with his ink palate.
  5. **Originals.** How are you going to deliver the copy that is to be printed? On a disk (be sure to include all the fonts you've used)? In camera-ready copy that is to be "shot" before print-ing? Are there photos that need to be scanned?
  6. **Deadline.** When do you need the finished product? The more lead time you can give your printer (try for at least a week), the more he'll appreciate you and the more money you'll save.

• Puppet Ministry

Can you find a text or incident in Scripture in which God used puppets? Probably not! But He did use some terribly strange animals and imagery that we wouldn't think of using today! A leopard with four wings and four heads. A red beast with seven speaking heads and 10 horns. A lion with eagle's wings. And then there was the talking donkey, a brass snake, trumpets, and tables of stone.

So why did God use such unusual things?

The answer to this question is the same as the answer to the question, "Why use puppets in <u>youth ministry</u>?"

God needed to catch the attention of people – then and now – to convey His truths. He needed to communicate a message that would not be easily forgotten and that worked well. God wanted to catch the imagination and interest of people throughout all time. And no question about it, He's done just that!

Some members of your <u>youth group</u> will take naturally to this ministry. Use them in writing scripts, designing puppets and backdrops, and performing in any of the following ministry ideas.

• Five Ways to Use Puppets in Ministry

1. **Storytelling.** Telling stories using a puppet can add interest. One storyteller uses a puppet to whisper a nature story into her ear. Then she tells the audience what the puppet tells her. The puppet never speaks to the audience.

    Once the storyteller forgot what she was to say next. Without missing a beat, she turned to the puppet and said, "Would you say that again? I didn't understand what you said." This gave her some time to collect her thoughts. No one was the wiser, and it actually made her story more interesting. Using a puppet in this manner doesn't require the puppeteer to develop a new voice or to have a puppet stage.

2. **Greeting.** One leader uses a puppet to welcome the children to Vacation Bible School or <u>Sabbath School</u>. This puppet is equipped with a rod attached to the wrist so that its arm can move. The leader and the puppet go about the room, speaking to each child and welcoming him or her. The rod allows the leader to shake hands with the child and to make meaningful gestures.

One puppeteer named his puppet Sam the Sabbath School Man. No effort was made to create a peculiar voice for the puppet. Children and adults find it difficult not to look at the puppet even when the puppeteer is clearly visible.

3. **Interacting With Children.** Another leader uses a puppet in a nonverbal manner to interact with the children. For example, she tells the story of Noah and God's care for the animals on the ark. To illustrate, she uses a giraffe puppet to "eat" the plastic greenery that the children bring to the front.

   Another leader uses a caterpillar puppet to eat the green leaves that the children have. Neither puppet speaks: they only act out the part. It's simple, but very effective.

4. **Interacting With Leaders.** A Sabbath School lesson dealing with God's plan for humans and Satan's lies consisted of the leader interacting with two puppets – a Sage, and Satan (in the form of a snake). The puppeteers were hidden by a stage, and the script has the leader talking with each puppet.

   During the program, the leader had individuals from the audience do certain activities. Although the leader deviated from the script, the puppeteers always knew when to speak next, as the leader would read the exact line before the puppet's line.

5. **Dialogue With Yourself.** One puppeteer prerecorded one voice of the dialogue using a different voice. Then, with an old tape recorder that has a microphone with a pause button, one of the voices was started and stopped with inconspicuous movements. Another puppeteer rigged an on-off foot switch. In this way, he could manipulate the puppet with one hand, turn the papers of the script with the other hand, read one part, and operate the tape recorder with his foot for the other voice. In this way he actually talked to himself!

We certainly can't find a text that says, "In the midst of the congregation a dramatic presentation was performed with six puppets to the exaltation of the Lord, and all fell on their faces and prayed for forgiveness." But God has made it clear that He is willing to use the common and the strange to communicate the truth of His love and <u>grace</u>. Puppets fit very nicely into the strategies that God has used.

• **Research**

In order to best understand your teens and what's happening in their lives and in your ministry, it's important to do research. That may mean just talking to your kids, asking them questions about their experience, their faith and their goals. Or it may mean getting a bit more formal and asking them to fill out research instruments.

There are many types of questionnaires and surveys available to assist you in developing your <u>youth ministry</u>, or as an aid in exploring certain topics. Many are available at no charge, and come with masters you can duplicate. Write to the <u>Hancock Center for Youth and Family Ministry</u>, or phone 1-800-785-HCYM for full information.

• *Eight Research Tools*

1. *Church Youth Program Evaluation Survey.* Identifies factors in the leadership and organization of youth ministries.
2. *Identifying Spiritual Gifts.* In helping teens gain a vision of their universal calling to ministry in the world this process assists the leader in identifying spiritual gifts, evaluating them, and clarifying their specific contribution to the local church.
3. *Leader Dedication Worksheets.* Realizing that time and talents must be made available to the church for the work of ministry this survey provides a focus on potential leaders
4. *Leadership Worksheets.* These worksheets help the youth ministry team evaluate leadership potential and clarify their needs in ministry and training.
5. *Learning Objective Worksheets.* Assists in focusing on specific content areas that behavioral outcomes target.
6. *Student Mission Activity Evaluation.* Pre- and post-tests for those involved in student helping activities such as short term mission trips.
7. <u>*Valuegenesis*</u>*: The Short Form.* A simple 35 minute survey that explores the faith maturity and religious life of your youth. The survey needs a minimum of 30 youth to be statistically accurate (often a number of local congregations join together to provide an adequate number). The cost is $1.50 per survey, plus $475 for data analysis done by the Hancock Center.
8. *Youth Program Evaluation Survey.* A true and false evaluation of the present condition of youth ministry in the local church.

Research

• Resiliency

Most of us know people we'd classify as survivors. Perhaps they were physically or sexually abused as children, raised by alcoholic parents, or exposed to hardships severe enough to make them unlikely candidates for success. But somehow these survivors emerge from their negative environments with hope and confidence.

The capacity to maintain competent functioning in spite of adversity or life stressors is called *resiliency*. Resiliency is the sense that adversity can be overcome, that there is life beyond the obstacles of today. Resilient individuals are those who, despite hardships and at-risk factors, learn to cope and even succeed.

Resiliency research suggests that certain characteristics persist in people who develop a resilient approach to life.

• Ten Characteristics of Resilient Individuals

1. A vibrant faith and the ability to use that faith to maintain a positive vision of a meaningful life.
2. A strong commitment to self.
3. A willingness to take action and deal with problems. They see life's obstacles as challenges that can be overcome.
4. A positive attitude toward their environment.
5. An easygoing temperament.
6. Verbal and communication skills.
7. A sense of direction or mission, such as evidence of a special talent, passion, faith, or strong interest.
8. A capacity to understand and respond to others' feelings.
9. A sense of humor.
10. The ability to think and act apart from troubled caretakers.

One factor emerges over and over again in resiliency research and literature: resiliency comes through supportive relationships! The most significant resiliency influence is a caring, warm and enduring relationship with an older adult or mentor. Unconditional love appears to provide young people with a positive, hopeful sense that the odds faced in life can be overcome. (Also see: Grace, Mentoring.)

More Great Discussion on Resiliency:
✔ V. Bailey Gillespie, Gary L. Hopkins, and Stuart Tyner, "Making Students Bulletproof," in *The Journal of Adventist Education* December 1988-January 1999, 10-14.

Resiliency

- **Resources**

Throughout the *ABZs of Adventist Youth Ministry* you'll discover entries about resources that will assist you in your ministry. But just to be sure you locate all of them, here's a collected listing.

- *Youth Ministry Newsletters, Magazines and Studies*
    1. Adventist View
    2. Cornerstone Connections
    3. CQ
    4. Dialogue
    5. FTC
    6. Gente Joven
    7. Giraffe News
    8. Group
    9. Insight and Insight/Out
    10. Listen
    11. Valuegenesis
    12. Youth Worker Journal
    13. Youth Worker Update

- *Youth Ministry Publishers*
    1. AdventSource
    2. Center for Youth Evangelism
    3. Group
    4. Hancock Center for Youth and Family Ministry
    5. Pacific Press Publishing Association
    6. Review and Herald Publishing Association
    7. Youth Specialties

- *Youth Ministry Resource Centers*
    1. Center for Creative Ministry
    2. Center for Youth Evangelism
    3. Hancock Center for Youth and Family Ministry
    4. National Black Youth Resource Center
    5. North American Division Youth Ministry
    6. PlusLine

☞ Also see: Resource People.

Resources

• Resource People

The following ministries are directed by experienced Adventist youth leaders, well-connected to the goals of Adventist <u>youth ministry</u>. In cooperation with your <u>conference youth director</u> they provide scheduled training events in all the active dynamics of youth leadership.

In addition, these busy people assist local <u>youth groups</u> as guest speakers, <u>worship</u> leaders, workshop and seminar presenters, week of prayer speakers, <u>drama</u> and music programmers, and resource developers. Case, Cornforth and Weeks are experts in organizing and leading short-term <u>mission trips</u>.

Each ministry will be happy to answer your questions, provide more information about their services, and discuss <u>budgets</u> with you.

• Big Face Grace
Timothy Gillespie, Jason Hutchinson, Roy Ice, Michael Knecht
    and Sam Leonor
4444 Beverly Drive
La Mesa, CA 91941
Phone: (909) 785-2091
FAX: (909) 785-2199
http://www.lasierra.edu/hcyfm/bfg/

• dre•am vision ministries
Deirdre and Allan Martin
http://www.tagnet.org/dvm
CServe: dream_VISION_ministries@compuserve.com

• Piece of the Pie Ministries
Steve Case
PO Box 2424
Carmichael, CA 95609
Phone and FAX: (916) 944-3928
http://www.pieceofthepie.org
CServe: 74617.3000

• Pieces of Eight Christian Drama
John Anthony
11762 Merida Place
Riverside, CA 92505

Phone: (909) 352-6622
E-mail: janthony@piecesofeight.org
http://www.piecesofeight.org

- ## Spirt Power Ministries
  Johnny Bennett
  3870 La Sierra Avenue, #157
  Riverside, CA 92505
  Phone: (909) 799-9896
  E-mail: mrjohnnyb@earthlink.net

- ## Youth and Young Adult Consultants
  Fred Cornforth
  PO Box 190167
  Boise, ID 83719-0167
  Phone: (800) 617-24998
  FAX: (208) 459-9692
  E-mail: fred@servicestation.org
  CServe: 74617.335
  http://www.servicestation.org

- ## Youth Outreach Unlimited
  George (Bucky) Weeks, Jr.
  341 Whipporwill Drive
  Riverside, CA 92507
  Phone: (909) 369-8485
  FAX: (909) 369-8684
  E-mail: youweeks@aol.com

More Resource People:

_____
_____
_____
_____
_____
_____
_____
_____

Resource People, continued

• Revelation Seminars

Prophecy Seminars (usually focusing on the books of Daniel or Revelation) can be an effective means of interesting people in <u>Bible study</u> and in discovering the <u>gospel</u> message at work in our lives today. <u>Youth leaders</u> can incorporate such seminars into the evangelism component of their <u>youth ministry</u>, using teens and <u>young adults</u> as teachers and <u>small groups</u> leaders.

Northwest Youth Challenge, an organization which regularly uses teens to teach Revelation Seminars, utilizes this format:

a. Mass mailing of professionally produced advertising brochures by zip code, giving subjects and time and places of meetings.
b. Set up tables in a church fellowship room or a rented hall.
c. Youth welcome and register guests and distribute materials.
d. One or two youth facilitators sit at each table.
e. Seat 6-8 guests at each table. Facilitators lead in a group discussion of the lesson. Sometimes facilitators give a quiz to review the previous lesson (or a local pastor may give the quiz).
f. Use a Revelation Seminar video series with Bible questions and answers as a 30-minute wrap-up.

Additional information on involving youth in Prophecy Seminars is available from:

Northwest Youth Challenge
20012 Bothel - Everett Highway
Bothel, WA 98012
Phone: (206) 481 - 7171
FAX: (206) 486-2310

Another Adventist source for Revelation seminar materials and direct brochure mailings is:

Seminars Unlimited
PO Box 66
Keene, TX 76059
Phone: (817) 641-3643 or 1-800-982-3344
FAX: (817) 641-3640

Revelation Seminars

Sabbath

The Sabbath is the day made holy and set aside by God during the creation week (Genesis 1, 2) for <u>worship</u>, celebration of God's presence and confession of God's <u>grace</u>.

- *Seven Ways to Treasure the Sabbath Gift*
  1. **Plan Ahead.** Read the manna story in Exodus 16. "Think ahead," God was telling the Israelites, and us as well. Make plans to enjoy the Sabbath gift. Don't just plan for a few hours, like 9:30 till noon on Saturday morning. Plan the entire 24 hours.
  2. **Make It Special.** In the middle of the Ten Commandments (Exodus 20:8-11) God reminds us of His gift of the Sabbath. "Don't do your everyday work on the seventh day," God tells us. By following His plan, we're not trying to buy His favor. Nothing we do can make Him love us more than He does already. We just want to be fully free to experience the incredibly wonderful presence of God and to enjoy being together with Him.
  3. **Do Good.** The Sabbath is not just about *not* working. <u>Jesus</u> taught us that we honor our Heavenly Father by doing good on the Sabbath (see Matthew 12:9-12).
  4. **Worship Together.** The practice of "going to church" on Sabbath was an example Jesus set for us during His life here on earth (see Mark 6:2 and Luke 4:16, 31, for example).
  5. **Discover Joy.** In some mysterious, wonderful way, the Sabbath gift imparts joy, filling our lives all through the week with deep trust in the goodness of God. Read Isaiah 51:11 and 58:13, 14.
  6. **Celebrate Salvation.** More than anything else, the Sabbath was to be a sign between the Creator and His people that it is God who saves us (see Ezekiel 20:12). The Sabbath points to the fact that we have given up on the idea of "working our way to heaven" (see Hebrews 4:9, 10). It reinforces the truth that there is nothing we can do to earn salvation. It reminds us every week that we are saved by the grace of God, and saved by grace alone (Romans 3:20-24).
  7. **Look Forward.** The Sabbath is not an earthbound tradition. The Bible makes it clear that when the history of this planet is over, the redeemed will continue to worship God every Sabbath in heaven (Isaiah 66:22, 23).
  - Adapted from *Walking On the Edge* (<u>AdventSource</u>, 1996).

Sabbath

Sabbath, continued

- **How Can a Youth Leader Enjoy the Sabbath?**
  1. **Get a head start.** Don't leave all your planning to Friday night. Start preparing <u>Sabbath School</u> early in the week. Make Wednesday or Thursday night your night for phoning participants, studying the lesson, preparing a bulletin, or practicing for the program.
  2. **Get up early.** Before everyone else in your house gets going, get ready for the day. Enjoy the quiet. Take a short walk outside while the air is still brisk. Don't rush. Plan to leave for church ten minutes earlier than you have to. Drive slowly.
  3. **Treat yourself.** Brew a pot of your favorite decaf. Eat a warm cinnamon roll. Read a chapter in a devotional book you don't read any other day. Listen to your favorite sacred music.
  4. **Make a big deal about Sabbath.** When you get to church, greet your youth with a warm, "Happy Sabbath." Comment about being thankful for Sabbath. Talk about the extra sweetness of Sabbath air, the additional intensity of Sabbath rain or snow, the special blueness of clear Sabbath skies, the deeper joy of Sabbath friendships. Wax eloquent!
  5. **Observe Sabbath all day long.** Don't stop thinking about the Sabbath when church is over. Keep a list of favorite Sabbath afternoon activities, play favorite Sabbath games, read together, enjoy a rest in the middle of the day, etc.

- *Super Sabbath Group Activities*
  1. **Cake Art.** Provide an undecorated sheet cake for each group of five or six people, as well as all the items necessary to decorate the cake. Once the cake is decorated, share it with people at a nursing home, or with little kids who could use a treat.
  2. **Midrash Walk.** Wander out in nature and find a place where you can comfortably interact. Talk in the form of the Hebrew *midrash*, equating two unrelated objects in order to learn and teach from the effort. For example, "How is the law like an overcoat?" or, "How is morality like the Alps?".
  3. **Scripture Acrostics.** Break your group into teams that represent an appropriate mix of age, maturity, skill, knowledge of the Bible, etc. After showing them a couple of examples, give each group the assignment to create ten Bible character acrostics. Here are a couple of examples:

NOAH   No land in sight
             Only water, water everywhere
             All the animals are restless
             Hold on! Here comes another wave.

PETER   Perhaps I'll try.
             Everyone else is afraid.
             There's another wave coming.
             Easy does it.
             Right now I wish I'd worked more on my backstroke!

These activities were taken from a wonderful book by Don Pate, *52 Sabbath Activities for Teen Groups* (Hagerstown, MD: Review and Herald Publishing Association, 1995).

It's interesting to note that the observance of the seventh-day Sabbath came to Adventists by way of the Seventh Day Baptists and the influence of a woman by the name of Rachel Oakes. In 1843 and 1844, Mrs. Oakes distributed Seventh Day Baptist literature to the members of the Christian Brethren Church in Washington, New Hampshire. Many of the members were followers of William Miller, who believed Jesus soon would return to earth. A Methodist minister in that congregation, Frederick Wheeler, studied the literature and began observing the Sabbath on Saturday. Soon others in the congregation joined him.

Within a few months, a curious visitor came to the New Hampshire congregation. He was Joseph Bates, a retired sea captain who had heard of the church members' interest in the Sabbath. In 1846 and 1847 Bates wrote a series of pamphlets in which he detailed his belief in the seventh-day Sabbath. These writings later were cited by James and Ellen White as influential in their decision to honor the Sabbath.

Beginning in 1848 the Advent believers held a series of retreats they called "Sabbath Conferences" in Connecticut, New York and Maine. During these meetings the members studied the Bible together and settled various points of doctrines, paving the way for a united statement of belief.

•   More Great Discussion on the Sabbath:
✔   Abraham Joshua Heschel, *The Sabbath* (New York, NY: Farrar, Strauss and Giroux, 1951).

☞   Also see: Grace Orientation.

Sabbath, continued

Sabbath School

• Sabbath School

Not long after the first Adventists began meeting regularly, the new members realized the need of systematic instruction of young people in their faith. In 1853, in Rochester, New York, James White organized a youth group and called it a *Sabbath School*. (Protestant *Sunday Schools* had existed in America since the late 1700s.)

Other Sabbath Schools quickly appeared here and there among the new believers, who at the time numbered almost a thousand in the state of New York, "several hundred in the Western States," besides a "goodly number" in Canada.

In 1877 the first State Sabbath School Association was organized, in California. By October, 1878, there were 12 such associations with around 200 Sabbath Schools and almost 6,000 members. (Today Sabbath School membership exceeds 10,000,000 all around the world.)

In those early years the emphasis in Sabbath School was on memorizing the Bible and on fostering an interest in world missions. Gradually a Sabbath School curriculum plan was developed and curriculum materials were produced. (See: *Cornerstone Connections*.)

- ### A Typical Youth Sabbath School Program
  1. Music   9:30
  2. Welcome and Opening Prayer   9:45
  3. Special Feature   9:50
     (Drama, Mini-concert, Interview, Mission Story, etc.)
  4. Lesson Study   10:10
  5. Benediction   10:45

- ### The Five Most Important Sabbath School Dynamics
  1. **The Welcome.** Are they catching your genuine love and care? Do they look forward to attending? Is this *their* Sabbath School?
  2. **The Level of Involvement.** Do your youth take part in every program element? Is there discussion? Are you listening?
  3. **The Meaning.** Check again to insure you are speaking out of their experience, their world.
  4. **The Spiritual Depth.** Does every element of your Sabbath School lead to Jesus? Everything else is secondary.
  5. **The Relevance.** Can your youth apply this worship experience to their lives on Saturday night and Monday morning?

• SDA Students in Public School

Like students everywhere, <u>Seventh-day Adventist</u> students who attend public schools face tremendous pressures, not the least of which is trying to maintain a vibrant Christian experience in a secular environment. <u>Youth leaders</u> can be of tremendous service to these students by creating a church atmosphere where they are welcomed and involved as full partners in the <u>youth ministry</u> program.

Understanding these students' educational choices, and knowing the challenges they face, are great places to start.

• *Seven Reasons Why Some Choose Public School*
1.   The distance to the nearest Adventist school.
2.   Religious differences between parents.
3.   Finances.
4.   Specific programs at the public school (which might mean sports, music, technology, special ed or honors).
5.   Personal freedom issues.
6.   <u>Diversity</u>.
7.   Wanting to witness to secular friends.

• *The Three Biggest Challenges*
1.   <u>Worldview</u>. Who wrote the textbooks? Who designed the <u>curriculum</u> plan? Who trained the teachers? Was it people with a Christian worldview? Or people with a secular worldview? Was it people who wanted the schooling to influence youth to be a better Christian? Or was Christianity not a part of the plan?
2.   <u>At-Risk Behaviors</u>. Certain lifestyle practices not only put people at risk for their health and physical well-being, they also undermine the opportunity to be a productive citizen. At-risk behaviors include smoking, drinking, taking drugs, sexual promiscuity, and <u>violence</u>.
     While no one would deny the many good things about public education, nor fail to admit that *every* school has its share of these problems, we cannot ignore the fact that at-risk behaviors are much more prevalent in public school settings.
3.   <u>Distancing</u>. Failing to take responsibility for one's own actions or beliefs, and giving the credit (or blame) for that responsibility to one's parents or to the church.

SDA Students In Public School, continued

In addition, many Adventists in public education feel their lack of knowledge in Bible backgrounds, in Adventist history and beliefs, and in the principles behind Adventist standards.

- *Seven Things You Can Do*
  1. **Talk About Worldview.** Teach your youth to study their textbooks and listen to their teachers with a discriminating ear. (See 1 Thessalonians 5:21.) Help them understand the Christian worldview. Help them learn how to express disagreement without being disrespectful to their teachers.
  2. **Discuss At-Risk Behavior.** Know the facts about the risks involved. Express the importance of choosing friends carefully (Research identifies friends as one of the most important factors in determining who gets involved in at-risk behavior and who doesn't.)
  3. **Penetrate Distancing.** Examine the reasons behind our beliefs and actions. Be positive about the Christian lifestyle. Make heroes of Christian students who are open about their witness and who are making a difference on their campuses.
  4. **Take Extra Time for Study.** Take your time with Bible study. Don't talk in phrases only older Adventists can understand. Establish a small group for these kids where you can explore Adventist history and belief without it being embarrassing to anyone. (*Walking On the Edge* from the Hancock Center and AdventSource was created specifically for this purpose.)
  5. **Establish Devotional Practices.** Teach your youth how to study the Bible and how to pray. Stress the importance of a strong spiritual life to successfully meeting the challenges of a secular environment.
  6. **Be Sure They're Involved.** Keep them busy at church. Make them an important part of your youth ministry. Commit yourself to no letting these kids slip away unnoticed.
  7. **Show Them How to Meet** Criticism. Many of these kids feel like second-class citizens in their own church family, frequently having to endure criticism for their educational choices. Teach them how to meet critical church people in a Christlike manner.

☞ **Also see:** Adventist Education; AMiCUS; Bible Study; Campus Advent; Climate Issues; Involvement; Spirituality.

• Service

> "I know your deeds, your love and faith, your service and perseverance." Revelation 2:19.
> "We have different gifts, according to the grace given us. If your gift is prophesying, use it in proportion to your faith. If it is serving, serve; if it is teaching, teach; if it is encouraging, encourage; if it is contributing to the needs of others, give generously; if it is leadership, govern diligently; if it is showing mercy, do it cheerfully." Romans 12:6-8.
> "Each one should use whatever gift he has received to serve others." 1 Peter 4:10.

Outreach. Evangelism. Witnessing. Sharing your faith. Spreading the gospel. Reaching out. Meeting people's needs.

We give many names to the efforts of God's people to tell the story of God's love for sinners as demonstrated in the life and death of Jesus. It is the common element of serving that brings all these activities together.

• Principles of Service

1. The Motivation for Service. "Christ's love compels us." 2 Corinthians 5:14.
2. The Reason for Service. "...that people may see your good deeds and praise your Father in heaven." Matthew 5:16
3. The Reward of Service. "If anyone hears my voice and opens the door, I will come in." Revelation 3:20.
4. The Many Ways to Serve. "God designs that in every place where the truth is introduced, different minds, different gifts, shall be brought in to exert an influence upon the work." Ellen White, *Gospel Workers*, 481.

The ABZs of Adventist Youth Ministry contains information on a wide variety of service activities. As you plan to put service to action in your youth group, be sure to read these entries and match them (and, of course, many others, as well) to the gifts, abilities and interests of your youth.

• Seven Service Activities

Service

• Seventh-day Adventists

What's a Seventh-day Adventist?

And why are we hearing an increasingly large number of <u>teens</u> saying that they want to be *Christians*, but they're not so sure any longer about being *Seventh-day Adventists*?

Our answer about who we are usually centers on one of two things: our *behavior* (Adventists are people who don't smoke, don't drink, don't dance, etc.) or our *belief* (Adventists are people who believe that Saturday, the seventh day, is the <u>Sabbath</u>, that <u>Jesus</u> is coming again, etc.).

Of course, there's a problem with both of these answers. In the first place, neither answer satisfies the requirement for being a definition: to state the *precise meaning or significance* of a word or phrase. The answers are true, but they don't *distinguish*. A lot of people who are not Adventists don't smoke, don't drink, don't dance. Thousands of people who are members of other churches honor the Sabbath. Millions of Christians look forward to the Second Coming.

In fact, Adventists share most of their beliefs and behaviors with others. Like most of the people on earth, Adventists accept by faith that we live in a universe that was intentionally created by a force or being larger than ourselves. Like millions of others religious people, Adventists revere the life and teachings of Jesus of Nazareth, whom we accept as the divine Son of God. Adventists trace their historical roots to the momentous 16th century Reformation, which makes us *Protestant* Christians instead of *Roman Catholic* Christians. Our corporate beginnings took place in America like many other Protestant churches. Today we have millions of members around the world, as do many of the other denominations that began in the United States.

The second reason why these typical answers are not good definitions is that they don't really describe the essence, the core of Adventist Christianity. I've never met anyone who says the primary reason they are Adventists is because they don't smoke, or because they believe caffeine is not good for you, or because they believe people don't go to heaven when they die. There must be something more.

When Moses talked about how others would know what was unique among God's followers, He pointed out that it was God's presence among the people that distinguished them (Exodus 33:15, 16). When Jesus discussed the topic, He said people would know we were His disciples if we loved each other (John 13:35). Peter explained that what makes us a chosen people, a holy nation, belonging to God is that we have received mercy (1 Peter 2:9, 10).

So let's help teens understand that Adventists are not people who have better truth than others have, or who behave more correctly than other people do. Rather, we are a group of sinners who have been forgiven by God's grace (receiving mercy), called out of darkness into God's wonderful light (daily walking in His presence), and given a share in telling the everlasting gospel (demonstrating our love for others). The more we experience this definition, the more Adventist we are.

Here's another definition, adapted from *Walking On the Edge* (AdventSource, 1996).

- ### God's At Work in the World

    Seventh-day Adventists are Christians who believe God is at work in the world. God has always cared about His message of love getting through. Sometimes He chooses individuals to tell the story. Sometimes He chooses nations. Sometimes He works through events as they take place. But always He's at work. Getting in touch with people, and through people, to tell people about His love.

- ### The Bible Reveals the Secrets

    Seventh-day Adventists are Christians who have accepted the idea that the Bible reveals the secrets, not only of eternal life with Jesus in the future, but also of successful living here on earth today. We're a people who stick to the Bible. We find our reasons for living in the pages of God's Holy Word. We find comfort in times of disappointment. Solutions for difficult circumstances. Hope for a life still to come.

- ### Jesus is At the Center

    Seventh-day Adventists are a people who have received a vision that places Jesus at the center of their life, that exalts Jesus as the core of their belief, and that gives Jesus as the reason for their behavior. All we believe, all we do, all we want to become is centered in Jesus.

☞   **Also see:** Doctrines; Sabbath; Ellen White.

Seventh-day Adventists, continued

• Sexuality Issues

The Bible tells us that our sexual natures were created by God prior to the entrance of sin into the world (Genesis 1:27-31) and that this intimate, satisfying arrangement was part of the plan pronounced by God as "very good." Adam and Eve, as husband and wife, were together in the Garden of Eden, "knowing" each other (to use the King James Version's euphemism for sexual intercourse), intentionally becoming "one flesh" (Genesis 2:24), experiencing sexual intimacy. They were "naked and not ashamed" (Genesis 2:25), a state which the Bible presents to us as natural, approved and encouraged by our Creator.

Physical love within a marriage is spoken of in the Bible in rapturous terms: rejoicing, satisfying and captivating us (Proverbs 5:15-19), bringing emotions that are delightful, eager, desirable and pleasing (see the Song of Solomon). We hear the beloved's almost-out-of-breath sigh, "I am faint with love" (Song of Solomon 2:5). And we smile with understanding at the poet's conclusion: "Love burns like blazing fire, like a mighty flame" (Song of Solomon 8:6).

Jesus tells the Garden of Eden story (Matthew 19:4-6), including the "one flesh" part. Paul counsels that intimacy in a marriage should be characterized by mutuality and equality (1 Corinthians 7:3-5). Isaiah uses the sexual relationship between husband and wife as a symbol of God's relationship His people (Isaiah 62:5).

But the Bible also presents frankly the power of sexual temptation to draw us away from God's ideal. Potiphar's wife attempts to seduce Joseph into an adulterous relationship. David lusts for Bathsheba. Brutality destroys the joy. Prostitution degrades God's creation and commercializes what should be the epitome of giving. In response, God has to issue detailed, strict commands to keep His people from descending into the most degrading, dehumanizing perversions, including incest and having sex with animals (Leviticus 18). And Jesus is forced to tell people that it would be better to gouge out their own eyes than to continue burning with lust (Matthew 5:27-30).

Today, hundreds of thousands of Christian teenagers are determined to follow biblical guidelines for sexual behavior. They have made this decision in spite of incredible pressure from the entertainment and advertising industries (for whom teenage sexuality is an acceptable, foregone conclusion with box-office appeal), and from friends and acquaintances who are sexually active (and who insist there's nothing wrong with sex and that there are only minimal risks involved).

This section of the *ABZs* deals with a number of issues raised within the topic of sexuality. Don't be reticent to deal head-on with these issues. Your positive portrayal of God's ideal, coupled with your frank discussion of those practices which draw us away from that ideal, will help your youth establish lifelong Christian principles of sexuality.

- ## The Statistics
    1. *Valuegenesis* research indicates that more than one fourth of Adventist eleventh and twelfth graders have already had sex.
    2. Of those who were sexually active, the greatest number reported having multiple experiences.
    3. 63% of *Valuegenesis* respondents admitted to looking at sexually explicit videos or magazines during the last 12 months.
    4. Only 50% of girls who have a baby prior to the age of 17 complete high school.
    5. 90% of teenage mothers are unemployed.

- ## Safe Sex
    In this generation in which <u>AIDS</u> is a horrifying reality, many counsellors have reduced sexuality to the level of *disease prevention*: "safe" sex is simply sex which does not lead to disease. Protected by use of a condom, sex suddenly becomes "safe." When discussing safe sex, ask questions such as these:
    1. What are the various dimensions of sex? Certainly there is the physical dynamic. Is there also an emotional side? A mental aspect? A spiritual dimension? Are there other dimensions?
    2. How does the term "safe" apply to each of these dimensions? Is there safe and unsafe *emotional* sex? How about safe sex in a *mental* or *spiritual* sense?
    3. In the physical realm, how safe is safe? How willing would any of us be to have sex with someone with AIDS? Why?
    4. Talk about abstinence as safe sex.

- ## Abstinence
    1. Why wait? What in the world could God have had in mind by telling us that sex is better in marriage than outside of marriage? Why would God even care about when we experience sex?
    2. Interview teens who have made the decision to save sex for marriage. What motivated them to make the decision? What

impact do friends have on being faithful to their decision?

3. Which of the following statements about abstinence reflects a position you'd be willing to take:

   a. "My reason for saving sex for marriage is because that's what God wants me to do."

   b. "Sex is the closest you can get with somebody physically, and I wouldn't want to get married having been that close with someone else."

   c. "Sex is so dangerous these days. But if two people save themselves for each other, you're not going to have to worry about it."

   d. "If you believe in God, then you know that He has a plan for our lives. That's something very sacred because you can commit totally to one person; your whole life is building up to that moment. I've saved myself my entire life, to share myself and be intimate with someone special. Why ruin it now?"[1]

• Abortion

Abortion rates are highest among young, unmarried, poor and minority women, but rates are also high for women in religious and ethnic groups that are generally thought to oppose abortion. The Alan Guttmacher Institute of New York City projects that nearly half of U.S. women in their childbearing years will have an abortion at some point in their lives.

Abortion seems to many to be an easy solution to an unfortunate problem - an accidental, unplanned or unwanted pregnancy. *American Demographics* magazine states that of the 1.5 million U.S. abortions each year, a high percentage come in pregnancies which were caused by a failed contraceptive device.

Among those who accept abortion, most insist on a woman's right to have "control" over her body by being able to have an abortion on demand. Opponents see abortion as the same as murder and an absolutely unacceptable method of birth control.

Here are the two most commonly given reasons not to have an abortion.

1. You're dealing with a live human being. Most pregnancies aren't detected until sometime in the sixth week. By then, your baby's heart has been beating for three weeks, brain waves can be read, the nervous system has been complete for about two

weeks and the baby is about to being moving. There are really two people to consider, the mother and the unborn child.

2. Knowing that you ended your child's life without giving her a chance can be a devastating emotional burden. Young mothers are often talked into a decision that they regret for years to come.

• Homosexuality

Counsellor Barbara Couden frequently deals with questions about the development of sexual orientation, about how to accept people whose lifestyle you reject, and especially about how parents and friends can demonstrate reconciliation and understanding. Here is a summary of eight points she says we know for sure.[2]

1. Christians have the responsibility of ministering in a loving manner.
2. Jesus moved closer to struggling people, not away from them. He loved them unconditionally.
3. Anyone identified by a label is seldom viewed as a real person. Labels keep us from knowing people individually.
4. We fail at restorative relationships whenever we become busy trying to act as a conscience for others who live or believe differently than we do. The tender conviction of the Holy Spirit is sufficient to guide all people.
5. Sexual orientation and behaviors are complex phenomena involving numerous factors. We have much yet to learn.
6. People with a different sexual orientation have often been frozen out of meaningful church relationships, excluded instead of included in a caring community of faith.
7. Support networks can be lifesavers for people facing all aspects of this issue. We don't need to withdraw from each other.
8. We are all subject to moral dilemmas and human weaknesses. Each one of us qualifies for membership in the group Jesus came to save.

• Sexual Harassment

1. Sexual conduct becomes unlawful when
   a. it is unwelcome, unsolicited and regarded as undesirable or offensive, and
   b. is either explicitly or implicitly made the basis of employ-

Sexualty Issues, continued

ment (although recent Supreme Court rulings indicate the unwanted behavior is enough to constitute harassment regardless of subsequent treatment at work, even promotion [3]), or

c. has the purpose or effect of reasonably interfering with an individual's work performance, or

d. creates an intimidating, hostile, or offensive work environment.

2. Sexual harassment includes unwelcome sexual advances, requests for sexual favors, and other verbal or physical conduct of a sexual nature. The victim may be a man or a woman, the individual harassed or anyone else who is offended by the conduct.

3. Sexually harassing behavior includes sexual teasing, jokes, remarks or gestures, pressure for dates, letters, phone calls, suggestive looks, deliberate touching, attempted rape or sexual assault, being spied on while dressing or showering and even being the victim of sexual rumors.

4. How to handle harassment:

a. **Ignore it**. Hope that it is a onetime only incident and that it will stop if ignored and not encouraged.

b. **Avoid it.** Stay away from the harasser. Don't frequent places where the harassment took place.

c. **Find a "protector."** Walk with other students. Talk to people who've dealt with such behavior before and will confront it.

d. **Protest it**. Begin with the harasser. Then move quickly to authorities at school, on the job or wherever the behavior is encountered.

e. **Find a safe environment.** If there is no official move to stop the behavior, move to another school, or quit the job. Don't risk physical danger.

1   Taken from Point of Grace, *Life Love and Other Mysteries* (New York, NY: Simon & Schuster, 1996), 39, 40.
2   Barbara Couden, "Unless We Know the Answers," in the *Adventist Review*, April, 1997.
3   Marianne Lavelle, "The New Rules of Sexual Harassment," in *US News and World Report*, July 6, 1998.

• Sexually Transmitted Diseases

Next to the common cold, sexually transmitted diseases are the most common infections among young adults today. Adolescent rates are skyrocketing. Millions of teens have STDs, and sexually active college-age men and women are at the highest risk for contracting them.

STDs are illnesses that are passed from one person to another by sexual intercourse or other intimate contact. There are more than 20 STDs, including AIDS, syphilis, chlamydia, gonorrhea, crabs, hepatitis B, genital herpes and genital warts.

Many STDs can be cured; others cannot. Antibiotics are effective against STDs caused by bacteria. Others, caused by fungi and parasites, also respond well to treatment. However, STDs caused by viruses can't be cured. In theses cases current treatments only help control symptoms and prevent recurrences. Drugstore remedies don't provide cures. Untreated STDs can lead to infertility, cancer and even death.

• Decreasing the Chance of Contracting an STD

1. Stay sexually abstinent until marriage.
2. Learn the dangers of premarital sex and multiple sexual partners.
3. Choose dating partners whose lifestyles are founded on sound Christian principles.
4. Discuss your sexual history with a prospective spouse.
5. Get tested if there is any chance of having an STD.

• Four Ways to Assist Someone Who Has an STD

1. **Offer comfort.** Having an STD will definitely affect how teens view themselves and their sexuality. It's very important that they don't feel rejected by God or see the STD as a punishment.
2. **Get medical attention immediately.** When diagnosed early and dealt with promptly, most STDs can be treated.
3. **Advocate honesty.** Because most STDs are spread through unprotected sexual contact with an infected person, encourage the infected person to talk to past partner(s), who will need to be checked immediately.
4. **Talk about sexual integrity.** Help your teens internalize a set of standards or values about sexuality, honesty, respect and responsibility which they can use as guides for their own sexual decision-making and behavior.

• Shared Experiences

Shared experiences are the contemporary, common occurrences, activities and needs of life, experienced by those in a designated age group within a particular culture, ethnic group or <u>community</u>.

Variations on the commonality of these experiences (such as the different compositions of our family structures) tend to reinforce the shared nature of the most basic life experiences.

• Examples of Common Life Experiences

1. Living in a family
2. Going to school
3. Experiencing emotions
4. Interacting with peers
5. Facing each new day
6. Having certain needs, such as for shelter, food, and friendship
7. Maturing.

Shared experiences can teach us spiritual principles. Our religious life "is not arrived at by successful mastering of factual material or by mere physical attendance at Christian or religious services even though that environment is educational and enculturation has a positive effect on values held. Religion (faith) is best seen in the give and take of people, situations, experiences, in moments of quiet reflection and noisy action, in the stress of anxiety and depression, in confrontations with the needy (unloved and unlovable)." [1]

Successful teaching in a religious setting begins with an appeal to concrete, shared experiences, taking advantage of the educational principle of "meaningfulness." This principle holds that effective religious instruction is that which is rich in personal meaning for the learner, and maintains that, if the learner's present and future religious experience is to have meaningfulness, then religion must "bristle with personal meaning and significance." [2]

1   V. Bailey Gillespie, *The Experience of Faith* (Birmingham, AL: Religious Education Press, 1988), 74
2   James Michael Lee, *The Flow Of Religious Instruction* (Birmingham, AL: Religious Education Press, 1973), 79.

• Small Groups

Real spiritual growth and relationship building happens best in a small group of people.

- ### • Five Ways to Attract People to Small Groups
  1. **Be Target Minded.** Try your best to keep your leaders, believers, and seekers in different groups so no one feels stupid or bored. Organize your content around the specific needs in the group.
  2. **Be Relationship Oriented.** Split your time 50/50 with a time to share personal stories and feelings and a Bible study that keeps a relationship with Christ central.
  3. **Be Equally Shared.** If you're doing all the talking, shut-up! Your job is to facilitate discussions and empower thinking, not to answer all your own questions (even though you know everything!). Eventually, young people should know enough from your example to start their own groups. Don't be afraid to ask your group for suggestions and criticism.
  4. **Be Christ Centered.** If it isn't, apologize and start over.
  5. **Be In the Now.** Make it relevant by applying Bible truths to today and offering practical challenges that can be lived out throughout the week.

- ### • Three Ways to Assure Small Group Success
  1. **Keep it short and small.** Our group should be able to finish in under 45 minutes to an hour. No points for overtime. If you need more time your group is too big.
  2. **Prepare to spawn.** Get a co-leader who can start a new group. When you're over a comfortable number of people (8-10), meet in the same place with separate groups.
  3. **Balance is the key.** Use the first 1/2 hour to go around the circle with a simple relational question like "What does Christ mean to you." Then use the second half hour to study what the Bible says about what Christ wants to mean to you.

- ### • Read These Verses on Small Groups
  1. Mark 3:14
  2. Acts 2:36-47

Spiritual Disciplines

• Spiritual Disciplines

Spiritual disciplines are activities that promote spiritual growth. They are habits we develop to help us "live the Christian life with authenticity, stamina and perseverance."[1]

Spiritual disciplines are the answers to the day-to-day spiritual challenges we all face. How can I become friends with God? How can I discover God's will for my life? How can I overcome temptations? How can I make the right decisions? How can I share my faith with others?

We don't seek the answers to these questions *in order to become* Christians, we seek them because *we are* the daughters and sons of God. We don't form spiritual habits *to convince* God to approve of us, we form them *in response* to our salvation, that our joy here on this earth might be full,[2] and that we more effectively can share God's grace with others.

Typically, spiritual disciplines are divided into two categories:

• The Disciplines of Activity

1. Bible study. Listening for God's voice to you in the Scriptures.
2. Prayer. Opening your heart to God as to a friend.
3. Worship. Responding to God's grace in all the areas of your life, with praise, adoration and thanksgiving.
4. **Confession**. Declaring where you stand. Making things right.
5. **Journaling**. Keeping track of your spiritual journey.
6. Community. Reflecting God's grace to other believers.
7. Service. Revealing God's grace to those who don't know Jesus.

• The Disciplines of Abstinence

1. **Solitude**. Spending time alone with God. Meditating.
2. **Silence**. Removing distractions so you can hear God's voice.
3. **Fasting**. Skipping a meal (or meals) and seeking spiritual strength and nourishment.
4. **Chastity**. Choosing to abstain from sexual pleasures.
5. Stewardship. Setting aside portions of your time, talents and income specifically for God's service.
6. **Giving**. Sacrificing part of your resources.
7. **Secrecy**. Avoiding self-promotion. Giving in secret.

1   See the *Willow Creek Small Groups Leadership Handbook*, 2nd Edition, 1994, 27.
2   1 John 1:4

Spiritual Gifts

Everyone who becomes a Christian is given a spiritual gift package. (Everyone. There are no exceptions. See 1 Peter 4:10.) God takes into consideration our personality, our environment and our passions in life. He gives us a gift (or gifts) that will make serving Him and others an exciting, renewing experience.

Encouraging Spiritual Gifts

1. **Model and use your own gifts.** Actively use your gifts. Talk about them. Talk about using them. Talk about how you feel when you are using your gifts as opposed to serving in areas in which you are not gifted.

    ("I don't call you during the week because my job description tells me I have to. I call you because God's given me the gift of shepherding and I just can't wait around till the weekend to see if you're doing okay!")

2. **Notice and appreciate other's gifts.** Find people in your church who are working in their gifted areas. Have them come and talk to your youth group about how it feels to serve in the way God created them to. Affirm gifts you see in action.

    ("I'm sure glad Jim has the gift of leadership. Didn't he do a great job of getting everyone excited and ready for the rafting trip?")

3. **Look for and encourage budding gifts** in the kids in your youth group. Instill a curiosity about gifts. Talk about how the group would suffer if they decided not to use their gifts.

    ("I really appreciate the way you took time to talk to Kate when she was down. She seems to feel better now. I think you probably have the gift of encouragement. What if you hadn't been willing to use your gift?")

The New Testament Speaks of Spiritual Gifts

1. Romans 12:1-8
2. 1 Corinthians 12:1-30
3. Ephesians 4:11-16
4. 1 Peter 4:8-11

Spiritual Gifts

Spirituality

Christian spirituality is concerned with the maturing response of believers to the saving grace of God; it is the deepening desire of the human heart to value the things that are valued by God. Spirituality implies progress and transformation in this life, "leaving behind the superfluous and becoming increasingly certain of the essential."[1]

When we explore spirituality with our youth we must always begin with and proceed from the uncompromising reality of God's absolute grace (2 Timothy 1:8-10). God speaks to us from the fullness of His grace (John 1:16), pursues us, wins us, adopts us as His children (Ephesians 1:4, 5) and places our feet on a path of freedom and hope (Galatians 5:1; Romans 15:4).

But not for a moment does God, having accomplished our redemption in Jesus (Romans 3:24), abandon us to walk that path alone (Matthew 28:20; Hebrews 13:5). On the contrary, God constantly nourishes and encourages us by building our faith in Him and in His ability to fulfill His promises (Romans 4:21).

Within this grace orientation then, spirituality focuses on those things we do to more fully realize God's presence and power. Without such a foundation, spirituality looks more and more like *heathenism*, like an attempt to exchange our religious efforts for the favors of a bartering God. [2]

Remember, we never catch God's attention, or earn His love, or merit our salvation by our actions, even when those actions are spiritual. God has already fully given Himself to us; spirituality is our increasing response to His gift of our salvation (1 John 5:11, 12).

- *Seven Common Themes of Christian Spirituality*
  1. **Seeking.** How God seeks us. How we seek God.
  2. **Symbols.** Holy places and holy time (including the Sabbath).
  3. Community. The influence of others. Corporate worship.
  4. **Solitude.** Reflection. Meditation.
  5. Bible study.
  6. Prayer.
  7. Spiritual disciplines.

1   Paraphrasing Peter Brown, *Augustine of Hippo* (Berkeley, CA: University of CA Press, 1967), 253.
2   See Ellen White, *The Desire of Ages*, 35.

Spirituality

• Standards

A standard is an acknowledged measure of comparison for something we hold as having value. In the Christian realm, a standard is a practical application of a biblical or philosophical principle which provides specific direction for behavior and clear goals for lifestyle issues.

Seventh-day Adventists have tended to group all lifestyle issues into one cluster. The music we listen to, the drugs we avoid, the clothes we wear, the way we keep the Sabbath – all these issues came under the one topic of standards. _Valuegenesis_ has shown that such a single grouping actually confuses the discussion instead of clarifying it.

Now we understand that, in practice, Adventists divide standards into three separate categories. These categories become crystal clear when we study responses to questions about the amount of personal agreement people hold with respect to each lifestyle issue.

• Three Types of Adventist Standards

1. **Substance Abuse Standards**
   a. Illegal drugs
   b. Tobacco
   c. Alcohol
2. **Adventist Way of Life Standards**
   a. Sabbath observance
   b. Exercise
   c. Unclean meat
   d. Sexuality
   e. Modesty
3. **Adventist Popular Culture Standards**
   a. Jewelry
   b. Caffeinated drinks
   c. Music
   d. Dancing
   e. Movies

Which of the three areas do you think Adventist youth agree with the most? Which area do you think has the highest percentage of disagreement? Which area is closest to the heart and mission of the Adventist church? Which area do we talk about the most?

For a full discussion of standards, see *Shall We Dance: Rediscovering Christ-centered Standards*, published by the Hancock Center.

- **Four Biblical Principles About Standards**
  1. **The War of the Ways**: the way of God and the way of the world are opposite. See 1 John 2:15-17.
  2. **The Spirit and the Letter**: the spirit of the Law exceeds the letter of the Law. See Matthew 5:21-30.
  3. **Offending and Tripping**: don't purposely offend others; and quit tripping over every little thing. See 1 Corinthians 8:9-113.
  4. **Protecting the Weak**: be accepting and tolerant, especially to those of weak faith. See Romans 14:1-4.
  - Adapted from *Shall We Dance*, pages 47-53.

The North American Division's Project Affirmation recommended that families, congregations and schools adopt the following approach to focusing on core values and clarifying Christ-centered standards.

- **Seven Ways to Evaluate Lifestyle Practices**
  1. **Identify** the relationship between core values and the specific practices that stem from them.
  2. **Establish** those practices that are central to the purpose and mission of the Seventh-day Adventist church in the local community.
  3. **Agree** on those practices that are useful and central in promoting faith in Christ and encouraging a life of service.
  4. **Establish** governance practices (in homes and schools) in accordance with good educational policy, positive effective discipline, and efficient human organization.
  5. **Eliminate** those rules and lifestyle practices that are not consistent with the four previous goals.
  6. Periodically **measure** faith maturity, values shifts, and attitudes regarding Adventist standards and lifestyle practices (by using, for example, a *Valuegenesis* survey modified for local use).
  7. **Seek out** and use methods and resources that directly contribute to focusing on core values.
  - Taken from *Risk and Promise*, pages 18 and 19.

Standards, continued

• Step By Step Praise Team System™

The Step By Step Praise Team System™ is an invaluable tool in leading dynamic praise and <u>worship</u> for your youth and <u>young adults</u>. The kit was designed as a turnkey system to help <u>youth leaders</u> empower their youth to get involved in the leading of praise <u>music</u>. This is done through several levels.

• *Six Step By Step Components*

1. **A Training Video.** This video not only helps your youth catch the vision, but provides a practical breakdown of how best to use the system.
2. **System Success Tips.**™ This comprehensive how-to resource covers everything from philosophy to feedback. It introduces a "P.L.A.N." for successful song leading. It also includes a technical support section, and job descriptions for each member of the praise team.
3. **Two Compact Discs.** Twenty of the best loved praise and worship songs are recorded on two digitally mastered compact discs. One disc is a learning tool, with complete vocal arrangements. The second disc is for performance, and contains full instrumental arrangements of each of the twenty songs.
4. **Transparencies & Lyrics Booklets.** Lyrics for each of the twenty songs are crisply and legibly reproduced on overhead transparencies for use by groups of more than twenty. For smaller groups, or groups that don't have access to an overhead projector, there are twenty booklets with lyrics provided.
5. **Lead Sheets.** Want to play along? Included are lead sheets with melody lines and chord progressions, so you can follow along with the arrangements. Guitar chord charts are also provided. There are even some tips on introducing the songs, along with a list of pertinent Bible texts.
6. **General MIDI Sequence Files.** MIDI files are included on Macintosh® and IBM® compatible disks for use with your General MIDI keyboard and sequencer. Also on the disk are Powerpoint™ presentation files of the song lyrics to use with a video projector or a slide film recorder.

The songs on the Step By Step CD's are divided into three sections for ease in planning an effective song service:

- ## Hot Starters
  1. Shine, Jesus, Shine
  2. Do Lord!
  3. Lean On Him
  4. Eat Right
  5. I Will Magnify The Lord
  6. We Trust In The Name (of the Lord Our God)

- ## Cool Praise
  7. How Majestic Is Your Name
  8. Soon And Very Soon
  9. Just For Today
  10. That's What Faith Must Be
  11. Ain't No Rock
  12. Hosanna
  13. Joyful, Joyful
  14. Thy Word
  15. He Who Began A Good Work

- ## Warm Worship
  16. He Is There
  17. Step By Step
  18. Welcome To Our Hearts
  19. Trinity Praise Song
  20. O Come Let Us Adore Him

You can order the complete Step By Step Praise Team System™ from _AdventSource_. Call 1-800-328-0525 for complete price and shipping information.

☞   **Also see:** Guitar; Leading Music; Music; Sabbath School.

Step By Step, continued

• Stewardship

For teens (and perhaps for most of the rest of us, as well), one of the most demanding standards of a maturing faith experience is that description of Christian behavior we call *stewardship*. This comprehensive principle of Christianity teaches us a perspective on daily living that runs strongly contrary to the secular worldview which suggests that we live life primarily to please and serve ourselves and that we are successful in life only when our hard work and effort result in big financial rewards and extensive material possessions.

• *Two Emphases of Christian Stewardship*
1. **Accepting.** All we have in life (our time, our talents and abilities, the things we posses, even the opportunities we have to improve) are gifts from a loving Creator (see 1 Chronicles 29:10-16). Acknowledging those gifts is an act of worship.
2. **Giving.** Taking part in and supporting ministry (giving our time, abilities, possessions, etc.) are investments we make in the kingdom of God which will result in happy dividends in the eternal joys of heaven.

God's children seek ways to improve their abilities to faithfully act as stewards of the generous gifts of our Heavenly Father. The foundation of true success lies in the recognition of God's ownership (see Ellen White, *Education*, 137). We build such character traits as honesty, integrity, diligence and thrift in order to honor God as the Originator of all our resources and to share those blessings with others who may benefit from them.

• *Five Ways to Apply Stewardship Principles*
1. Give first priority to God's kingdom. Matthew 6: 25-34.
2. Serve others in love. Galatians 5:13. Matthew 25:40. Acts 2:44, 45.
3. Conserve the resources of the earth. Genesis 1:26-30. Genesis 2:15.
4. Give tithe and offerings. Leviticus 27:30, 32. Malachi 3:10.
5. Work at all things with diligence, honesty and integrity. Proverbs 22:29. Leviticus 19:36. 2 Kings 12:13-15.

Stewardship

• Student Missions/Task Force

One of the most exciting moments in a youth worker's life is the day one of her or his own youth expresses an interest in sharing their developing faith with others in their world. This sharing can be accomplished by inviting a next-door neighbor to church, by volunteering at the local homeless shelter, by spending time reading books to children at a hospital, or simply by being willing to offer prayer or special music for the church service.

However, when kids get involved with serving others and begin to realize the potential for seriously affecting the world around them, you've got a snowball on a slippery slope on your hands. They'll want to discover more and more new areas in which to exercise their gifts.

A more intensive way for young people to become involved in service for God is to volunteer as a Student Missionary or Task Force Worker. The North American Division operates a program of mission work for young people. This program provides positions all over the United States and the world for mission terms from three months to up to two years. Youth can teach elementary school in the Marshall Islands, run a Campus Ministries program in Colorado, serve as an Assistant Dormitory Dean in Iceland, teach Physical Education in Tennessee, become an English as a Second Language teacher in Korea, and list goes on and on.

Requirements for each position vary, sometimes including language skills or a certain level of education completed. But with hundreds of calls available each year, it is generally possible to find a position that fits the need of your youth group member interested in service.

And, as most returned Student Missionary and Task Force workers will attest, the time spent serving God through helping others is a dramatic, life-changing experience.

- • *Two Ways to Sign Up*
    1. Each Adventist college has a World Missions department on their campus. Contact the college Chaplain's office for information.
    2. Contact the NAD YouthNet office at (800) 331-2767 or http://www.cuc.edu/sdaorg/youthnet/mail.html

• Suicide

Teen suicide is on the rise. Currently, suicide is the second leading cause of death from ages 13-24. (Only accidents cause more deaths and many of those are believed to be the result of suicidal impulses.) Over 50,000 teen suicide attempts occur annually in the U.S. alone.

Valuegenesis tells us that Adventist homes are not immune; 58% of Adventist youth report considering suicide at least once (close to the national averages in both Canada and the U.S.). The number soars to 74% when kids are growing up in an unhappy home.

People usually attempt suicide to end unbearable emotional pain. Suicidal people often feel terribly isolated, without friends or anyone to turn to, and with no other choice to deal with their problem. Often a suicide attempt is a tragic cry for help.

• *Four Myths About Suicide*

1. MYTH: **"You can't help suicidal people because all suicidal people are crazy."** Suicidal thoughts are not an indication of mental illness, but a revelation of acute distress and probably depression. In a society in which there is so much fear about mental illness, a suicidal person may feel that it is hopeless to reach out to others for help in a crisis.

2. MYTH: **"People who talk about suicide don't do it."** Studies have found that, in the weeks and months prior to the event, more than 75% of those who committed suicide behaved in ways that should have indicated to others that they were in deep despair. Anyone expressing suicidal feelings needs immediate attention.

3. MYTH: **"If someone is going to kill themselves, nothing can stop them."** The suicidal person is ambivalent; part of him or her wants to live, part wants the suffering to end. If a suicidal person turns to you, it's likely they see you as a caring person who knows how to cope and is willing to honor their confidence. Don't turn them away.

4. MYTH: **"Talking about suicide may encourage someone to do it."** Suicide is a constant item in our news, and, in the world of the teenager, a frequent visitor to their culture. Talking to teens about suicide doesn't introduce the idea to them, in fact, it may save their lives. Give the person the opportunity to discharge penned up and painful feelings.

Suicide

Suicide, continued

- **Ten Major Warning Signs of Suicide**
  1. Talks about feeling hopeless.
  2. A friend or family member dies or is experiencing a terminal illness.
  3. Stops associating with close friends.
  4. Suffers from major depression.
  5. Experiences significant mood changes.
  6. Gives away meaningful possessions.
  7. Talks about feelings of worthlessness.
  8. Interest declines in friends or activities previously enjoyed.
  9. Neglects personal appearance.
  10. Inappropriately says good-bye.

  (Note: Many teens experience only a few of the conditions listed above. All indications of suicide need to be taken seriously.)

- **Relating to Someone Who Is Thinking About Suicide**
  1. Listen.
  2. Tell them, "I don't want you to die."
  3. Try to form a "no-suicide contract."
  4. Ask them to phone you whenever the temptation arises.
  5. Invite the assistance of an experienced counsellor, pastor, psychologist, social worker or physician.

- **Relating to Someone Who Has Attempted Suicide**
  1. Visit them in the hospital as soon as possible. Don't wait until they come home.
  2. Acknowledge what's happened without dwelling on it.
  3. Treat them with love.
  4. Treat them with understanding.
  5. Treat them with compassion.
  6. Don't be afraid to acknowledge the subject of suicide.
  7. Don't allow their friends to avoid them. Encourage support.
  8. Allow them to talk openly about their feelings.
  9. When the person is ready (check with their doctor or counsellor first), give them a "We Love You" party.
  10. Be yourself.

Sources: The B.C. Council for the Family, Vancouver, British Columbia, Canada; The Oxford University Libraries Newsgroups – Psychological Services.

• Summer Camp

During the formative years of <u>youth ministry</u> in the <u>Seventh-day Adventist</u> Church, the idea of summer camps began to grow. The very first camp was held in Australia in 1925. In the North American Division, Grover Fattic, MV Secretary for the Michigan Conference, held the first summer camp in 1926 in Townline Lake, Michigan. Wisconsin held a camp in 1927, Illinois in 1928, and other conferences followed their example.

Today conference owned and operated camps exist in most every conference in North America. Summer camp programs are usually divided by age groups. Many conferences offer a variety of camps which focus on interests or activities, such as aquatics, <u>drama</u>, backpacking, water sports, rock climbing, arts and crafts, photography and horsemanship.

• A Typical Day at Summer Camp

1. Rise and shine. (Get up early for warm showers!)
2. Clean up the cabin; inspection held later in the day.
3. Line call; raise the flag. ("All present and accounted for.")
4. Breakfast.
5. Worship, classes and activities.
6. Mail call.
7. Lunch.
8. Rest time (counsellors decide on absolute quiet or conversations permitted).
9. Rotations – try other activities.
10. Free time (go to the camp store, write letters home, go to the nature center, etc.).
11. Dinner.
12. Recreation.
13. Evening program.
14. Lights out!

Write the numbers below of your nearest summer camp.

Name: _____

Address: _____

Phone Number: _____

Summer Camp

Technology

It's no secret that technology is becoming an increasingly integrated part of every aspect of life. Gone are the days when a film strip or a 16mm movie in the classroom was considered a special occasion. We've come to expect exciting, attention grabbing audiovisual productions, full of special effects.

Today technology is being used in a variety of creative ways to help youth leaders communicate stories and ideas. Computer generated effects, video editing consoles and interactive programs have replaced the overhead projector. The challenge is to find the products that work for your group and then learn to use them.

Getting Acquainted With the Technology

1. Contact the media services department at a local college or university.
2. Look in the yellow pages under Audio-Visual Equipment.
3. Contact to the audiovisual person at a large church in your city or town.
4. Do a search of the World Wide Web for Audio-Visual Technology.

Using Technology in Your Presentations

1. **Know your potential.** Audiovisual technology should do more than fill space in a meeting. Take the time to develop a program that uses the audiovisual technology to it's full potential.
2. **Know your audience.** Make sure that you keep your audience in mind as you consider the technology that you are going to be using.
3. **Know the equipment.** Schedule a rehearsal so that you can feel comfortable with the audiovisual equipment. Use this time to work out the rough spots and transitions so that you can do a first-class production.
4. **Remember the details.** Things like power cords, patch cables, monitors, screens and outlets may seem like small details, but they have also been know to hold up many a presentation. Be sure that you have all the accessories that you need.

Technology

• Teens

After early <u>adolescence</u> comes the infamous teen years, a time when spiritual interest diminishes and takes a secondary place to the much stronger developmental aspects of physical and social growth.

• Physical Development

Puberty heralds the release of a whole range of hormones that radically change the young person. Physically he or she is now moving into adulthood. The individual experiences rapid growth spurts. The change in body shape brings with it a new self awareness and the young person can be very sensitive about how he or she looks and concerned about what is normal. With the release of the sex hormones the adolescent becomes increasingly more aware of the sexual dimension and most often teens become acutely aware of the opposite sex.

• Emotional Development

The teen years see the onset of a crisis of identity. At this stage there is a new sense of self-consciousness. This is the time when the young person starts to break away from the family and traditional ties in an attempt to establish his or her own identity.

• Moral Development

Since many youth have not achieved the ability to think abstractly, it is unlikely they will *naturally* develop the ability to exercise mature moral judgement and develop mature moral <u>values</u>. Devotional modules, discussion of issues, sermons, prayers, songs, etc., should reflect, as often as possible, a more concrete thought form, and relate biblical concepts to the life-situation in which youth exist.

• Faith Development

In the movement towards maturity, adolescence is the optimum age for identity formation; it is also the optimum age for the development of a belief system and for the adoption of a personal set of values; it is the stage of faith in which an individual sees deep meaning behind faith issues.

As a child, the beliefs and values of those that they regard as significant are accepted literally. In adolescence there is a tendency to view the meanings of these beliefs and values and an attempt to apply them in their widening sphere of experience. Beyond adolescence the individual engages in a critical assessment of these previously held beliefs and values.

• Building a Ministry to Meet Teens

There is little doubt that the teenage period is a most critical stage of development. During these years families and the church must assume the heavy responsibility of nurturing the youth in such a way that they will emerge from adolescence with a mature faith and relationship with Jesus. A separate and distinctive style of church ministry is usually necessary if this is to happen. This should take the form of a balanced youth ministry plan that includes the four basic elements of grace, worship, community and service.

• Five Teen Characteristics to Keep in Mind

1. **Flexibility.** Teens will respond to that which appeals without the cluttering effect of traditional hang-ups.
2. **Creativity.** Teens of this generation particularly appreciate and respond to the creative - a consequence of being second generation "TV kids."
3. **Impatience.** Teens tend to be impatient with what appears to them to be irrelevant and obsolete.
4. **Intolerance.** Teens tend to be intolerant when issues have a negative impact on them. In the area of religion, youth appear to withdraw rather than do battle with authorities. For example, they will leave the church because of harsh criticism, hypocrisy, perceived irrelevancies, etc.
5. **Idealism.** Teens are typically idealistic and are particularly perceptive when inadequacies or irrelevancies exist, or hypocritical attitudes are persistently held.

– Adapted from Barry Gane, *Building Youth Ministry: A Foundational Guide* (Riverside, CA: Hancock Center for Youth Ministry, 1997).

☞ Also see: Faith Development.

Teens, continued

Teenspeak

Is it still cool to be an awesome dude? Or is that totally bogus old skool stuff these days? Like, I'm really clueless, okay?!

One of the biggest challenges of ministry to <u>teens</u> is the constant reminder that we speak a different language. Call it by a proper-sounding linguistic term like *adolonics,* or just refer to it as *slang* – teenspeak is the informal, nonstandard, unconventional group of words and phrases currently popular and common among teenagers.

All subcultures tend to create communication shortcuts. Mountain bikers, surfers, computer hackers, religious people, church administrators, all utilize "insider" terms which reflect the experiences, beliefs and values of its speakers. Teens may do it better than anyone else.

Why Teens Use Slang

1. **It's cool.** Teanspeak conveys a certain sense of style. When we speak, we communicate not only a specific content, but also a message about who we think we are. Using the latest phrase says we are contemporary, in tune with the times.
2. **It's acceptable.** Typically, teenspeak is used in informal environments, with communication partners who accept and know the language, and avoided in more formal settings, such as the classroom or the workplace, where its use may lead to a negative evaluation (by a teacher or supervisor).
3. **It's fun.** Teenspeak can be creative and humorous, almost like a form of play. Often it is entertaining and amusing.

Probably the best advice to <u>youth leaders</u> about teenspeak is to have fun with it, laugh about how you used to say things, admit your ignorance, and *don't try to speak it.*

Three Reasons Not to Use Teenspeak

1. **You can't keep up.** Master the slang of the summer and by fall you'll be out of date.
2. **You'll get embarrassed.** Sooner or later you'll use a word that was perfectly acceptable the last thing you knew, but today means something you absolutely don't want to say.
3. **You model the permanent.** Don't be stuffy. Just keep pointing your youth away from the transitory toward the everlasting.

Teenspeak

• Television

Many <u>youth leaders</u> advise tossing out the television altogether, on the basis of the notion that so much of the programming has become contrary to our <u>values</u>. This is certainly one way to solve the problems of watching too much TV or watching things that aren't good for us as Christians. But such a solution is unlikely to go down well in most families or in your <u>youth group</u>.

An alternative is to use television as a means of teaching teens how to identify and process their values, and deal with the challenges television presents. With all the temptations out there in the world, it's never too soon for kids to begin using <u>critical thinking</u> skills and putting their values to work in weeding out the trash. It's *easier* to draw a line at *zero* tolerance, but it's also less productive. Discrimination is much more difficult, but it ends up being more rewarding.

Begin lively discussions with your youth about television. Start with the underlying assumptions about media's potential influence on the Christian experience. Then talk about what constitutes good programming, and why.

• Ten Tantalizing Topics for TV Talk

1. **TV News.** Does it give a distorted view of the world (sensationalism; creates fear by making crime seem ubiquitous; emphasis on the visual and the local— whatever makes a good picture; ratings determine priorities; bottom-line thinking of TV execs)?

2. **Sitcoms** — Yesterday and Today. Are they better or worse? Funnier or dumber? How has the language changed? Are the innuendoes more obvious? Are we laughing at things that really aren't funny? How are Christian values portrayed? Or are they?

3. **The V-Chip.** Is this technology really a solution? Or is it parental abdication? How can the viewing habits of the very young be controlled? When should we be allowed to see anything we want to see?

4. **Soap Operas.** Why are they so popular? Why are they so addictive? Is there anything redeeming about them? Do we really want this much sex?

5. **Crime Shows.** How real are they? Do they contribute to the

idea that everything can be or should be solved in an hour? Do we know how to separate fact from fiction? Do we really need this much explicit violence?

6. **Contextual vs. Gratuitous** – Language/Violence/Sex. Is the degree of language/violence/sex essential to the story line? Or does it seem to be added just for shock value? How does/ should this affect your tolerance of these things?

7. **If You Were the Parent.** How will you treat these subjects when you have kids of your own? What would you want them to watch? What will you do the same way as your parents? What will you do differently?

8. **Could Jesus Watch this With You?** This is an old standby question, but it's still a thought-provoker! Do you think it's an appropriate measure of our standards?

9. **How Hooked Are You?** Could you give up TV for a week or two? How about for a month? Would this be a good way to find out how hooked you are. What would you miss the most? Why? What could you learn from such an experiment?

10. **Ratings.** Have television producers done a good job in defining their own programs? Do the ratings make you more or less interested in a program? Should TV producers go further in explaining the content of their programs?

- *More Notes On Television Viewing*
  1. By the time they graduate from high school, most kids have watched 20,000 hours of television.
  2. By some estimates, television contains more than 14,000 sexual references and innuendoes annually.
  3. Most children will have seen 100,000 acts of violence on television by the time they enter the 6th grade.
  4. Kids see about 20,000 TV commercials each year.
  5. Seventy percent of TV viewers say they watch television for escape. Only 1 in 10 seek intellectual stimulation.

Television Notes:

_____

_____

_____

_____

Television, continued

• The Three:20 Zone

The Three:20 Zone is a one or two day training event for all the good people involved in <u>youth ministry</u>: local church <u>youth leaders</u>, <u>youth pastors</u> and senior pastors, teachers and parents. The Zone includes workshops, general sessions, devotionals and a <u>worship</u> service designed to demonstrate how to involve youth in <u>church</u>.

The Zone is a cooperative venture between your conference youth ministry director and the <u>Hancock Center for Youth and Family Ministry</u>, with a faculty of active youth ministry professionals.

- *Four Practical Workshop Tracks*
  1. **Basic Youth Ministry Strategies**. If you're a brand new youth leader and you need to know exactly where to start and how to proceed, here's where you'll find help.
  2. <u>Programming</u>. For all those who's primary responsibilities involve local church youth programming, here's a wealth of ideas.
  3. **Youth Ministry Issues**. What are the key issues facing today's kids? How can you assist them in the challenging task of being a Christian in a secular society?
  4. <u>Parents</u>. With the probability that you are going to be the single most important spiritual influence in your children's life, wouldn't it be nice to approach the task with understanding and insight? Here's the insight you're looking for.

- *How to Schedule a Three:20 Zone*
  1. Call your <u>conference youth director</u>. Ask him or her if there are any training events already scheduled. Tell them about the Three:20 Zone.
  2. Ask the youth director to contact the Hancock Center at (800) 785-HCYM. We'll talk about the size and duration of the event you'd like to plan, discuss Zone details, and establish a date and place. Then we'll send you all the publicity materials you'll need (Union paper ads, bulletin inserts, posters, news releases, etc.).

- *Where did the name "Three:20 Zone" come from?*
  You'll have to show up to find out! (Be sure to bring your Bible.)

Time Management

What is it that *wastes* most of your time? Bad committee meetings? Misplaced notes? Forgotten appointments? A cluttered desk?

With all they do, youth leaders just don't have any time to waste. So let's tackle several of the biggest challenges that attack your time.

How to Keep Up With All Your Projects

1. **Take Inventory.** Set aside an hour early one Sunday morning for this necessary first step. Use a time management application (such as IN CONTROL or Now Up-to-Date), or, if you prefer, write on a blank sheet of paper. List every project, program, appointment, deadline, duty and chore you can think of. Consult your master calendar to jog your memory.

2. **Categorize.** Now go back over your list and shuffle each entry into a project category. You might include categories such as family-related items (visits to the dentist, graduation, recitals, etc.), work-related items (meetings, business trips, etc.), and certainly youth ministry-related items (programs, social activities, etc.). Place every item into a category.

3. **Prioritize.** Assign a priority to each item in each category. For example, give some items a number 1 priority, which means this has to be done immediately. A number 2 priority means you need to get to this item as soon as possible. Number 3 means a deadline is not pressing, but it needs to be done soon.

4. **File.** Organize your files to match your priorities. Create a file folder for each item on your list. Place all your notes, receipts, addresses and phone numbers for that activity in the file. When the activity is completed, make a decision: if the activity will be repeated keep the file in a new category for review. If you can't see any future need, be unsentimental and toss the file.

5. **Stick to it.** The longer you stay with your system of organizing, the better it will work for you. Make the necessary adjustments (you may need more than three priorities, for example) and stick to the job of managing your time.

Don't forget to delegate; build a youth ministry *team*, rather than attempting to do it all yourself. Try to control interruptions while you're working. And most of all, simplify your life.

• Tobacco

Historically, <u>Seventh-day Adventists</u> have held such a strong anti-tobacco position, that not smoking has become part of the definition of who we are. Now, it seems the rest of the world (with the exception of corporate attorneys and politicians from the tobacco-producing states) has joined the crusade.

There's a lot more to this discussion than stained teeth, premature wrinkles and disturbed sleep (all related statistically to smoking!). But, whatever you do, *don't connect it with salvation*! This is an addiction problem (nearly one third of everyone who tries a *single* cigarette develop a dependence on tobacco), a self-esteem problem, a peer pressure problem, and an advertising challenge, not an entrance requirement for heaven. Never make the mistake of telling a young smoker that Jesus won't love them if they keep smoking.

Help kids who are tempted or addicted to get help. Give them the facts. Build their confidence. Help them succeed. Keep them close to you. Keep talking about the problem.

• Who Smokes?
1. About 61 million U.S. adults, or 29% of the U.S. population smoke. There are an estimated 3.2 billion smokers worldwide.
2. More men than women smoke.
3. Almost 5 million youth in the U.S. (age 12-17) smoke.
4. Approximately 80% of adult smokers started smoking before the age of 18.
5. Every day nearly 3,000 youth under the age of 18 become regular smokers.

• What are the Health Risks?
1. Smoking is the single greatest preventable cause of illness and premature death in the United States.
2. Tobacco use is blamed for nearly one in five deaths in the U.S.
3. Worldwide, about 3 million people a year die as a result of smoking. By 2020, the total is predicted to be approximately 10 million, and smoking will be the single largest cause of death, according to a World Health Organization study, released in September, 1996. A person dies as a result of tobacco use EVERY TEN SECONDS.

Tobacco

4. On average, a smoker loses 15 years of life.
5. Men who smoke have a 22-times greater risk of dying of lung cancer than do men who have never smoked.
6. Lung cancer continues to increase in women as more and more women begin smoking. Since 1987, more women have died each year from lung cancer than from breast cancer.
7. While the associations between smoking and lung cancer — as well as smoking and heart disease — are well-known, there are other cancers associated with smoking. Among them: cancers of the mouth, pharynx, larynx, esophagus, pancreas, cervix, kidney and bladder.
8. Smoking is associated with a higher risk of miscarriage and inhibited child development, and is a factor in sudden infant death syndrome and higher rates of respiratory illnesses including bronchitis, colds, and pneumonia in children.
9. Smoking kills more people each year than AIDS, alcohol, drug abuse, car crashes, murders, suicides and fires - combined!

In China, cigarette consumption per adult is on the rise. If current trends persist, approximately 50 million of the young people under twenty years of age alive today in China will die prematurely from the consequences of smoking.

The World Health Organization now refers to smoking as "the tobacco epidemic."

- ## The Cost of Smoking
  1. A World Bank economist has estimated that the use of tobacco results in a net loss worldwide of $200 billion per year.
  2. Members of the European community put more money into *promoting tobacco production* EACH DAY ($3.8 million) than the total spent by the European Commission on Tobacco Control in A YEAR.
  3. Medical costs for smokers in the U.S. are $50 billion annually, plus an additional $47 billion for indirect expenses, such as time lost from work and disability.

- ## Quitting Smoking
  1. Nearly 70% of adults who smoke want to quit.
  2. Overall, fewer than 3% of smokers quit successfully, but that

Tobacco, continued

percentage increases dramatically if there is a health risk or a formal cessation program.

3. The Centers for Disease Control urges smokers to:
   - Be committed. Be aware that breaking nicotine addiction isn't easy and takes a significant individual effort.
   - Discuss nicotine replacement therapy and smoking cessation programs with your doctor.
   - Set a quit date; do not try to "taper off."
   - Create a support network of family and friends who will encourage your efforts to stop smoking.
   - Learn how to cope with situations that make you want to resume smoking.

- ## Eight Important Anti-Tobacco Contact Points
   1. Centers for Disease Control and Prevention, Office on Smoking and Health. Phone: (409) 639-3311. http://www.cdc.gov/
   2. American Cancer Society. Phone: 1-800-ACS-2345. http://www.cancer.org
   3. World Health Organization. http://www.paho.org/english/address.htm#hdqt
   4. US Department of Health and Human Services. Phone: (202) 619-0257. http://www.os.dhhs.gov/about/contacthhs.html
   5. The Foundation for a Smoke-Free America. Phone: (310) 277-1111. FAX: (310) 657-1822. http://www.tobaccofree.com/
   6. Laboratory Centre for Disease Control, Ottawa, Ontario, Canada. Health Protection Branch. http://www.hc-sc.gc.ca/hpb/lcdc/hp_eng.html
   7. Adventist Youth to Youth
   8. Breathe Free. General Conference Health and Temperance Department. (301) 680-6702. http://www.adventist.org

Sources: *Los Angeles Times,* September 18, 1996; Centers for Disease Control; World Health Organization.

More Notes on Tobacco:

_____

_____

_____

_____

_____

_____

Tobacco, continued

• Transportation

Here's the problem: your <u>youth council</u> meets Sunday night at 6:30 at the church. You've got two kids whose parents can bring them as far as the school, but you've got to get them to church and then home again. One more member needs to be picked up after work at Taco Bell. And two more will attend the meeting if you pick them up at home.

Should you start early and make several trips yourself in your old car? Should you ask a couple of kids with cars to help you? Or should you try to convince the pastor and church board that you need a 12-passenger van and a permanent volunteer driver?

Then there's the question of providing transportation for kids who can't take part without you. Do you take them to <u>Sabbath School</u>, to service projects on the other side of town, and to the <u>pizza</u> party next Saturday night? Is it feasible within your <u>budget</u>? Is it possible with your staff of helpers? Is it safe?

• *Six Transportation Rules for Youth Leaders*

1. **Check local guidelines.** There are considerable variances from state to state and province to province in requirements for transporting groups. Investigate your local liabilities and requirements before you finalize any transportation plans. Follow the standards and procedures established by your area.
2. **Check vehicle maintenance.** Schedule regular maintenance of all the vehicles you use. Before a trip check the air pressure in the tires, the lights and brakes, and start out with a clean windshield.
3. **Enlist volunteer help.** Establish a core group of parents and church members who have adequate insurance and will devote their time to <u>youth ministry</u> by getting the kids where they need to go.
4. **Insist on seatbelts.** Never start any portion of a trip until everyone is buckled up.
5. **Obey all traffic laws.** Hold to the speed limit. Be extra safe at intersections. You are carrying precious cargo.
6. **Take phone numbers with you.** Make a list of names, addresses and phone numbers of parents or guardians. Keep your cell phone nearby. Be prepared to notify the appropriate people in case of an emergency.

Transportation

• T-Shirts

In the 1930s the Hanes Company and Sears Roebuck began producing plain, white undershirts with short sleeves and crew necks. The manufacturers marketed the new product as both inner and outer wear, called the garments "T-shirts," and sold them for 24 cents each. From this humble beginning the T-shirt became a teenager's most indispensable garment, what one observer of <u>youth culture</u> has called "the alpha and omega of a teenager's fashion alphabet."

No one knows for sure when the product was transformed from an unpretentious, utilitarian piece of clothing to a glamourous fashion statement. Many point to youthful sailors in the Second World War, strolling through distant ports-of-call in their all-cotton Ts. Some insist it was Elvis Presley and James Dean who succeeded in fully popularizing the teen-idol, anti-status symbol. Others say the T-shirt industry didn't really take off until a handsome millionaire war-hero named John Kennedy, newly married and newly elected to the U.S. Senate was pictured in *Life* magazine relaxing in a T-shirt in his Georgetown townhouse.

At any rate, the industry today is a ubiquitous presence at sporting events, political rallies, computer shows and evangelistic crusades. White and tye-died. Slashed and ripped. Beaded and gilded. Shrunken and oversized. With simple logos and complex art work. With blue jeans and tuxedoes. Nothing identifies youth culture more than a T-shirt.

• Three Ways to Use a T-Shirt

1. Have your youth group design your own line of T-shirts. You might decide on a logo that identifies your group. Or choose a Bible phrase (such as, "Don't Be Afraid," or "I Am With You Always"). Give every member a shirt as a token of belonging. Present the T-shirt to new members whenever they join the group.

2. Advertise an upcoming event using T-shirts. Print the name of the event, the location and the date on the shirt and hand them out. Kids who wear the shirts to the event get in free!

3. Create an extra-extra-extra-extra large T-shirt out of old bed sheets. Make it big enough for all your kids to fit into. Take a group picture, have everyone autograph the picture and hang it in your Sabbath School room.

• Urban Embrace

In the heart of East L.A. a summer tutoring program named Urban Embrace gives city kids a shot at good grades and an escape from gang life. Now gearing up for another summer at the White Memorial Church, Urban Embrace boosts pride in the barrio.

Like most inner-cities, this one needs help. Jobs and lifestyles lack glamour and the locals, for the most part, struggle with English in a community long abandoned by big investors. Without daring projects like Urban Embrace , most kids here stand no chance of college success. Nearby schools, starved of cash and space, dangle the thinnest of ropes for kids climbing out of poverty.

Back in 1994, the Hancock Center at La Sierra University created a solution - the Urban Embrace day camp. Each June college-aged counselors spend 10 weeks teaching kids to read, play ball, encounter Jesus, and build their community in a church setting.

- ● *Urban Embrace Funding*
  1. Parents with kids aged 6 through 14 sign-up at bargain prices.
  2. Local businesses subsidize the project.
  3. Local schools provide free lunches.
  4. The church donates space, time, and evangelism dollars.
  5. The camp coordinator, with a stipend from the White Memorial Church, plans each summer months ahead of time.

- ● *Urban Embrace Follow-Through*
  1. Each kid has a file-folder.
  2. They're written to and encouraged during the year.
  3. Volunteers continue tutoring once camp's out.
  4. Pathfinders and youth programs offer year-round contact.
  5. Parents see the church as a friend.

For information on getting involved, or on starting a sister-project in your town, call or write to:

Urban Embrace Coordinator, White Memorial Church
401 North State Street
Los Angeles, CA 90033
Phone: (213) 264-2170
FAX: (213) 264-6012

Urban Embrace

- ## *Valuegenesis*

  - What makes some teenagers religious while others are not?
  - What are the primary influences that determine the values of teenagers?
  - How are Adventist youth today relating to traditional Adventist standards?
  - Do Adventist youth understand and agree with Adventist doctrines?
  - Why do young people leave the church?

  Because Adventist <u>youth leaders</u> need the answers to questions like these in order to effectively minister to young people, and because so little <u>research</u> had been done specifically about Adventist youth, the North American Division Office of Education funded a massive research project to find some answers. The project was called *Valuegenesis*, an investigation into the faith, values and commitment of <u>Seventh-day Adventist</u> youth.

  The research was created and first implemented across North America in 1989, and has been ongoing in other world divisions and in specific North American conferences, schools and churches ever since.

  The original sample exceeded 15,000 6th through 12th grade students in Adventist schools, as well as samples of youth in public education, student's parents, teachers, administrators, and pastors. Well over 22,000 people took part in the original research, making it, at the time, the largest research project any denomination had ever conducted about its youth. Statisticians tell us that the sampling methods, combined with the huge size of the population sampled, make the results extremely accurate.

  - ## The Areas of Valuegenesis Study
    1. Mature Faith
    2. Denominational Loyalty
    3. Denominational Orthodoxy
    4. <u>Standards</u>
    5. <u>Adventist Education</u>
    6. Adventist Teaching
    7. Service Activities
    8. Personal Religious Practices and Behaviors

  In addition to these well documented areas of religious life, information was processed which focused on four dynamic areas of religious life and growth, areas which are influenced by our homes, schools and churches.

A. <u>Grace</u>—a more grace-oriented approach to religious life and understanding of God would enhance the faith experience.
B. <u>Worship</u>—a renewed focus on worship and the human response to God was suggested as youth and adults relearn what it means to worship their God.
C. <u>Community</u>—suggestions were made regarding changing the actual climate and thinking atmosphere in local congregations and schools which enrich the faith experience.
D. <u>Service</u>—significant information was seen that supported increased involvement in helping activities by all targeted in the research.

For detailed information and the implications of this research see the publications listed below. All the publications may be ordered by calling the <u>Hancock Center</u> at 1-800-785-HCYM.

- Roger Dudley with V. Bailey Gillespie, *Faith in the Balance* (Riverside, CA: La Sierra University Press, 1992).
- V. Bailey Gillespie, editor, *Perspectives on Values* (Riverside, CA: La Sierra University Press, 1993).
- Roger and Doris Larson, V. Bailey Gillespie, editor, *Teaching Values* (Riverside, CA: Hancock Center Publications, second edition, 1996).
- Steve Case, editor, *Shall We Dance: Rediscovering Christ-Centered Standards* (Riverside, CA: Hancock Center Publications, 1996).
- Stuart Tyner, *The Colors of Grace in Our Homes* (Lincoln, NE: <u>Advent*Source*</u>, 1996).
- Gail Rice, *The Textures of Grace in Our Schools* (Lincoln, NE: Advent*Source*, 1996).
- V. Bailey Gillespie, *The Sounds of Grace in Our Churches* (Lincoln, NE: Advent*Source*, 1996).
- Stuart Tyner and V. Bailey Gillespie, *Walking On The Edge: 13 Interactive Study Guides for Adventists in Public Schools* (Lincoln, NE: Advent*Source*, 1996).

☞ **Also see:** Effectiveness Factors; Research; Standards.

Valuegenesis, continued

- ## Values

A value is a goal or a characteristic we think is desirable or worthwhile.

For example, good health is a value. I want to enjoy life as much as I can, and I know that in order to do that I have to be healthy. I think that being healthy is worthwhile, so I value good health.

Other values might include experiencing meaningful friendships, having a moral character, living in a free country, and enjoying the benefits of being a part of a community of faith.

– Taken from *Walking On the Edge* (Lincoln, NE: AdventSource, 1996).

- ## *Three Strategies for Talking About Values*

1. **Watch for Samuel's Invitation.** (See 1 Samuel 3.) Be ready for the teachable moments when someone asks you a question about faith. Such questions usually indicate an open mind, minimal distractions and clear focus. Generally, the moments should be initiated by the learner.

   To encourage teachable moments, do the following:
   a. Create a friendly atmosphere. Relax. Don't argue. We do very little learning in the middle of conflict.
   b. Take your time. Values are built over a lifetime by many moments just like this.
   c. Watch your tone of voice. Don't start preaching. Don't sound worried. And don't stamp your feet!
   d. Give reassurance of your positive feelings. Don't condemn.
   e. Focus. Concentrate. Listen.
2. **Avoid Peter's Perspective.** (See Matthew 14:22-33.) As long as Peter continued to look at Jesus, his behavior was miraculous. But the moment Peter took his eyes off Jesus and looked down at what he was doing, he sank beneath the water.

   The formula for success is the same for us today as it was for Peter: focus on Jesus, and walk on the water. Focus on walking on the water, and sink.
3. **Listen to the Conversation with Nicodemus.** (See John 3:1-21.) Jesus cut through the surface conversation, asked the right questions, and focused on the real issue.
   – Adapted from, *Perspectives On Values* (Riverside, CA: Hancock Center for Youth and Family Ministry, 1993), 270-279.

• Violence

Violence is physical, verbal or emotional force exerted for the purpose of coercion, debasement, abuse, or injury.

We encounter violence in arrogant, aggressive behavior and in the sullen disregard for the well-being of others. We see it in a violent person's posture and hear it in his or her language. We're at first embarrassed by it when we recognize it in the play of children, but later we pay to be *entertained* by it in countless R-rated movies.

Violence is part of the human fabric, as old as Cain and Abel. It is as pervasive as the evening news and as local as our morning newspaper. It is personal, domestic, gang-related, ethnic, racial, sexual and political. It happens on the plains of Montana and in the taxi cabs of New York City, on the playgrounds of elementary schools and in the federal buildings of Oklahoma City, on our inner-city streets, in the video games we buy at toy stores, and in the skies above our shorelines.

But Christians insist that violence stands in direct opposition to everything that the love of God represents. "The exercise of force is contrary to the principles of God's government. He desires only the service of love; and love cannot be commanded; it cannot be won by force or authority." Ellen White, *The Desire of Ages*, 22.

• What Can We Do About Violence?

1. **Talk about it.** Don't pretend that it doesn't exist.
2. **Don't be intimidated by it.** See Psalm 91:5; Matthew 10:28; and Romans 8:35-39.
3. **Be sensible.** Don't walk alone after dark. Don't ever get in a car with strangers. Don't challenge people on the freeway. Avoid convenience stores and ATMs late at night.
4. **Eliminate the risk factors.** For example, alcohol plays a part in 95% of all college campus rapes. If for no other reason than the connection between alcohol and violence, don't drink!
5. **Model nonviolent behavior,** beginning at home. Violence usually takes root in early childhood.
6. **Be intentional about your entertainment values.** Don't learn to laugh at violence. Don't become insensitive to the victims.
7. **Make nonviolent people your heroes.**
8. **Support local and national efforts** against the spread of violence in our culture.

Violence

violence, continued

- ## Martin Luther King, Jr.'s Six Nonviolent Truths

  1. Nonviolence is not a method for cowards; it does resist.
  2. Nonviolence does not seek to defeat or humiliate the opponent, but to win his friendship and understanding.
  3. Nonviolence is directed against forces of evil rather than against persons who happen to be doing the evil.
  4. Nonviolence is a willingness to accept suffering without retaliation, to accept blows from the opponent without striking back.
  5. At the center of nonviolence stands the principle of love. The nonviolent resister not only refuses to shoot his opponent but he also refuses to hate him.
  6. Nonviolence is based on the conviction that the universe is on the side of justice.

- ## Thomas Merton's Seven Nonviolent Conditions

  1. Nonviolence must be aimed at the transformation of the present state of the world.
  2. Nonviolence must be for others not just for self.
  3. Nonviolence must avoid self-righteousness.
  4. Nonviolence must be based on trust in God and not in one's own ingenuity or tenacity.
  5. Nonviolence believes that the manner in which the conflict for truth is waged will itself manifest or obscure the truth.
  6. Nonviolence keeps an open mind to the ideas of others.
  7. Nonviolence must be optimistic, maintained in the purity of Christian hope.

- ## And don't forget. . .

  It won't always be this way! Isaiah 60:18 promises us:

  "No longer will violence be heard in your land, nor ruin or destruction within your borders, but you will call your walls Salvation and your gates Praise."

Visioning

Visioning is a group process by which people determine the goals and priorities for a project or program.

In youth ministry, visioning helps a pastor or youth leader bring a congregation together in its support of youth ministry, assists the youth leader in building community among a team of volunteers, helps focus a philosophy of youth ministry into specific strategies, and serves youth group members by providing a model of how to approach challenges and make the most of opportunities.

In a youth ministry setting, the steps of visioning would typically include expressing dreams about youth ministry, sharing those dreams with others, determining the actions that need to be taken to make the dreams come true, prioritizing those actions, determining who should be involved and making a commitment to taking the necessary steps.

The process can be accomplished in a long afternoon, or, more ideally, it can take place over a weekend, perhaps in a retreat setting. Time should be given to answering each of the following questions and for sharing the answers with the others present.

Questions for a Youth Ministry Visioning Process

1. What is your vision, your dream, for youth ministry in your church?
2. What *pleases* you about youth ministry in your church? What successes have you had? What strengths do you exhibit?
3. What *troubles* you about youth ministry in your church? Where have your failures been? What weaknesses exist?
4. What *opportunities* do you currently see for establishing your vision in your church?
5. What *challenges* to effective youth ministry in your church do you see at this time?
6. What steps do you need to take to accomplish your vision for your church? (To strengthen the things that please you. To eliminate the things that trouble you. To take advantage of the opportunities. To meet the challenges.)
7. How would you prioritize the steps you have determined? What should come first? Which step is most important to fulfilling your goals? Which will be most helpful in making your youth ministry dreams come true?

8. What time frame should you attach to each of these prioritized steps? How long should it take you to accomplish the step?

9. Who is best suited to take the steps you've prioritized? What interest do you think each of those people have in working with your youth ministry team? What part are you willing to play in accomplishing your vision?

10. How and when and how often should you evaluate your progress?

- *Three Reminders for Accomplishing Your Vision*

1. **Set challenging, but attainable goals.** "I want 500 enthusiastic, dedicated kids packing my programs every week" is NOT REALISTIC. These goals are more like it:

   a. By the end of the summer, I want my kids to have a clear and unmistakable understanding of grace.

   b. By Christmas I want each of my kids to have brought one unchurched friend to an activity.

   c. By the end of this year, I want my five student leaders to be leading out in Sabbath School.

2. **Set definite steps toward reaching your goal.** Your vision should set the tone for all the interim activities.

   a. Are your worships illustrating grace in a tangible way?

   b. Do you talk about the importance of reaching out to people beyond our church community?

   c. Do you model this by bringing your unchurched friends and introducing them to your kids?

   d. Are you giving our student leaders more and more responsibility?

3. **Find a catchy way to present your vision.** A ten-page paper on the need for spiritual growth will not be remembered by the time you finish presenting it. But a phrase like "It's time for another Growth Spurt" probably will. Especially when it's all over the bulletin boards, repeated in your talks and newsletters and illustrated in all your programming.

Visioning Notes:

_____

_____

_____

_____

visioning, continued

• **Volunteers**

You can't do it all yourself!

Youth leaders wear too many hats: Sabbath School programmer, lesson teacher, AYS leader, social director, newsletter editor, mission trip sponsor, friend, counsellor, pastor – and the list goes on!

Obviously, one person can't do all that work alone. But more than the human impossibility of the demand, it's not good for youth ministry to be dependent on just one person. It deprives church members of the joy of involvement. It turns what should be a creative endeavor with much variety into a monochromatic, one-dimensional picture.

What's more, when youth ministry is built around one person (even if that person is a youth pastor), it usually ends up failing. Ultimately burnout occurs, or the youth leader moves to another location, and the kids suffer, having been uninvolved and untrained to establish their own youth ministry.

How much better to use the team approach. Look to the members of your youth group to get involved. Then find members of your larger congregation who have the skills you need to be successful.

- *Three Ways to Utilize Volunteers*
  1. **One Talent at a Time.** Find volunteers who have the specific talents your program needs. For example:
     a. People who are organized can keep your master calendar.
     b. Members who are good teachers can lead out in the lesson study.
     c. Writers and editors can help with the newsletter and write press releases and bulletin announcements.
     d. People who do well financially can become your budget advisors.
  2. **One Project at a Time.** Ask for volunteers to be in charge of just one event (a banquet, fund-raiser, service project, mission trip, etc.). Give them both the responsibility and the authority they need to get the job done well.
  3. **One Youth Group Member at a Time.** Ask volunteers to take special interest in individual members of your youth group; to pray for them, remember their birthdays, invite them home for Sabbath dinner, and just be available to talk and listen.

Volunteers

• Luther Warren and Henry Fenner

Many early Seventh-day Adventist leaders were teenagers just like the kids in your youth group. Students. Committed young Christians with a consuming vision. Eager to serve. Ready to go wherever God led them. Willing to devote their lives to a well-defined mission.

Ellen Harmon was 16 when she was first drawn to the Advent message. Within weeks of her 17th birthday in 1844, God began to use her to give encouragement to a discouraged group of believers who needed to hear that God still cared. (See: Ellen White.)

John Loughborough was 16 in 1848 when he started preaching. It was before the time when ministers received regular salaries, so John worked during the week at whatever job he could find and then preached his heart out on the weekends.

Annie and Uriah Smith, sister and brother, became Adventist Christians while they were teenagers. Annie turned out to be a noted poet and hymn writer. Uriah started editing church publications in 1853. He was 21 years old.

John Andrews was already part of the picture when he was 15. He began a career as a minister when he was 21. And he passed along his youthful enthusiasm to his children. When he left the U.S. in 1874 to become the Church's first missionary, he was a single parent (his wife had died two years earlier) with two teenagers, Mary, 13, and Charles, 17.

Luther Warren was only 14 in 1879 when he and a 17 year old friend, Harry Fenner, decided the church needed an organization to encourage and support the youth. They called their new group a "young people's society." Within ten years the church structure was beginning to follow their lead. In 1889 the Ohio Conference became the first to form a conference-wide youth organization. It was known as Christian Volunteers. And in 1907 the General Conference Youth Department was formally organized.

Remember, God doesn't ask us how old we are, whether we're male or female, how well we've done in school, or what life's been like at home. He just tells us how much He loves us and how eager He is for us to join His team in telling the good news of the gospel of His grace to others.

–Adapted from *Walking On the Edge* (Lincoln, NE: AdventSource, 1996), 20, 21.

• Ellen White

Following the Great Disappointment (October 22, 1844), when <u>Jesus</u> did not return to earth as Adventist believers had expected, individual Christians picked up the pieces of their shattered lives and started all over again. The small group found encouragement in each other's company. Rededicated to understanding the Bible, to praying for guidance, to doing their best in this world, they continued to meet together, to study and pray.

On a cold December morning in 1844, five young women were having worship together on the second floor of a country house in South Portland, Maine. [1] While the women were praying, one of them, Ellen Harmon, felt incredibly overpowered by the Holy Spirit.

"I was wrapped in a vision of God's glory," she later recalled, "and I seemed to be rising higher and higher, far above the dark world." [2]

During this "vision," which <u>Seventh-day Adventists</u> believe was a miraculous gift from a loving God, Ellen saw the discouraged Advent believers walking along a path which led to heaven. Behind the travellers was a light, identified as the events they had just experienced. Ahead of them, at the end of the path, was the New Jerusalem, the heavenly city where they would enter eternity.

Whenever the believers would become disheartened, Jesus would encourage them by raising His right arm. A glorious light would shine on the pathway, and the Advent people would shout, "Hallelujah!"

The message of the vision was clear. Ellen shared her understanding later: "If they kept their eyes fixed on Jesus, who was just before them, leading them to the city, they were safe." [3]

It wouldn't be the last time God sent encouragement through Ellen. For the next 70 years Ellen listened to God's voice and spoke to the growing church of His will for our lives. Ellen and her husband, James White, became leaders in the church. They travelled around the world, preaching, teaching, helping to establish schools and hospitals, writing dozens of books and scores of magazine articles, and sharing their vision for Seventh-day Adventists.

At every step of the way, through acceptance and opposition, through endorsement of her ministry and misunderstanding of her purpose, Ellen's message stayed the same: *keep your eyes on Jesus.*

"Do not allow your minds to be diverted from the all-important theme of the righteousness of Christ," Ellen cautioned us in 1892. [4]

"There is one great central truth to be kept ever before the mind in

Ellen White

the searching of the Scriptures – Christ and Him crucified. Every other truth is invested with influence and power corresponding to its relation to this theme." [5]

"I can never doubt my mission," she wrote in 1903, "for I am a participant in the privileges and am nourished and vivified [made alive], knowing that I am called unto the grace of Christ. Every time I set forth the truth to the people, and call their attention to eternal life which Christ has made possible for us to obtain, I am as much benefited as they with most gracious discoveries of the grace and love and the power of God in behalf of His people."[6]

– Taken from *Walking On the Edge* (Lincoln, NE: <u>Advent*Source*</u>, 1996), 24, 25.

- *Notes From Ellen's Life*

1. Ellen Gould Harmon and her twin sister, Elizabeth, were born on November 26, 1827 in Gorham, Maine.

2. Ellen's and Elizabeth's parents, Robert and Eunice Harmon, already had six children when the twins were born. The Harmon family attended the Chestnut Street Methodist Church.[7]

3. When Ellen was nine years old, a schoolmate threw a rock in anger which struck her in the face, causing a concussion and breaking her nose. Ellen was in a coma for three weeks. Most people thought she would die. When she recovered and first saw her disfigured face in a mirror, she wanted to die.[8] Later in the school year, Ellen attempted to return to school. But her health had been permanently weakened; she dropped out of school, ending her formal education.

4. Ellen married James White in Portland, Maine, on Sunday, August 30, 1846. James was 25, Ellen was 18. The couple was married for 35 years, until James' death in 1881. James and Ellen had three children, all boys: Henry, Edson, and Willie.

5. Ellen died on July 16, 1915 at Elmshaven in northern California.

1   Arthur L. White, *Ellen G. White: The Early Years, Vol. 1, 1827-1862* (Hagerstown, MD: Review and Herald Publishing Association, 1985), 55.
2   Ellen White, *Early Writings*, 13.
3   Ellen White, *The Day-Star*, Jan. 24, 1846.
4   Ellen White, *Review and Herald*, April 5, 1892.
5   Ellen White, *MS 31*, 1890 (*Ellen White Comments on the Bible Commentary*, 1084).
6   Ellen White, *MS 174*, 193 (*Selected Messages, Volume 3*, 76).
7   Arthur L. White, *Ellen G. White: The Early Years*, 18, 32.
8   Ellen White, *Spiritual Gifts, Vol. 2*, 9.

Ellen White, continued

• Women in Youth Ministry

Regardless of the current debate within the Adventist Church concerning women in ministry, youth workers will find themselves surrounded by women called and committed to ministry to young people. Women are serving as pastors, religion teachers, school administrators, hospital and school chaplains, writers and editors.

Jesus said, "The harvest is plentiful but the workers are few. Ask the Lord of the harvest, therefore, to send out workers into his harvest field." (Matthew 9:37, 38) Anyone who has worked with young people will understand the need for more and more willing people to join the ranks of God's fieldhands! These kids need all the time and love we can give to them.

Therefore, utilize as many men *and* women as you can in your <u>youth ministry</u>. Of course, not everyone is cut out for youth work, but don't pass up the opportunity of recruiting help from anyone who is talented and willing simply because of their gender.

Another benefit from incorporating women into your youth ministry is the effect such an example can have on the future career choices of the girls in your youth group. If they never see a woman serving in a ministry role, they will tend to disregard the possibilities for themselves in the future. Losing the potential ministry of those young women would be tragic. We want to encourage as many workers as possible to join the battle for turning the hearts and lives of our youth to Christ.

- • More Great Discussion on Women in Ministry:
- ✔ Pat Habada, editor *The Welcome Table* (Langley Park, MD: TEAMPress, 1995).
- ✔ Caleb Rosado, *Women, Church, God* (Riverside, CA: Loma Linda University Press, 1990).

Notes:

_____

_____

_____

_____

_____

_____

_____

_____

Working With Your Pastor

Your pastor can be your biggest ally in <u>youth ministry</u> in your church. And because of that potential strength, <u>youth leaders</u> need to be careful to ask for and listen to the pastor's counsel, and to be aggressive in keeping the pastor informed, involved and active as a member of your youth ministry team.

Here a few tips on how to work successfully with your pastor.

Seven Ways to Work With Your Pastor

1. **Create a Regular Appointment Time.** You should meet with your pastor *at leal* once a month.
2. **Clear Calendar Items.** Stay *at least* six months ahead of major events, projects and programs. The more advance notice, the better.
3. **Discuss Your Strategies.** Talk about your <u>philosophy of youth ministry</u>, your goals, your overall approach to ministry. Ask for advice and support.
4. **Reveal Specific Plans.** Give your pastor a list of the <u>Sabbath School</u> and <u>AYS</u> leaders and teachers for the coming month. Discuss details of projects, special events and programs, social events, and personnel.
5. **Work on Budgets.** Go over your <u>budgets</u> together, line by line. Explain the financial support you need, the ways you intend to raise the necessary funds and what help you need from the church.
6. **Give Personal Invitations.** Be sure to invite your pastor to attend programs and events, give devotions to your <u>youth group</u>, and make appearances, even when he or she can't stay for the entire event.
7. **Evaluate.** Ask for your pastor's opinion on specific events and programs. Listen carefully. Take notes. Make the changes you can agree with.

Notes:
_____
_____
_____
_____
_____

Working With Your Pastor

• World Religions

"Some of my best friends are Buddhists," reports an Adventist teenager who attends a public high school. "How can I share my faith with them without being offensive to their religion?"

Increasingly, Adventist young people are becoming aware of the great religious systems of the world. As their <u>youth leader</u>, you are likely to be asked questions about key elements of these religions, including backgrounds of the founders, significant beliefs and practices, special festivals and rituals and their sacred writings.

Here are a few primary facts, some clues for sharing with others, and a bibliography for further study.

• Buddhism

Buddhism is one of the oldest of the world religions practiced today, and it is claimed by 250 million people. The founder was a man named Siddhartha Gautama, who was born near the present-day border between Nepal and India in the sixth or fifth century BC. He was given the title Buddha, which means, the Enlightened One. Buddhists follow a clear "path" in order to become free from suffering and desire, ultimately to "nirvana," a release from desire and reincarnation.

• Hinduism

The Hindu religion, practiced today by most of the people in India, has over 330 million gods, but Hindus believe each person has his or her own special god. They believe in a higher spiritual goal of freedom from the cycle of death and suffering in this world, and that they will be reborn someday, according to their "karma," which is a kind of fate. The *Bhagavad-Gita* is the single most influential Hindu text.

• Islam

Followers of the religion of Islam and the prophet Muhammad (who lived from 570-632 AD), are known as Muslims. They worship on Friday, usually in a mosque. They believe in one God, Allah, and are committed to doing good in their lifetime in order to be judged positively by Allah. They pray often during the day, facing their most holy city, Mecca, which all Muslims hope to visit during their lifetime on a pilgrimage known as a Hajj. Most Muslims observe a holy month, Ramadan. The "Bible" of Islam is called the Quran (also spelled Koran).

World Religions

World Religions, continued

• Judaism

Being Jewish is both a nationality and a religion. Some Jews are very conservative in their faith. Others are not religious at all. History is very important – from Abraham to the Exodus, through the Old Testament, to the horrible persecutions, including the Holocaust in World War II. Worship takes place in a synagogue. Sabbath is a very special day, as are a number of holidays and feast days. The Jews are still looking for a Messiah who will come and finally put things right.

• Roman Catholicism

A billion people in the world today are Roman Catholic Christians. They trace the beginnings of their church structure to Peter's ministry in Rome. The leader of the church is known as the Pope. Local ministers are priests, respectfully called "Father." Catholics are baptized as infants, and attend "mass" on Sunday. They pray to Jesus and to "saints," especially Jesus' mother, Mary. Both the Bible and the teachings of the church throughout its history are highly respected.

• Sharing Your Faith With Members of Other Religions

1. **Discover common points of faith**, such as, your belief in God, in God's communicationl humanity , and in the idea that God wants us to be happy here and to have eternal life.[1]
2. **Express genuine interest in traditions.** Talk about the historical and spiritual significance of holidays. Find ways you can join their celebrations. Share Christian traditions with them.
3. **Ask for the best spiritual advice.** Listen to words from their scriptures. Affirm your belief that "every good and perfect gift is from above," (James 1:17). Share your favorite Bible verses.
4. **Share your love for Jesus.** Express your admiration for His life and your appreciation for His words.
5. **Focus on grace.** This is probably the biggest difference between your religious systems, as well as the most attractive feature of Christianity. Let Jesus' amazing, unconditional love be a drawing point (John 12:32).

[1]   "Speak to them, as you have opportunity, upon points of doctrine on which you can agree." Ellen White, *Gospel Workers*, 119, 120.

•   **More Great Discussion on World Religions:**
✔   Christopher Blake, editor, *A Reason To Believe* (Hagerstown, MD: Review & Herald, 1993).

• Worldview

Worldview simply means the way we look at the world. It is the bottom line for our interpretation of events. The way we understand history. The perspective that colors our view of the future. Our worldview is the overarching factor that influences our decisions.

A Christian worldview includes the understandings that God is a loving, personal Being, that He is active in our world, that forces of evil are powerful in opposition to God's activity, and that God's ultimate victory is assured.

Christian young people need to learn skills which will help them recognize and reject worldviews which compete with the Christian worldview. Some of these oppositive worldviews are blatant in their opposition to the government of God. They include the Satanic, the occult, the addictive lifestyles of illegal drugs, <u>alcohol</u>, prostitution, etc. Some oppositive worldviews are subtle and seemingly inconsequential. Most of the avenues of our popular culture, including much of the entertainment industry, are built upon secular worldviews, which, if not openly opposed to the spiritual life, usually refuse to bring God into the picture.

• *Seven Ways to Distinguish Worldviews*

1. Is room made for the spiritual dimension of our life? Or is the spiritual excluded?
2. Is the spiritual dimension integrated into or segregated from the remainder of life?
3. Is God active or distant or nonexistent?
4. Is God portrayed as harsh, vindictive, judgemental and to be feared? Or as gracious, forgiving, accepting and to be loved?
5. Are spiritual people caricatured or stereotyped? Or do they appear as they really are, as real people?
6. Are the heroes ever those who hold spiritual <u>values</u>? Or are the heroes always non-spiritual?
7. Are spiritual responses to life's challenges ever considered? Or do things such as <u>Bible study</u>, <u>prayer</u>, <u>worship</u>, <u>community</u> and <u>service</u> never inform people's decisions?

• World Wide Web

In addition to the web sites listed elsewhere in this resource, here are a few websites to help you get started surfing on the web, or to widen your cyberworld. At the time we went to press each of these were active and helpful.

We've found all of these to contain lots of good information, and to lead us into myriads of other pages. (Of course, just because we've listed a site here doesn't mean that we take responsibility for everything that's presented, or even that we agree with 100% of what you'll find. You visit the site and decide for yourself on how helpful the resource is in your setting.)

• Five Web Sites With Search Engines

1. **Communication** Resources
   http://www.comresources.com/
2. Gospel **Online Services**
   http://www.goshen.net
3. **National Network of Youth Ministries**
   http://www.nnym.org
4. **NetCentral**
   http://www.netcentral.net
5. Youth Pastors
   http://www.youthpastor.com

• Fifteen Web Sites with Additional Links

1. **Adventist Connections**
   http://www.andrews.edu/inst.html
2. **American Academy of Ministry**
   http://www.preaching.com/ministry/index.html
3. **Christian** Music **Links**
   http://www.m8.com/christian/
4. **Christian Spotlight on the** Movies
   http://www.christiananswers.net/spotlight
5. **Christian Telecommunications Toolkit Home Page**
   http://www. bible.acu.edu/ctt
6. Contemporary Christian Music **(online magazine)**
   http://www.ccmcom.com/

World Wide Web

7. Free Cartoons and Art for Church <u>Newsletters</u>
   http://www.goshen.net/calebproject/toons.htm
8. Gospel Communications Network
   http://www.gospelcom.net
9. Institute for Christian Leadership
   http://www.iclnet.org/
10. InterVarsity Christian Fellowship
    http://www.gospelcom.net/iv/
11. Preaching Magazine
    http://www.preaching.com/preaching/index.html
12. Worldwide Resources for Christian <u>Small Groups</u>
    http://www.smallgroups.com
13. The <u>Worship</u> & Music Ministry Resource Center
    http://www.getnet.com/%7Emusicmin/
14. The Worship Leader
    http://www.kuesterlaw.com/worship/
15. Youth Ministry Central: <u>Drama</u> Resources
    http://www.gospelcom.net/ys/central/drama.html

More of Your Favorite WWW Sites:

_____

_____

_____

_____

_____

_____

_____

_____

_____

_____

_____

_____

_____

_____

_____

_____

_____

World Wide Web, continued

- ## Worship

Worship, most simply defined, is our response to God's goodness, our response to God's invitation to love and to adore Him – an initiative that springs not from our goodness or worthiness, but purely from God's grace, His incredible love and compassion for us as His children. A thankful life is a response of our worship of God.

The apostle Paul, in Romans 12:1, reminds us that our spiritual service is an act of worship. The youth class we teach, our work with the homeless, the time we spend on the church board – our daily lives will be revolutionized when we realize that this involvement is offered to God as a gift of worship.

One of the most significant needs in youth ministry is to help our young people understand that worship is far more than simply going to Sabbath School and church. How can we, as youth leaders, enable our young people to see that God longs for worship to have priority in their everyday lives? Here are five key considerations.

- ### Five Worship Considerations
  1. It's clear that young people have an inherent ability to worship. If you've ever attended a rock concert or sporting event and witnessed the adulation of young fans, you know that young people *can* worship. We must ask ourselves some hard questions as to why our worship services are so often experienced by our young people as "boring."
  2. In this day of nonstop MTV, our youth long for an approach to worship that takes into consideration their social and spiritual needs. At times we complain that it seems all our youth are interested in is each other. Yet it's important for us to recognize that their particular social needs, when met, can help us meet their spiritual needs as well.

     Senior highers appreciate a variety of worship and musical styles, and enjoy helping to lead out in worship. Symbolism, varying prayer experiences, and small-group interaction appeal to their developing mental and emotional needs.

     It's imperative to remember that adolescents have the acute ability to distinguish between true and false worship. They are able to sense whether the adults who are working with them really believe what they are saying.[1]

worship

3. Young people want to belong. It's evident by the way they dress and by the way they interact with each other. A church that longs to effectively minister to its youth will be a church that finds creative ways to help its young people know that they are needed and wanted; a place where they are challenged to think and where their responses will be thoughtfully considered.

    We need to remember, as well as model, that it is in <u>community</u> that we have reason to sing louder, to pray more fervently, and to be more caring and compassionate. When we hear others speak of God's goodness, we sense how good He has been to us; when we hear of one another's struggles and hurts, we sense God's healing in our own lives, and the renewed desire to be instruments of care. For this reason, community will be emphasized in youth worship.

4. Young people want *to be* the church. One of the ways this is most easily accomplished is to not only *tell* them that they are needed, but also to *use* them. Involving them in the life of the church says far more about our commitment to their nurture than mere words can ever do.

5. To worship God means to serve Him. The youth of our church can show us how to do this.

Today, God is still willing to place His confidence in young people. We are powerfully reminded of this as we listen to the words of Joel:

> *I will pour out my Spirit on all people. Your sons and daughters will prophesy, your old men will dream dreams, your young men will see visions. Even on my servants, both men and women, I will pour out my Spirit in those days.*[2]

How do youth worship? Young people worship best in the context of a stimulating community—one in which the walls of indifference and mediocrity are broken down and grace is modeled by caring adults. A context where youth are challenged to worship with their whole being, creatively and radically living out their lives as disciples of <u>Jesus</u> – and in the process, invigorating the church with their vitality and vision.

---

1   John Dettoni, "Worship That Fits the Worshipper," in *Youthworker* (Spring 1990): 30-34. A very helpful source dealing with the way in which faith is developed over the entire life cycle is V. Bailey Gillespie's *The Experience of Faith* (Birmingham, AL: Religious Education Press, 1988).
2   Joel 2:28,29.

Worship, continued

• **Young Adults**

Young adults are individuals who are between 18 and 35 years of age. Situated beyond the youth group, but not yet fully comfortable with the mainstream adult scene, college and career young adults often have difficulty finding their place in a church that has not created a natural niche for them.

Although the world calls them Generation X, young adults can stand for something excellent in your church. With consistent efforts to pray for, nurture, and empower young adults, your ministry can make a positive spiritual impact in their lives.

• *Five Characteristics of Young Adults*

1. In general, they are better educated than the average member.
2. They are usually single or recently married.
3. They are highly mobile.
4. They are progressive in their thinking, aware of and sensitive to social issues.
5. They are looking for a congregation that will provide a varied, quality program of meaningful, relational activities.

• *Five Ways You Can Minister to Young Adults*

1. **Empower them to minister to each other.** Unlike youth ministry where an adult is more central, young adults are more inclined to lead their own groups, meetings, and projects. Ownership is important to them. Give them responsibilities based on individual talents and interests, then step to the side, providing support from an advisor vantage point.
2. **Be practical.** Young adults are pragmatic; look towards practical projects with local relevance. Also make sure there are tangible results that are evident to your young adults.

    Doing homeless feedings or shelter work, blood drives, and big "sibling" programs are examples of programs close to home that make an impact. Young adults get excited about these opportunities.
3. **Relationships are a primary concern.** Beyond their peers, young adults are also looking for authentic, mutual relationships with adults. Select some empathic adults to initiate personal rela-

tionships with one or two of your young adults. Start a mentorship program in your church. Create social events that are more relationally structured and less program structured. Intentional ministry efforts to get to know young adults personally will make a substantial difference.

4. **Niche ministries.** A successful way to involve young adults in your ministry is to look first at the talents of your young adults. Rather than plug them into a church job description, create "niches" where they can use their expertise or develop their interests.

   Videography for Sabbath School discussion starters, developing a desktop-published newsletter for the church, and initiating relations for the church with social action agencies; These are examples of simply empowering young adults to employ their abilities of the church.

5. **Focus group consult.** Young adults are very diverse, and no doubt your ministry to and by them will need to be custom-tailored. An excellent way to involve them is to create a focus group or advisory council made up of young adults. Regularly meet with them to check your ideas, to get their advice, to ask for their help.

   Gradually, based on their comfort, enlist their leadership into the very core of church life. Taking this route will help them acclimate to the occasional "tempests" that emerge in church boards and other arenas of church leadership. But keep the focus group to hone your young adult ministry vision.

☞ **Here's a Great New Young Adult Resource:** *Scanner* is a publication of the Glendale City Seventh-day Adventist Church Young Adult Program. You can get in touch with *Scanner* at the following addresses: *Scanner*, 610 E. California Avenue, Glendale, CA 91206; phone (818) 244-7241; fax (818) 240-9485; E-mail - Scanner - gc7ac@earthlink.net; http://www.glendalecitysda.com.

- **More Great Resources About Young Adults:**
✔ George Barna, *The Invisible Generation: Baby Busters* (Glendale, CA: Barna Research Group, Ltd., 1992).
✔ N. Howe and W. Strauss, *13th gen: Abort, Retry, Ignore, Fail?* (New York, NY: Vintage Books, 1993).
✔ W. Mahedy and J. Bernardi, *A Generation Alone: Xers Making a Place In the World* (Downers Grove, IL: InterVarsity, 1994).
✔ *Adventist Review*, Cutting Edge edition, William G. Johnsson, editor, 12501 Old Columbia Pike, Silver Spring, MD 20804-6600, (800) 456-3991, e-mail: 74617.15@CompuServe.com.
✔ *Build Magazine*, Dara Mayers & Naadu Blankson, editors, DO Something, 423 W. 55th Street, 8th floor, New York, NY 10019, (212) 523-1175, F AX: (212) 582-1307, Email: Daramay@aol.com.
✔ *Regeneration Quarterly*, W. Bradford Wilcox, editor, P.O. Box 3000, Denville, NJ 07834-9369, (800) 783-4903, e-mail: r egeneration@csgi.com.

young Adults, continued

Youth Church

One of the secrets of continuing local support for your <u>youth ministry</u> program is to keep your youth visible to the entire congregation. And one of the best ways to accomplish that is to hold a regularly scheduled youth church, a regular <u>worship</u> service presented entirely by the youth. Here are a few points to keep in mind in your planning process.

Five Planning Points for Youth Church

1. **Schedule.** Meet with your pastor and ask for a date for a youth church. After you've had two or three successes with youth church, ask for a regular appointment, such as twice a year or once a quarter.
2. **Program.** Meet with your <u>youth council</u> and discuss ways to involve as many youth as possible in the church service. For example, use several kids to lead the music, two kids to read the scripture reading, a group for special music, and two or three to present the sermon.
3. **Participants.** Ask for volunteers, or nominate members of your youth group to take part. Ask each person to take part and schedule a meeting of all participants.
4. **Theme.** Talk to the participants about the goals of your worship service. Choose a theme around which the participants can plan their part of the program. Choose music, a scripture passage and a sermon topic that fit the overall theme.
5. **Practice.** While most church members (especially <u>parents</u> and grandparents) will be thrilled to see their kids involved in church, some members may be critical. So take the time to practice each part. Give appropriate respect to the responsibility of leading a congregation in worship to God.

What to Do After Youth Church

1. **Greet the Congregation.** Have all the members of your <u>youth group</u> join the program participants in greeting the members of the congregation. Line both sides of the church foyer, smile and shake everybody's hand.
2. **Evaluate.** Within a week of youth church talk to your youth group about the service. Ask for tips on doing a better job next time. Discuss creative ways to enhance the worship.

Youth Church

• Youth Council

A council is a group of people brought together for a specific purpose: to discuss issues, give advice, evaluate, make decisions, plan, or administer a project or program.

In youth ministry, there are two types of youth councils: a *local* youth council, made up of the local church youth leader and kids from a church's youth group; and, a *general* youth council, usually an areawide (conference, union, division) group of youth leaders or youth ministry professionals or a combination of lay and professional youth ministry people.

• Five Functions of a Local Youth Council

1. Evaluating a local church's current philosophy of youth ministry, its strategies, personnel, programs and projects.
2. Visioning; establishing the goals of a local youth ministry.
3. Planning, budgeting and scheduling the local youth ministry program.
4. Administering the local youth ministry, preparing for programs and events, fulfilling marketing strategies, accomplishing projects, etc.
5. Staffing, seeking volunteers and enlisting help for the local youth ministry.

• Five Tasks of a General Youth Council

1. Evaluating the philosophy, strategies, personnel, programs and projects of a designated system segment (e.g., a conference, union or division).
2. Visioning; working with the leader of a designated system (such as a conference youth director) to establish youth ministry goals for the entire system.
3. Making plans for system-wide youth ministry activities or projects, establishing a system-wide master calendar, working on a budget for major endeavors.
4. Fulfilling assignments, empowering local youth ministry.
5. Working on job descriptions for the leader of the designated system segment, searching for qualified people to fill employment openings.

• Youth Culture

If you had just accepted a call to serve as a missionary to Papua New Guinea, you would be advised to learn everything you could about the culture of the people to whom you were going to minister. For committed youth leaders, the same advice holds true: we must learn everything we can about the young people we are to serve.

Mark Senter, in describing youth ministry, states that ministry to young people "begins when adults find a comfortable way of entering a student's world."[1] This is particularly true when it comes to youth culture. Just like our missionary to Papua New Guinea, we do not have to *accept* all areas of the culture of those to whom we would minister; however, we should not be *surprised* by what we might hear or experience. If young people are to be comfortable in talking with us, we must be open to the realities of their world.

• Five Clearly Visible Revealers of Culture
1. Clothes
2. Music
3. Language, especially popular phrases
4. Hair styles
5. Heroes

Each of us belong to a variety of subcultures (our particular ethnic makeup, our church affiliation, our age-category, etc.). Youth culture, however, tends to be a global culture that intentionally challenges adults, as well as many of the institutions they care about, and personally identify with (i.e. the church).

In North America youth culture is multifaceted. One of the best places to experience the culture is at the local mall as crowds of young people gather to hang out, eat, watch movies, and walk through the shops that want their business. (Note: young people are the primary consumers of entertainment and related areas – a fact easily noticeable by looking at the advertising campaigns of those who would sway the youth market.)

• Five Other Places to Experience Youth Culture
1. MTV. No longer do young people simply listen to music – they experience it in a variety of visual ways.

Youth Culture

2. A current issue of VIBE or SPIN magazines.
3. Observing the rows and rows of video games at the local K-Mart.
4. A local high school. Sit in your car, across the street from the school, either first thing in the morning when kids are arriving, or when school is getting out for the day.
5. Sitting down with a young person and asking some thoughtful questions.

It doesn't take long to note that the postmodern values (everything is relative, . . .) that scream from the well-oiled and all-entertaining media machine directed at our young people are often in direct opposition to the Christian values we would share with them.

H. Richard Niebuhr once challenged the church with his view of *Christ Transforming Culture* by suggesting that the church is to take what the culture offers and transform it into something usable for the sharing of the gospel. The challenge we face as youth leaders is to find appropriate ways to encourage our young to take those things from the culture that can be used to promote God's kingdom, and to discard those things which can only hurt God's cause or His people.

Jesus' involvement in the culture of His day likewise challenges us as we are confronted by our own discomfort with particular areas of youth culture. His example demands that we find new ways to reach the young people of our community who do not yet know Him as we do, amid their wide-range of life experiences and situations.

1 Mark Senter, *The Complete Book of Youth Ministry* (Waco, TX: Word, 1989), 10.

More Notes on Youth Culture:

_____
_____
_____
_____
_____
_____
_____
_____
_____
_____
_____

youth culture, continued

• Youth Group

Youth ministry is primarily relational. Youth ministry *relations* are primarily between the youth leader and individuals. But youthful individuals primarily prefer interactions in *group* settings. Consequently, the most effective support system in youth ministry, the social dynamic most helpful to youth leaders, is an active, growing youth group.

A hundred years ago, youth "societies" were a novel idea, just being introduced in nondenominational circles. Gradually the idea caught on as individual churches and denominations formed their own "youth fellowships," usually centering on an evening "young people's meeting," which dealt with different concerns than the biblical subjects being presented in the church's religious education curriculum.

Today the concerns of those evening meetings have become the core dynamics of youth ministry itself.

• Seven Core Youth Group Dynamics

1. Forming Identity
2. Building Relationships
3. Enjoying Social and Recreational Expressions
4. Developing a Maturing Faith in the Contemporary World
5. Worshipping Together
6. Serving Others
7. Finding a Spiritual Home

The local church youth leader assumes the primary responsibility for establishing, building and nurturing the youth group. Necessary skills include communicating, marketing, and programming.

• What Kids Are Looking For In a Youth Group

1. Acceptance
2. Friendships
3. Involvement
4. Challenge
5. Support

☞ **Also See:** Attachment; Attendance; Building Your Youth Group; Climate Issues; Community; Effectiveness Factors; Listening Skills; Newsletters.

Youth Group

• Youth Leader

Working with teenagers is a challenging path that requires dedicated people, committed to Jesus, who care personally for the youth. Being a youth leader is not for everyone, but it is for those to whom God has given the following gifts.

• 15 Qualities of a Youth Leader

1. Is convicted of God's call to youth ministry.
2. Has a sense of responsibility, commitment and devotion to youth. (See: Confidentiality.)
3. Is genuinely sympathetic and friendly.
4. Is positive and enthusiastic.
5. Is developing excellent listening skills.
6. Understands team effort.
7. Knows the importance of continuing to learn. Attends training seminars, subscribes to youth ministry journals, reads youth ministry books (owns a personal copy of The ABZs of Adventist Youth Ministry!).
8. Plans ahead. Delegates. Organizes.
9. Monitors other youth programs with a view to improving his or her own program. Talks to other youth leaders, looking for creative ideas that may work in his or her own setting.
10. Manages time.
11. Holds high standards of personal behavior.
12. Is never too busy to serve.
13. Develops leadership skills in a wide area of activities.
14. Works constantly toward the fulfillment of goals.
15. Is a person of prayer. Youth ministry without prayer is like breathing without air.

Notes about Being a Youth Leader:

_____

_____

_____

_____

_____

_____

_____

Youth Leader

Youth Leadership Convention *(vertical, left margin)*

• Youth Leadership Convention

A Youth Leadership Convention is a weekend training event designed to inspire, encourage, teach, and network <u>youth leaders</u> throughout a designated territory.

For example, the REV Youth Leadership Convention of the Florida Conference is held once a year to foster leaders who will be better equipped and committed to REVolutionizing youth for Christ. Key elements include <u>worship</u> sessions, training seminars, round table discussions, hands-on learning activities, and a relaxing banquet.

• 12 Ways to Make Your Convention Run Smoothly

1. Pray! Pray! Pray! Stay connected with Christ's creativity, strength and love throughout the whole process.
2. Understand your purpose for the convention, and keep coming back to it throughout each step.
3. Start earlier than you think you need to (no matter what the area— planning, advertising, setting up, scheduling, etc.).
4. Surround yourself with a core group of dependable people. Delegate and follow up.
5. Write down everything while brainstorming and evaluating (and be sure to put the list where you can find it when you need it!).
6. Do everything you can possibly do ahead of time, because there will be plenty of surprises to fill up the last minute.
7. Schedule speakers and special guests far in advance.
8. Allow room for each participant's creativity (musicians, seminar speakers, artists, etc.).
9. Advertise way in advance, and don't stop promoting. (For REV conventions we begin five months in advance, and follow a bell-shaped pattern for advertising: we begin with simple announcements and increased information [posters and brochures] until we reach the peak. Then, we taper off with more letters, postcards, and phone calls for reminders and encouraging registration, ending the promotion two weeks prior to the convention.)
10. Keep your focus on creating moments where leaders can come in contact with the Greatest Teacher through seminars, worship, and play. You can't go wrong when the focus is Christ.
11. Keep it as simple as possible.
12. Make it FUN!

Youth Ministry

According to *Harper's Encyclopedia of Religious Education*, "Youth Ministry" refers to "all the activities of planning, support, and leadership within a religious community that are intended to engage and nurture youth in the outlook and priorities of that community."

The *Encyclopedia* points out that "the contemporary emphasis in youth ministry assumes that youth are genuine members of the religious body and, therefore, not just recipients of ministry but participants in the total congregational life and mission. A congregation implementing this point of view will think in terms of ministry *with* and *by* youth as well as *for* youth." – From *Harper's Encyclopedia of Religious Education* (San Francisco, CA: Harper & Row, 1990), 712.

Eight Components in a Youth Ministry Model

1. Theological and philosophical foundations regarding what is believed, valued, and shared in mind and purpose.
2. A description of the specific youth involved. Where are they developmentally? What is their subculture? What are their characteristics and needs?
3. Intended outcomes. What do we hope to accomplish? How will we know if a youth ministry is effective?
4. The elements of ministry and program: instruction, worship, fellowship, and service. What will we do in each element?
5. The roles of both youth and adults. Who are the leaders? What specific roles will they play?
6. Organization that is interrelated, interdependent, and well-articulated.
7. Analysis, evaluation, and feedback for the purpose of correction, improvement and change.
8. A means to participate, observe, analyze, introduce change, evaluate, lead others in the group, follow leaders of the group, help others to lead, and make improvements in the model.
   – From John M. Dettoni, *Introduction to Youth Ministry* (Zondervan, 1993), 39, 40.

"Youth are that part of the church which is moving through a particularly sensitive period of personal development," says Barry Gane. "They are faced with a set of issues, problems and tasks that younger or older members do not face with the same intensity. As a result, they have a range of needs that require a distinct ministry that is especially directed towards meeting those needs." – From Barry Gane, *A Foundational Guide to Youth Ministry* (<u>Hancock Center for Youth and Family Ministry</u>, 1997), 2.

- *Three Common Adolescent Dilemmas*
  1. **"Why do I keep messing up everything?"** One of the major immobilizers of teenage Christians is the sense that they simply do not measure up, physically, academically, intellectually, or spiritually. They are getting older, and they *aren't* getting better.
  2. **"But that's not right..."** It's called apparent contradictions. Life itself causes doubt. Life raises questions. Building in students a durable faith means working through the questions with them.
  3. **"I'm just not sure what I want to do."** The reality of responsibility. Part of the freedom of childhood is the absence of difficult decisions concerning day-to-day living. But most of that kind of freedom ends during adolescence. It is exchanged for the more authentic and risky freedom of being able to choose one's own restrictions and boundaries.
  – From Duffy Robbins, *The Ministry of Nurture* (Youth Specialties, 1990), 144-149.

- *The Coming Revolution in Youth Ministry*

"The time has come for a revolution – a total restructuring of youth ministry. Continued modifications of the current system simply will not keep up with the changes in the world in which we live. Youth ministry has grown old. Leaders have become conservators of treasured memories. Ownership of property, advanced degrees, and successful youth ministry business ventures have minimized risk-taking and cultivated a desire for respectability.

"The problem which must be faced is, who will lead the revolution and what will the resulting forms of youth ministry look like?" – From Mark Senter, III, *The Coming Revolution in Youth Ministry and Its Radical Impact on the Church* (Wheaton, IL: Victor Books, 1992), 29, 30.

Youth Ministry, continued

In *The Complete Book of Youth Ministry* (Benson and Senter, Chicago, IL: Moody Press, 1987, 202-223), Mark Senter presents a dozen axioms, propositions or self-evident truths which "isolate ministry principles that apply in all the models of youth ministry." Whether you are in a large or small church, conducting <u>inner-city ministry</u> or live out in the country, are a <u>youth pastor</u> or a lay youth leader, a Bible teacher, chaplain or parent of a teen, these axioms will assist you in discipling your youth.

- *Twelve Axioms of Successful Youth Ministry*
  1. Youth ministry begins when a Christian adult finds a comfortable method of entering a student's world.
  2. Youth ministry happens as long as a Christian adult is able to use his or her contact with a student to draw that student into a maturing relationship with God through <u>Jesus</u> Christ.
  3. Youth ministry ceases to happen when the adult-student relationship is broken or no longer moves the student toward spiritual maturity.
  4. The influence of the student's family on his or her value system will exceed the influence of the youth worker on most occasions.
  5. Most youth groups reach peak effectiveness when <u>attendance</u> reaches twenty to thirty high school students.
  6. Long term growth of a youth ministry is directly dependent on the ability of the youth worker to release ministry responsibilities to mature and qualified lay <u>volunteers</u>.
  7. A high school student will not be theologically mature until he or she is sociologically comfortable.
  8. The most effective youth ministries are those that rapidly move students into ministry postures.
  9. Student ownership of youth ministry guided by respected Christian adults is essential for the ministry to remain healthy.
  10. A youth ministry will reflect the <u>vision</u> of its adult leaders.
  11. In youth ministry the group performs three functions: identification, contribution, and consolation.
  12. The development of a youth ministry will not exceed the public communication skills of the primary adult leader.

- ## YouthNet

YouthNet isn't really a *thing*, it's a movement. It's a network of <u>service</u> opportunities. Kind of like one-stop shopping, only for volunteer opportunities.

Say, for instance, you've always wanted to fly a plane over the Amazon. Well, who do you talk to to find out if there even is such a thing?

Or, maybe you've always wanted to live within a North American Native Nation and witness there. Who do you call?

Suppose you want to make your own project and simply need <u>volunteers</u> to fill it. Who do you call?

You call *YouthNet*.

The point of YouthNet is to connect those wanting to serve with places who need their help. Naturally, YouthNet has a bunch of ways you can get into service (it's a NET work, get it?). As a member of YouthNet you can do any of the following stuff:

- ### Eight YouthNet Opportunities
  1. <u>Student Missions</u>. Foreign service of ten months or more.
  2. **Task Force.** Service within North America of ten months or more.
  3. **Young Pioneers.** Partner up with another volunteer to:
     a. Plant churches in areas where no <u>Seventh-day Adventist</u> churches exist.
     b. Pastor and help revitalize diminishing churches.
     c. Begin evangelism on secular college campuses.
  4. **Messengers.** Enter Native American Nations and begin churches or pastor existing churches.
  5. **Youth Emergency Services (Y.E.S.).** Youth Emergency disaster response teams trained to be deployed with Adventist Community Services credentials during natural disasters.
  6. **YouthNet Partners.** Partners put you into service doing short- or long-term ministry either in North America or overseas. Examples of YouthNet Partners are Maranatha and <u>ADRA</u>.
  7. **YouthNet Hosts.** Adventist schools or churches that join YouthNet, sponsoring day-long, short- or long-term mission projects, either foreign or domestic.
  8. **YouthNet Volunteers.** You can develop your own service projects and hook up with other hosts or volunteers.

YouthNet

- **Why Would You Want to Join YouthNet?**
  1. **For Networking and Inspiration.** You can call the people at YouthNet and they can hook you up with just about any kind of project you can imagine — and some you probably had never even thought of. YouthNet has the tools to get you ready for your great adventure with training materials, inspirational reading, and contacts with those who have already done it.
  2. **To Discover and Develop a Stronger Relationship with God.** To tell you the truth, that's YouthNet's ultimate goal. And along the way, you'll be helping other people who need you.
  3. **Adventure.** Sure, you'll do some fun stuff at home this weekend (like eat Cheetos in front of the TV). But wouldn't you rather be riding an elephant? Sleeping in a hammock on a boat floating the Amazon? Or how about hanging out on a street corner talking about the meaning of life with kids who really need someone to look up to. (Cheetos seem kinda stale, huh?)
  4. **Involvement in *Real* Christianity.** Remember how Jesus did it? He almost always put *doing* ahead of *saying* when it came to ministering to people's needs. You can, too.
  5. **Direction, Purpose and Focus to Life.** Don't ask how it happens, but it does. If kind of just *grows* from the inside out, and before you know it, you know it.
  6. **Make Friends.** When you're out there working side by side with other volunteers doing the same kind of thing, well, it's a great way to make really good friends.
  7. **Network with Similar-Interest People.** It's like Internet chat rooms come to life. Honestly, why live your life through a keyboard? Get out there and meet people who like doing the same stuff you do.
  8. **Be the Boss.** Sure. Why not form your own crew and do something? Try something that's different (holding babies in a hospice, driving around in an awesome 4WD with chains and picks — and digging people out of the ditches on snowy nights). Be creative. Be the boss.
  9. **Invest in Eternity.** What are you going to take to heaven with you? Your sneakers? Your GameBoy? Why do we spend so much of our time trying to get stuff that has a "lifetime" warranty at best? Come on, go for the stuff that has a "beyond lifetime" warranty. The value is way better. Why not take some friends to heaven?

YouthNet, continued

10. **Win**. YouthNet decided to join the winning side. You know, the battle against good and evil. When you get involved in YouthNet and get out there and *do* something, you're part of an honest-to-goodness winning team. When you get down and meet people where they are, live where they live, actually look at life through their eyes, you'll see why it's called a war — and you'll see that with the help of Jesus Christ, you're winning.

11. **Travel**. There are short-term trips to south (or north) of the border; big-city projects; yearlong domestic calls; neighborhood events; and long- and short-term foreign opportunities. Try new foods, see new dimensions of nature, and experience different holidays.

12. **Give**. That's right. In a world of getting; we're going to give. (But here's a little secret: those who return from serving always say they've *gotten* more out of it than they put in — even though they're giving all they can!)

13. **Grow in God**. Remember, this is about more than volunteer work. This is also about discovering and developing a stronger relationship with God. The growing part isn't limited to those you're working with — it happens inside you, too.

- *Seven Reasons Why Youth Leaders Appreciate YouthNet*

1. **Materials and <u>Resources</u>**. YouthNet has leadership resource materials, training opportunities, and a wealth of connections and great ideas to tap into, before blazing your own trail.

2. **Updates**. You and your group can receive up-to-the-minute news on foreign and domestic service opportunities — or you can advertise for others to join you.

3. **Church Growth**. Volunteer service experiences build your church from the inside out by involving the youth today. No need to wait until tomorrow to make them the church's leaders.

4. **Evangelizing**. Invigorate spiritually bored kids through the transforming power of service.

5. **Establishing**. Solidify the faith of youth through the practical nature of Christianity.

6. **Equipping**. Give youth the tools, motivation, and experience they'll need to mature and take individual ministry as a mission for the rest of their lives.

7. **Enabling**. In every youth group, there are leaders to make. Each young person has a unique potential for leadership to develop.

YouthNet, continued

- *The History of YouthNet*
  1. The whole concept of an Adventist Youth Service Network was brought to the division at the 1993 NAD Year-end Meeting by the NAD Youth Evangelism Taskforce as one of its four recommendations. In order to empower "youth and young adults to exercise fully their faith through innovative, relational witnessing," the Taskforce specifically proposed:
     a. Locating and recruiting volunteers;
     b. Placing and screening applicants;
     c. Training workers;
     d. Spiritually nurturing volunteers in the field; and,
     e. Financially supporting volunteers with a stipend or living allowance, college scholarships, and approved government community service allotments.
  2. On January 24, 1995 in St. Louis, the 74 people present at the NAD Youth Ministries Advisory reviewed and approved a proposal document for the Adventist Youth Service Network, at the time referred to as The Adventist Youth Service Corps. The advisory further voted an enabling action for the <u>NAD Youth Ministries</u> Department to launch the Adventist Youth Service Network once the necessary elements were in place.
  3. NAD administration voted to approve the launch of YouthNet on December 20, 1995. There were many administrative details that required time to resolve delaying the official launch until the late Spring of 1996.
  4. That same Spring the <u>General Conference</u> approached YouthNet to request that volunteers not be limited to people under age 30. This led to a major new role for YouthNet.

YouthNet has now grown to be the official volunteer agency of the Seventh-day Adventist Church in North America. YouthNet is a volunteer agency which serves not only youthful interests but also the broader participation of volunteers of all ages across the NAD.

YouthNet is not a program, it is a movement of people coming together to serve in a large variety of outreach efforts. Whether it be social action, traditional evangelism, or a host of other creative expressions of outreach, YouthNet is becoming the network.

For more information concerning YouthNet, call 1-800-331-2767.

YouthNet, continued

• YouthNet eXtreme Rig

The Center for Youth Evangelism is an active partner in the North American Division's youth mission entity, YouthNet, and has embraced the challenge of equipping NAD youth to reach others for Christ.

One aspect of this equipping is the new YouthNet eXtreme Rig, developed to train, inspire and network youth and young adults. The YouthNet Rig is a touring ministry, using Christ-centered young adults, to share the gospel, call for revival, and connect young people to a network of exciting ministry options. The high energy and talented Christian team provides excellent role models for youth.

Since June 1998, the YouthNet eXtreme Rig has been travelling year round, visiting academies, summer camps, national and international events, Bible conferences, conventions, Pathfinder events, youth rallies, campmeetings and Adventist colleges and universities.

YouthNet Rig programs include dynamic speakers, training seminars for drama, puppet ministry, small groups, public school ministry, Sabbath School programming, Bible study, nature ministry, health education, street evangelism, and Christian music concerts.

In addition the YouthNet eXtreme Rig provides a variety of recreational opportunities, including basketball tournaments, velcro walls and inflatable "sumo" wrestling, etc.

For more information and scheduling, contact the YouthNet eXtreme Rig people at the numbers below.

YouthNet eXtreme Rig
    Center for Youth Evangelism
    8903 S. US 31
    Berrien Springs, MI 49103-0904
    Phone: (616) 471-9881 or 1-800-Youth-2-U
    FAX: (616) 471-9883
    e-mail: cye@andrews.edu
    http://www.YouthNet-eXtreme.com

YouthNet eXtreme Rig

• Youth Pastor

A youth pastor is someone who loves young people, understands their developmental process, has an interest in sharing the gospel with them in a dynamic and contemporary manner, and is committed to breaking down the barriers that keep young people separated from their families and from their church.

Young people tell us that it doesn't really matter if their youth pastor is a woman or a man, is young or old, or can name the top five songs on their favorite radio station. Young people *are* quick to note if a pastor is really committed to them, has an incredible interest in their individual stories, and has an undying enthusiasm for life and for the way God will use them in the present.

A youth pastor's ultimate role model is Jesus.

• Five Identifying Features of Our Role Model
1. He came to our planet in a way we could understand.
2. He chose to live life with integrity and compassion.
3. He loved people no matter where He found them.
4. He was an active participant in the culture of His day.
5. He used discipleship as the strategy to help people learn how to minister to others.

As long as there are young people who need direction, there will be men and women who will seek to follow Jesus and provide the kind of ministry to young people He so ably demonstrated.

More Youth Pastor Notes:

_____

_____

_____

_____

_____

_____

_____

_____

_____

_____

Youth Pastor

Youth Specialties

For over 25 years now, Youth Specialties has worked alongside Christian youth ministry people of just about every denomination to provide quality resources and training events for youth workers throughout North America and the world. "We're here to help you," the Youth Specialties web site says, "whether you're brand new to youth ministry or a veteran, whether you're a volunteer or a career youth pastor."

- ## Four of Our Favorite Youth Specialties Resources

1. **The *Ideas* Library.** This growing collection of field-tested, proven, creative ideas for youth ministry is all you'd ever need for games, programs, special events, fund-raisers, service projects and more. Now 56 volumes containing over 3,500 ideas.

2. ***Edge TV.*** Faced-paced, discussion-launching videos that grab kids' interest and help them open up about their own lives and the challenges they face. Each 45-minute video contains several segments (dramas, lighthearted pieces, interviews, stories and a music video), and comes with a 32-page leader's guide. Call 1-800-616-EDGE to join the *Edge TV* video club.

3. **TalkSheets.** Interactive lessons on the hottest adolescent topics. Formatted as reproducible handouts filled with questions and activities, they can be easily photocopied and distributed to your kids. TalkSheets provoke thinking about issues and consider a biblical perspective. Use them to supplement your curriculum, to lead to lively, relevant discussions, or as the focus of a youth retreat.

4. **National Youth Workers Convention.** The Youth Specialties convention is held in two locations each year, one site in the east and one in the west. Call (619) 440-2333 or e-mail nywc@youthspeciaties.com.

Youth Specialties
1224 Greenfield Drive
El Cajon, CA 92021-3399
Phone: (619) 440-2333 or (800) 776-8008 (Order Center)
FAX: (619) 440-8542
http://www.youthspecialties.com

Youth Specialties

• Youth Summit

Youth Summit is teens reaching teens. It's the most energetic <u>Sabbath</u> your young people will have experienced in a long time; it's learning through active participation; it's experiencing God in new and interesting ways. Youth Summit actively combines witness with the incredible potential of service. It comes with your choice of four topics: Love, Freedom, Honesty and Communication.

Youth Summit is on the move! As of 1998, over 10,000 young people have experienced this dynamic Sabbath experience for themselves, and more conferences and churches are sponsoring Youth Summits than ever before!

• Youth Summit FAQs

1. Who's the Youth Summit target? It's for <u>teens</u> between 13 and 19 years of age. It's for public school students. It's for private school students. It's for the youth in your conference or region.

2. How can you help us? Youth Summit is a chance for your local youth group to be involved in evangelism. In other words, it's a chance for them to invite their unchurched friends to experience God in an unthreatening, provocative way.

3. How much does it cost? Most groups that have hosted a Youth Summit have done so relatively cost free. Hard to believe? Call us and we'll fill you in on the details.

4. When can I have a Youth Summit? Any time you want to have a major regional teen emphasis.

5. How can I get more information on having a Youth Summit in my church? Call the <u>Center for Youth Evangelism</u> for a complete information pack.

Youth Summit
  Center for Youth Evangelism
  8903 S. US 31
  Berrien Springs, MI 49103-0904
  Phone: (616) 471-9881 or (800) Youth.2.U
  FAX: (616) 471-9883
  e-mail: cye@andrews.edu
  http://www.andrews.edu/CYE

• *Youthworker Journal*

Youthworker journal is a professional journal for youth workers, written by youth workers. Published every other month, each thematic issue focuses on specific challenges that your ministers (church, parachurch, and volunteer) face every day with practical help and "fodder for thought." Some recent themes include: Expectations, Conflict, Intimacy, Music in Ministry, and Growing Up. Youthworker also keeps you in touch with important youth culture trends.

Youthworker Journal
PO Box 636
Mt. Morris, IL 61054-0636
(800) 769-7624
Youthworker Update newsletter

Index